COMPUTER GRAPHICS AND MULTIMEDIA

COMPUTER GRAPHICS AND MULTIMEDIA

By

EHTIRAM RAZA KHAN
Sr. Lecturer
Deptt. of Computer Science
Jamia Hamdard University
New Delhi

HUMA ANWAR
Assistant Director
IPM Ghaziabad
Uttar Pradesh

UNIVERSITY SCIENCE PRESS
(An Imprint of Laxmi Publications Pvt. Ltd.)
BANGALORE • CHENNAI • COCHIN • GUWAHATI • HYDERABAD
JALANDHAR • KOLKATA • LUCKNOW • MUMBAI • PATNA
RANCHI • NEW DELHI

Published by :
UNIVERSITY SCIENCE PRESS
(An Imprint of Laxmi Publications Pvt. Ltd.)
113, Golden House, Daryaganj,
New Delhi-110002

Phone : 011-43 53 25 00
Fax : 011-43 53 25 28

www.laxmipublications.com
info@laxmipublications.com

Price : ₹ **175.00** *Only.*

First Edition : 2008
Reprint : 2009, 2011

OFFICES

✆ **Bangalore**	080-26 75 69 30	✆ **Chennai**	044-24 34 47 26
✆ **Cochin**	0484-237 70 04, 405 13 03	✆ **Guwahati**	0361-251 36 69, 251 38 81
✆ **Hyderabad**	040-24 65 23 33	✆ **Jalandhar**	0181-222 12 72
✆ **Kolkata**	033-22 27 43 84	✆ **Lucknow**	0522-220 99 16
✆ **Mumbai**	022-24 91 54 15, 24 92 78 69	✆ **Patna**	0612-230 00 97
✆ **Ranchi**	0651-221 47 64		

UGC-9243-175-COMPUTER GRAPH & MULTI-KHA **C—3039/011/02**

Typeset at : Shubham Composer, Delhi. *Printed at* : Sanjeev Offset Printers, Delhi.

CONTENTS

PREFACE

There was a time when computers were boring and we kept on keying commands after commands to accomplish our tasks—but with the advancements in Graphics technology, GUI (Graphical User Interfaces) took over and now everything is in Graphical form. GUI based packages are always easy to understand and work upon. Even a mouse click can do wonders for us.

This advancement in Computer technology has been possible because of application of principles of Computer Graphics. The subject of Computer Graphics is important to all of us because it can be used in an interactive manner enabling a programmer/designer to view instantly, the effect of modifying certain parameters. Multimedia, Videogames, Cartoons, CAD, Interactive websites etc., are all areas that use Computer Graphics.

Computer Graphics is not only a subject but a philosophy and a way of life. It gives us an honest path for exploration and innovation in almost any field. Computer Graphics is an attitude and hence this book has been prepared with all honesty and hard work.

The purpose of this book is to provide an insight into the fundamentals, principles and applications of Computer Graphics. This book contains text, principles, algorithms and programs written in C/C++ that are often used in this area.

This book covers topics like introduction to Computer Graphics, Graphics Primitives & devices, Drawing Geometry, 2-D Transformations & Graphics operations, 3-D Transformations & Hidden surfaces, Interaction, Rendering & Illumination, Curves & Animation Multimedia.

The salient features of this book are:

1. Latest concepts and real life applications have been incorporated in this book.
2. Algorithms have been implemented in C/C++ Programming language for the benefit of students.
3. Solved numerical problems have been included to facilitate the students.
4. Questions and exercises have been provided to check the progress of students.
5. Additional topics on Multimedia, AutoCAD and Animation tools.

This book has been designed keeping in mind the syllabus of various universities like Hamdard University, Delhi, Guru Govind Singh Inderprastha University, Delhi, Uttar Pradesh Technical University, Lucknow, Ch. Charan Singh University, Meerut etc.

The book contains various references and questions from the notes of my respected professors that they use to give in the classroom when I was a student like you.

Note: The term "He" refers to "user" in general and therefore shouldn't be considered as any favour to male or offence to female gender.

—Authors

ACKNOWLEDGEMENT

First of all , we would like to thank the Almighty for giving us everything in life. We would like to thank Chotti Badi Sarkar, Hazrat Nizam Uddin Aullia Sb., Kazi Kutub Sb., Hazrat Haji Ali for having positive influence on our family and being our strength throughout.

We would like to thank Laxmi Publications for giving us the opportunity to write the book for them. We would like to thank Prof. Afshar Alam, HOD Computer Science Deptt., Jamia Hamdard, Delhi and Prof. Vikas Verma, Director IPM Ghaziabad for always being co-operative and helpful.

We are thankful to Prof. Diwakar Pandey and Prof. Mridul Pandey from Ch. Charan Singh University and Prof. Vinod Batura Ex. Director Global for helping us whenever we needed their help.

We are thankful to all our family members for supporting us in whatever we do, the list includes our parents, brother, sister and loving son Shahi Raza Khan (SRK).

We would like to thank our colleagues, staff members and students for all their help and support without which this book wouldn't have been possible. Special thanks to our students Mohit Sharma, Yasir, Faizan, Ahmad, Muqudas, Saurab, Shariq, Rafi, Sadiq, Kashan, Rafiq, Sudesh, and Kamaldeep for being available throughout the writing of this book.

—Authors

1

Introduction to Computer Graphics, Graphics Primitives & Devices

OVERVIEW OF COMPUTER GRAPHICS

Introduction

Computer technology has progressed rapidly over the years. Starting from machine languages, we are into the world of high level languages like C, C++ and Java. Keeping pace with these developments is the field of Computer graphics.

Computer graphics is the field of Computer Science in which we are interested in generating objects and images using pixels (picture elements). It started with elementary programs like point, line and circle generation. Earlier Graphics systems used primitives to generate simple graphics. But with the development of interactive input and output devices and the technology, it is possible virtually to design anything on the computer system. Animation and cartoons have reached high quality with the use of Advanced Graphics. The scene showing Titanic sinking in the sea was possible through Graphics designing with Maya. The movies like Spiderman, Superman, Hanuman etc have generated special effects using Computer Graphics.

Multimedia, CAD and CAM have all been possible because of Computer graphics.

According to computer terminology, computer program is the collection of algorithm and data structure. In the same convention computer graphics has been defined as the collection of data structure, graphic algorithms and any higher level language. We can use any of the higher level language like C, C++, Java or any of the Graphics packages like Maya, 3-D Max or Flash to generate graphics of our choice.

Simplest application of graphics is to plot a point (pixel) on the screen of any resolution (VGA or SVGA) or to plot a line or plot a circle. Algorithm are already defined and given by the scientists/

researchers and students are just required to implement those algorithms in the programming language of their choice.

Computer Graphics need a logical mind and mastery over a programming language to succeed. This field is becoming popular day by day and there are a larger number of opportunities to be explored. There are different types of Computer Graphics like Passive and Interactive Graphics.

Computer Graphic is the discipline of producing picture or images using a computer including modeling - creation, manipulation, and storage of geometric objects and rendering – converting a scene to an image, or the process of transformations, rasterization, shading, illumination, and animation of the image.

Computer Graphics has been widely used, such as graphics presentation, paint systems, computer-aided design (CAD), image processing, simulation & virtual reality, and entertainment. From the earliest text character images of a non-graphic mainframe computers to the latest photographic quality images of a high resolution personal computers, from vector displays to raster displays, from 2D input, to 3D input and beyond, computer graphics has gone through its short, rapid changing history.

SURVEY OF COMPUTER GRAPHICS

PreHistory

The foundations of computer graphics can be traced to artistic and mathematical "inventions," for example,

- Euclid (circa 300-250 BC) who's formulation of geometry provides a basis for graphics concepts.
- Filippo Brunelleschi (1377-1446) architect, goldsmith, and sculptor who is noted for his use of perspective.
- Rene Descartés (1596-1650) who developed analytic geometry, in particular coordinate systems which provide a foundation for describing the location and shape of objects in space.
- Gottfried Wilhelm Leibniz (1646-1716) and Issac Newton (1642-1727) who co-invented calculus that allow us to describe dynamical systems.
- James Joseph Sylvester (1814-1897) who invented matrix notation. A lot of graphics can be done with matrices.
- Schoenberg who discovered splines, a fundamental type of curve.
- J. Presper Mauchly (1919-1995) and John William Mauchly (1907-1980) who build the ENIAC computer.

Early History

I would like to date the history of computer graphics from the Whirlwind Project and the SAGE computer system, which were designed to support military preparedness. The Whirlwind Project started as an effort to build a flight simulator and SAGE was to provide an air defense system in the United States to guard against the threat of a nuclear attack. The SAGE workstation had a vector display and light pens that operators would use pinpoint planes flying over regions of the United States. You can see a SAGE workstation at the Boston Computer Museum. The display is a large radar screen with a wire frame outline of the region being scanned. The light pens are like old large metal drills. A SAGE computer is on display on the corner of "Hollywood and Vine" at IBM in Kingston New York.

Besides the being the age of the first vacuum tube computers, the 1940's was when the transistor was invented at Bell Labs (1947). In 1956, the first transistorized computer was built at MIT.

The Age of Sutherland

In the early 1960's IBM, Sperry-Rand, Burroughs and a few other computer companies existed. The computers of the day had a few kilobytes of memory, no operating systems to speak of and no graphical display monitors. The peripherals were Hollerith punch cards, line printers, and roll-paper plotters. The only programming languages supported were assembler, FORTRAN, and Algol. Function graphs and "Snoopy" calendars were about the only graphics done.

In 1963 Ivan Sutherland presented his paper ***Sketchpad*** at the Summer Joint Computer Conference. Sketchpad allowed interactive design on a vector graphics display monitor with a light pen input device. Most people mark this event as the origins of computer graphics.

The Middle to Late '60's

Software and Algorithms

Jack Bresenham taught us how to draw lines on a raster device. He later extended this to circles. Anti-aliased lines and curve drawing is a major topic in computer graphics. Larry Roberts pointed out the usefulness of homogeneous coordinates, 4×4 matrices and hidden line detection algorithms. Steve Coons introduced parametric surfaces and developed early computer aided geometric design concepts. The earlier work of Pierre Bézier on parametric curves and surfaces also became public. Author Appel at IBM developed hidden surface and shadow algorithms that were pre-cursors to ray tracing. The fast Fourier transform was discovered by Cooley and Tukey. This algorithm allows us to better understand signals and is fundamental for developing antialiasing techniques. It is also a precursor to wavelets.

Hardware and Technology

Doug Englebart invented the mouse at Xerox PARC. The Evans & Sutherland Corporation and General Electric started building flight simulators with real-time raster graphics. The floppy disk was invented at IBM and the microprocessor was invented at Intel. The concept of a research network, the ARPANET, was developed.

The Early '70's

The state of the art in computing was an IBM 360 computer with about 64 KB of memory, a Tektronix 4014 storage tube, or a vector display with a light pen (but these were very expensive).

Software and Algorithms

Rendering (shading) were discovered by Gouraud and Phong at the University of Utah. Phong also introduced a reflection model that included specular highlights. Keyframe based animation for 3-D graphics was demonstrated. Xerox PARC developed a "paint" program. Ed Catmull introduced parametric patch rendering, the z-buffer algorithm, and texture mapping. BASIC, C, and Unix were developed at Dartmouth and Bell Labs.

Hardware and Technology

An Evans & Sutherland Picture System was the high-end graphics computer. It was a vector display with hardware support for clipping and perspective. Xerox PARC introduced the Altos personal computer, and an 8 bit computer was invented at Intel.

The Middle to Late '70's

Software and Algorithms

Turned Whitted developed recursive ray tracing and it became the standard for photorealism, living in a pristine world. Pascal was the programming language everyone learned.

Hardware and Technology

The Apple I and II computers became the first commercial successes for personal computing. The DEC VAX computer was the mainframe (mini) computer of choice. Arcade games such as Pong and Pac Mac became popular. Laser printers were invented at Xerox PARC.

The Early '80's

Hardware and Technology

The IBM PC was marketed in 1981 The Apple Macintosh started production in 1984, and microprocessors began to take off, with the Intel x86 chipset, but these were still toys. Computers with a mouse, bitmapped (raster) display, and Ethernet became the standard in academic and science and engineering settings.

The Middle to Late '80's

Software and Algorithms

Jim Blinn introduces blobby models and texture mapping concepts. Binary space partitioning (BSP) trees were introduced as a data structure, but not many realized how useful they would become. Loren Carpenter started exploring fractals in computer graphics. Postscript was developed by John Warnock and Adobe was formed. Steve Cook introduced stochastic sampling to ray tracing. Paul Heckbert taught us to ray trace. Character animation became the goal for animators. Radiosity was introduced by the Greenberg and folks at Cornell. Photoshop was marketed by Adobe. Video arcade games took off, many people/organizations started publishing on the desktop. UNIX and X windows were the platforms of choice with programming in C and C++, but MS-DOS was starting to rise.

Hardware and Technology

Sun workstations, with the Motorola 680x0 chipset became popular as advanced workstation a in the mid 80's. The Video Graphics Array (VGA) card was invented at IBM. Silicon Graphics (SGI) workstations that supported real-time raster line drawing and later polygons became the computer graphicists desired. The data glove, a precursor to virtual reality, was invented at NASA. VLSI for special purpose graphics processors and parallel processing became hot research areas.

The Early '90's

The computer to have now was an SGI workstation with at least 16 MB of memory, at 24-bit raster display with hardware support for Gouraud shading and z-buffering for hidden surface removal. Laser printers and single frame video recorders were standard. UNIX, X and Silicon Graphics GL were the operating systems, window system and application programming interface (API) that graphicist used. Shaded raster graphics were starting to be introduced in motion pictures. PCs started to get decent, but still they could not support 3-D graphics, so most programmer's wrote software for scan conversion (rasterization) used the painter's algorithm for hidden surface removal, and developed "tricks" for real-time animation.

Software and Algorithms

Mosaic, the first graphical Internet browser was written by *xxx* at the University of Illinois, National Center for Scientific Applications (NCSA). MPEG standards for compressed video began to be promulgated. Dynamical systems (physically based modeling) that allowed animation with collisions, gravity, friction, and cause and effects were introduced. In 1992 OpenGL became the standard for graphics APIs In 1993, the World Wide Web took off. Surface subdivision algorithms were rediscovered. Wavelets begin to be used in computer graphics.

Hardware and Technology

Hand-held computers were invented at Hewlett-Packard about 1991. Zip drives were invented at Iomega. The Intel 486 chipset allowed PC to get reasonable floating point performance. In 1994, Silicon Graphics produced the Reality Engine: It had hardware for real-time texture mapping. The Ninetendo 64 game console hit the market providing Reality Engine-like graphics for the masses of games players. Scanners were introduced.

The Middle to Late '90's

The PC market erupts and supercomputers begin to wane. Microsoft grows, Apple collapses, but begins to come back, SGI collapses, and lots of new startups enter the graphics field.

Software and Algorithms

Image based rendering became the area for research in photo-realistic graphics. Linux and open source software become popular.

Hardware and Technology

PC graphics cards, for example 3dfx and NVIDIA, were introduced. Laptops were introduced to the market. The Pentium chipset makes PCs almost as powerful as workstations. Motion capture, begun with the data glove, becomes a primary method for generating animation sequences. 3-D video games become very popular: DOOM (which uses BSP trees), Quake, Mario Brothers, etc. Graphics effects in movies become pervasive: Terminator 2, Jurassic Park, Toy Story, Titanic, Star Wars I. Virtual reality and the Virtual Reality Meta (Markup) Language (VRML) become hot areas for research. PDA's, the Palm Pilot, and flat panel displays hit the market.

The '00's

Today most graphicists want an Intel PC with at least 256 MB of memory and a 10 GB hard drive. Their display should have graphics board that supports real-time texture mapping. A flatbed scanner, color laser printer, digital video camera, DVD, and MPEG encoder/decoder are the peripherals one wants. The environment for program development is most likely Windows and Linux, with Direct 3D and OpenGL, but Java 3D might become more important. Programs would typically be written in C++ or Java.

What will happen in the near future -- difficult to say, but high definition TV (HDTV) is poised to take off (after years of hype). Ubiquitous, untethered, wireless computing should become widespread, and audio and gestural input devices should replace some of the functionality of the keyboard and mouse.

You should expect 3-D modeling and video editing for the masses, computer vision for robotic devices and capture facial expressions, and realistic rendering of difficult things like a human face, hair, and water. With any luck C++ will fall out of favor.

Ethical Issues

Graphics has had a tremendous affect on society. Things that affect society often lead to ethical and legal issues. For example, graphics are used in battles and their simulation, medical diagnosis, crime re-enactment, cartoons and films. The ethical role played by a computer graphicist in the use of graphics programs that may be used for these and other purposes is discussed and analyzed in the notes on Ethics.

More History of Computer Graphics

In the **1950's**, output were via teletypes, line printer, and Cathode Ray Tube (CRT). Using dark and light characters, a picture could be reproduced.

1950 : Ben Laposky created the first graphic images, an Oscilloscope, generated by an electronic (analog) machine. The image was produced by manipulating electronic beams and recording them onto high-speed film.

1951 : UNIVAC-I: the first general purpose commercial computer, crude hardcopy devices, and line printer pictures.

1951 : MIT - Whirlwind computer, the first to display real time video, and capable of displaying real time text and graphic on a large oscilloscope screen.

In the **1960's**, beginnings of modern interactive graphics, output are vector graphics and interactive graphics. One of the worst problems was the cost and inaccessibility of machines.

1960 : William Fetter coins the computer graphics to describe new design methods.

1961 : Steve Russel -- Spacewars, first video/computer game.

1963 : Douglas Englebart – first mouse

Ivan Sutherland – Sketchpad, interactive CG system, a man-machine graphical communication system, it features:

- pop-up menus
- constraint-based drawing
- hierarchical modeling
- utilized light pen for interaction

He formulated the ideas of using primitives, lines polygons, arcs, etc. and constraints on them; He developed the dragging, rubber banding and transforming algorithms; He introduced data structures for storing. He is considered the **founder of the computer graphics.**

1964 : William Fetter-- first computer model of a human figure.

1965 : Jack Bresenham – line-drawing algorithm

1968 : Tektronix – a special CRT, the direct-view storage tube, with keyboard and mouse, a simple computer interface for $15, 000, which made graphics affordable

Ivan Sutherland – first head-mounted display

1969 : John Warnock – area subdivision algorithm, hidden-surface algorithms

Bell Labs – first frame buffer containing 3 bits per pixel

In the early 1970's, output start using raster displays, graphics capability was still fairly chunky.

1972 : Nolan Kay Bushnell – Pong, video arcade game

1973 : John Whitney. Jr. and Gary Demos – "Westworld", first film with computer graphics

1974 : Edwin Catmuff – texture mapping and Z-buffer hidden-surface algorithm

James Blinn – curved surfaces, refinement of texture mapping

Phone Bui-Toung – specular highlighting

1975 : Martin Newell – famous CG teapot, using Bezier patches.

Benoit Mandelbrot – fractal/fractional dimension.

1976 : James Blinn – environment mapping and bump mapping.

1977 : Steve Wozniak -- Apple II, color graphics personal computer.

1979 : Roy Trubshaw and Richard Bartle – MUD, a multi-user dungeon/Zork.

In the **1980's** output are built-in raster graphics, bitmap image and pixel. Personal computers costs decrease drastically; trackball and mouse become the standard interactive devices.

1982 : Steven Lisberger – "Tron", first Disney movie which makes extensive use of 3-D computer graphics

Tom Brighman – "Morphing", first film sequence plays a female character which deforms and transforms herself into the shape of a lynx.

John Walkner and Dan Drake – AutoCAD

1983 : Jaron Lanier – "DataGlove", a virtual reality film features a glove installed with switches and sensors to detect hand motion.

1984 : Wavefron tech. – Polhemus, first 3D graphics software

1985 : Pixar Animation Studios – "Luxo Jr.", 1989, "Tin toy"

NES – Nintendo home game system

1987 : IBM – VGA, Video Graphics Array introduced

1989 : Video Electronics Standards Association (VESA) - SVGA, Super VGA formed

In the **1990's**, since the introduction of VGA and SVGA, personal computer could easily display photo-realistic images and movies. 3D image renderings are become the main advances and it stimulated cinematic graphics applications.

- **1990 :** Hanrahan and Lawson - Renderman
- **1991 :** Disney and Pixar – "Beauty and the Beast", CGI was widely used, Renderman systems provides fast, accurate and high quality digital computer effects.
- **1992 :** Silicon Graphics - OpenGL specification
- **1993 :**
- University of Illinois -- Mosaic, first graphic Web browser
- Steven Spielberg – "Jurassic Park" a successful CG fiction film.
- **1995 :**
- Buena Vista Pictures – "Toy Story", first full-length, computer-generated, feature film
- NVIDIA Corporation – GeForce 256, GeForce3(2001)
- **2003 :** ID Software – Doom graphics engine

CLASSIFICATION OF COMPUTER GRAPHICS

This is also called types of computer graphics. Computer Graphics has been classified into two categories according to the application domain and requirements. They are Passive and Interactive Computer graphics.

1. **Passive Computer Graphics :** This is also called Off-line graphics. Once the graphics program is developed, the user has no control over the display even if he wishes to change the display. Development takes place independently in Off-line mode. Example of passive graphics can be compared to static web page (Using HTML) where user has no control over the contents on the monitor. The screen will be static with no marquees flying on the screen or no advertisements changing or no color change on mouse movements etc.

   The displays are generally calligraphic in nature and are printed by line printers, plotters etc.

2. **Interactive Computer Graphics :** This is also called On-line graphics. User can dynamically control the display on the monitor. Displays are controlled by mouse, trackball, Joystick etc. This is termed as Interactive Computer Graphics (ICG) because the user can interact with the machine as per his requirements. ICG is the case in which user can dynamically control the picture contents, formats, sizes or the color on the display surface by means of interaction devices such as keyboards, light pen, mouse etc.

   Cartoons, special effects in movies (remember Dinosaurs of Jurassic Park), video games and dynamic web sites(Using dynamic HTML) are all making use of ICG.

   ICG affects our lives in a number of indirect ways. For example

   (*i*) Flight simulators helps us to train the pilots of our airplanes. These pilots spend a lot of time for their training not in a real aircraft but on the ground at the controls of a flight simulator. Flight simulator has many advantages over real aircraft for training purposes including safety, fuel saving and ability to familiarize the trainee with different aspects and technology of aircraft.

   (*ii*) Architects can explore alternative solutions to design problem with Interactive Graphics. Design programs like CAD help designers, engineers, draftsmen etc. to complete the tasks associated with hand drafting of designs easily and more efficiently.

   (*iii*) Micro-processor based video-game processors attached to home TV's

   (*iv*) Cartoons, Animation and special effects in movies and TV serials are all possible with the use of computer graphics.

COMPONENTS OF COMPUTER GRAPHICS

Interactive Computer Graphics consists of three components namely digital memory buffer, TV monitor and display controller. Using these components, we are able to see the output on the screen in form of pixels(picture elements). Following is the explanation of these components:

1. **Digital Memory Buffer :** This is the place where images or pictures are stored as an array (matrix of 0 and 1, 0 represents darkness and 1 represents image or picture). This is also called Frame Buffer. In today's terms, frame buffer is called V-RAM (Video RAM) and it helps to store the image in bit form. It helps to increase the speed of graphics (Sometimes we watch movies on our Computer system and the movie run slowly. System engineer is then called for. He comes and fits in V-RAM(in Mega bytes) into our system and the movie runs perfectly).
2. **TV Monitor :** Monitor helps us to view the display and they make use of CRT technology (Cathode Ray Tube) will be discussed in Output devices. Raster scan and random scan monitors are also discussed in graphics devices section.
3. **Display Controller :** It is an interface between Digital Memory Buffer and TV Monitor. Its job is to pass the contents of Frame buffer to the monitor. This passing has to be fast for steady display on the monitor (depending on the material of the system). The image must be passed repeatedly to the monitor to maintain a steady picture on the screen. The display controller reads each successive byte of data from the FB memory and converts 0's and 1's into corresponding video signal. This signal is then fed to the TV monitor to produce a black and white picture on the screen. In today's terms, display controller is recognized as display card and one of our choices can be VGA card with a resolution of 640×480. (Display controllers are also capable of displaying image in colors and will be discussed in colored display section). Several graphics systems have been designed this way.

Fig. 1.1 *Frame buffer (bit Pattern of 0 & 1)*

Throughout the book certain questions will again and again be asked or encountered and they are very important to be discussed right now. The questions are like:

1. How to display straight lines and curved lines?
2. Why speed is important for graphics displays?
3. How pictures are made to grow or shrink on the screen?
4. What happens if the picture is too large to fit in the screen?
5. Can we directly draw on screen?
6. How is analog form of data converted into digital form so that the computer system can understand it?

My Professor would ask these questions regularly in class and once these questions were clear to us, graphics became an easy subject for us.

Ans 1. Straight lines can be drawn using algorithms that have to be implemented in any programming language. There are two methods of drawing lines (as we will study later) DDA (Digital Differential Analyzer) and Bresenham's line algorithms. These algorithms have been used to generate lines.

Curves can be drawn by breaking them into several straight lines. Then the algorithm of straight line drawing can be applied to these straight lines. Curves can also be generated if function of the curve is known or curve fitting techniques are also used to generate curves.

Ans 2. Speed is important because we are talking of Interactive graphics and in this type of graphics, speed of transfer of entire picture contents from FB to monitor must very fast Also we need fast responses in ICG so speed is important. A slow graphics system will not be acceptable even to a small child who would want his cartoons to be at the best possible speed. A powerful processor can do the trick aided with additional V-RAM in the system.

Ans 3. Pictures can be made to grow and shrink according to our needs using mathematical techniques like

- Co-ordinate Geometry
- Matrix method
- Trigonometric functions

Using these techniques, various 2-D or 3-D transformations are possible. They are:

1. Changing the scale (scaling to magnify or shrink)
2. Shifting the position (translating to move to new position on the screen)
3. Rotation (rotating the object by some angle)

These transformations are achieved through equations implemented in algorithms and hardware. Transformation like shearing and reflection are also important in computer graphics.

Programs for scaling, translation and rotation are given in this book.

Ans 4. It sometimes happens that image is too large for the screen. We will study the concepts of Clipping and Windowing in this regard. Clipping is the process in which the big whole picture is chopped into small portions and only a portion inside the window is displayed. Clipping divide the picture into visible and invisible parts and rejects invisible parts and displays them.

We will study Cohen Sutherland and Sutherland Hodgeman algorithms for clipping of lines and polygons respectively.

Ans 5. Yes, we can directly draw on screen. Haven't we seen cricket live coverage and seen Geoffrey Boycott or Sunil Gavasker or Ravi Shastri drawing directly on the screen when they mark the fielder or the trajectory of the ball. Devices like light pen, mouse, tablets etc. helps us to draw on the screen directly.

Light pen, mouse or tablets will be covered later in Interactive devices.

Ans 6. Analog to digital conversion has to be performed since the computer is a discrete digital device, while most data in the world outside the computer is continuous. The data must be therefore converted to enable the computer to use it. The conversion of continuous analog data to discrete data is called analog to digital conversion or simply A/D conversion.

The computer graphics programmer must have some knowledge of A/D conversion because many graphics input devices are analog devices and A/D conversion can affect the accuracy of data collected even while exhibiting a high degree of degree of precision. Typically, A/D conversion is performed either by hardware devices incorporated in the computer's input circuitry or by means of firmware that directly interfaces with computer's input circuitry.

GRAPHICS PRIMITIVES

Regardless of the differences in display devices, most graphic systems offer a similar set of graphic primitive commands (although the form and syntax may differ from system to system). The first primitive command is that for drawing a line segment. These primitives are widely used in CKS and CORE graphics packages. While a segment may be specified by its two endpoints, it is often the case that the segments drawn will be connected end to end. Primitive commands were very important when Random scan was being in graphics systems but now in Raster scan devices, primitives are no longer used.

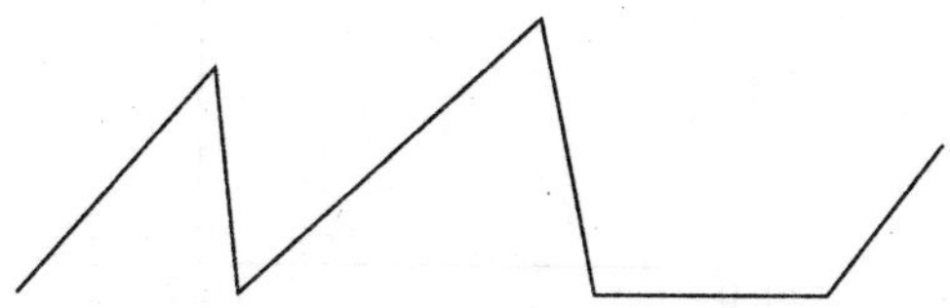

Fig. 1.2

LINEABS (X, Y) is called an absolute line command because the actual co-ordinates of the final positions are passed. Most of the graphics packages offer this line primitive. Even in C language, definition of this primitive has been picked up. **Lineto (*x*, *y*)** in C language refers to LINEABS (*x*, *y*) only. This command is used to pass the final co-ordinates of the point.

LINEREL (DX, DY) is called relative line command because in this command we only indicate how far to move from the current position.

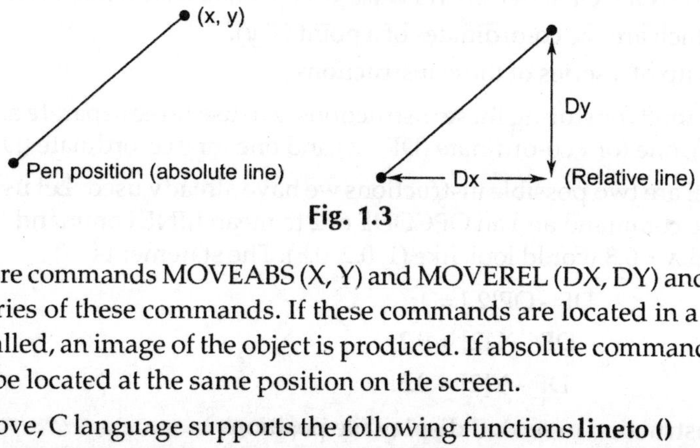

Fig. 1.3

We have two more commands MOVEABS (X, Y) and MOVEREL (DX, DY) and we can construct a line drawing by series of these commands. If these commands are located in a function then each time a function is called, an image of the object is produced. If absolute commands are used then the house will always be located at the same position on the screen.

As discussed above, C language supports the following functions **lineto ()**

For example **lineto(1, 1)** draws a line from current pen position to (1, 1).

In C language, there are built -in functions like :

```
linerel (Int x, Int y)
moverel (Int x, Int y)
setlinestyle ()
```

And their definitions have been taken from Graphics primitives.

Graphics primitive commands are stored in **Display file**. Display file is a file storing all primitive commands and when this file is interpreted, visual image is displayed on the screen. We need to study normalized co-ordinates, display file and interpreter for a better understanding of the system.

NORMALISED DEVICE CO-ORDINATES

Different display devices may have different screen sizes as measured in pixels. If we wish our program to be device independent, we should specify co-ordinates in some units other than pixel and use the interpreter to convert the co-ordinates to the appropriate pixel for the particular display we are using.

Device independent units are called normalized device co-ordinates.

Fig. 1.4

Screen measure 1 unit wide, 1 unit height

DISPLAY FILE & ITS STRUCTURE

Each display file command contains two constituents:

1. Operation code (OPCODE) which indicates what kind of command it is (Example Line, move)
2. Operands which are the co-ordinates of a point (x, y).

Display is made up of a series of these instructions.

One possible method for storing these instructions is to use three separate arrays: one for operation code (DF – OP), one for *x* co-ordinate (DF – X) and one for *y* co-ordinate (DF – Y).

MOVE and LINE are two possible instructions we have already used. Let us define an OPCODE of 1 to mean a move command and an OPCODE of 2 to mean LINE command. Then a command to move to X = 0.2 and X = 0.8 would look like (1, 0.2, 0.8). The statements

DF – OP[2.] = 1;

DF – X [2] = 0.2;

DF – Y[2] = 0.8;

will store this instruction in second display file position.

DF-OP	DF-X	DF-Y
1	0.2	0.8

THE DISPLAY FILE INTERPRETER

Line and Move commands store their information in display file. We then use information in the file to create the image. The display file will contain the necessary information to construct the picture. Saving instructions such as these usually takes less storage than saving the picture itself.

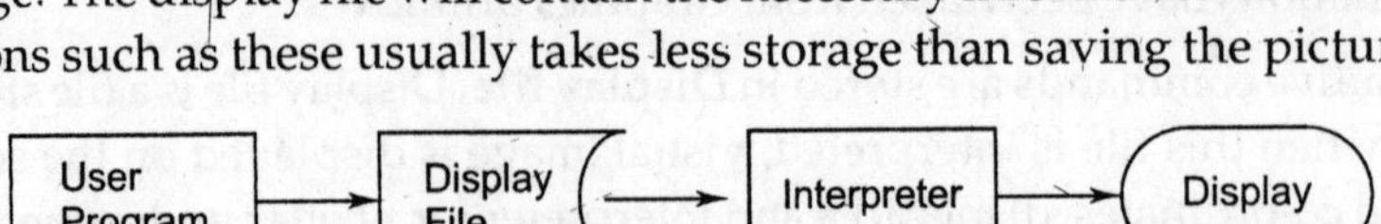

Fig. 1.5

Graphic file interpreter serves an interface between our graphic program and the display device. Interpreter may be thought of as a machine which executes these instructions. The result is a visual image.

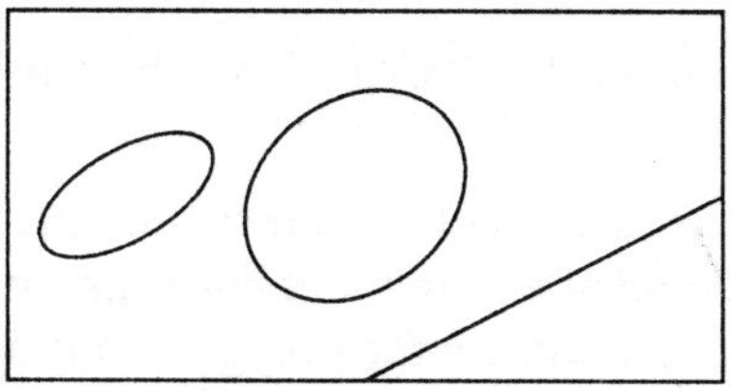

Fig. 1.6

There are many more Graphics primitive commands other than Line and Move. They are Text, Linestyle and polygon primitives. Their detail is given below.

TEXT PRIMITIVE

Another primitive operation is that of text output. Most graphic displays involve textual as well as graphical output data, labels (giving scale values etc.), instructions, commands, values, messages and so on may be presented with the image.

The primitive command involved here is the output of a character or a string of characters. The character themselves may be drawn by either the dot matrix or the stroke method. Their patterns are copied from memory into frame buffer or created by special character generation hardware.

Ex. Text ('My first graphic program') would output this on screen.

LINE STYLE PRIMITIVE

Many display devices offer a selection of line style. Lines may be continuous or they may be dashed or dotted. One may be able to select the color of the line or its intensity or thickness. It is desirable to be able to change the line style in the middle of the display process. We therefore need a display file command for changing line style. When the interpreter encounters such a command, the line style is changed and all subsequent lines are drawn in this new style.

For example, SETLINESTYLE (2) would give us broken line

SETLINESTYLE (0) would give us solid line.

Other options are

0 Solid line
1 Dotted line
2 Broken line
3 Dashed line

POLYGON PRIMITIVE

So far discussion has dealt with only the lines. The world might seem rather dull if it were made out of straight lines. How interesting is the world of patterns, colors and shading. Unfortunately, much of the early graphics dealt with line drawings only. This was because the available devices (DVST,

Plotters etc.) were line drawing devices. Raster display can display solid patterns and objects with no greater effort than that involved in showing their outlines. Coloring and shading is possible with raster technology.

We introduce new graphic primitive, the Polygon. We shall discuss what polygons are and how to represent them?

We wish to be able to represent a surface. One basic surface primitive is a polygon, a many sided figure. A polygon may be represented as a number of line segments connected end to end to form a closed figure. The line segments that make up the polygon boundary are called sides or edges. The endpoints of the sides are called the polygon's vertices. The simplest polygon is the triangle, having three sides and three vertex points.

Polygon can be divided into two classes: Concave and Convex. A Convex polygon is a polygon such that for any two points inside the polygon, all points on the line segment connecting them are also inside the Polygon. A concave polygon is the one which is not convex. A triangle is always convex and so are the shapes shown below :

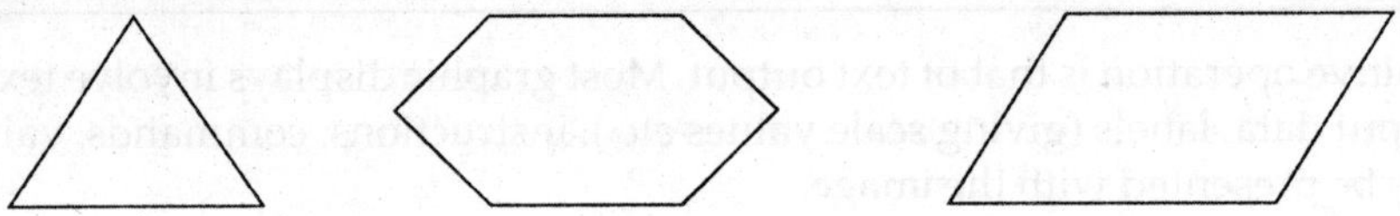

Fig. 1.7

Some concave polygon shapes are shown below:

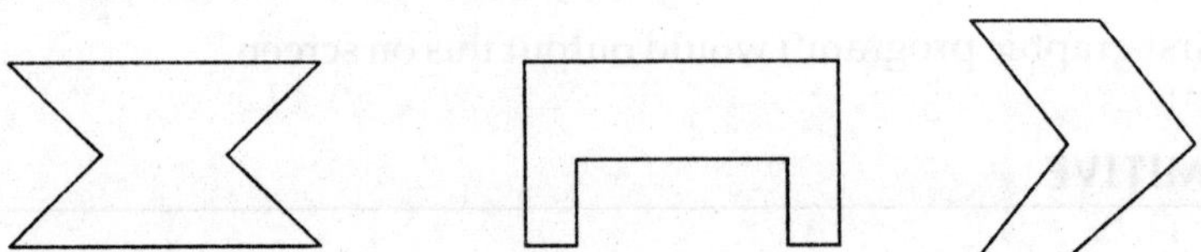

Fig. 1.8

POLYGON REPRESENTATION

If we want to add polygons to our graphics system, we must first decide how to represent them.

Some graphics, devices have polygon drawing primitive to directly draw polygon shape. There is trapezoid primitive also and a polygon can be drawn as a series of trapezoids.

Now the question is what should a polygon look like in a display file?

We introduce a new command into the display file. This new command will tell us how many sides are in the polygon so that we'll know how many of the line commands are part of the polygon. Upon interpretation this new command will act like a move to correctly position the pen for drawing the first side.

Let's talk about the Operation code 3 or greater. We can use these codes to indicate polygons. The value of the operation code will indicate the number of sides in a polygon. The X and Y variables of the polygon will be the co-ordinates of the point where the first side to be drawn begins. Polygons are closed figures so it will also be the final endpoint of the last side to be drawn.

Let's work out an example of a polygon given below and look at its display file

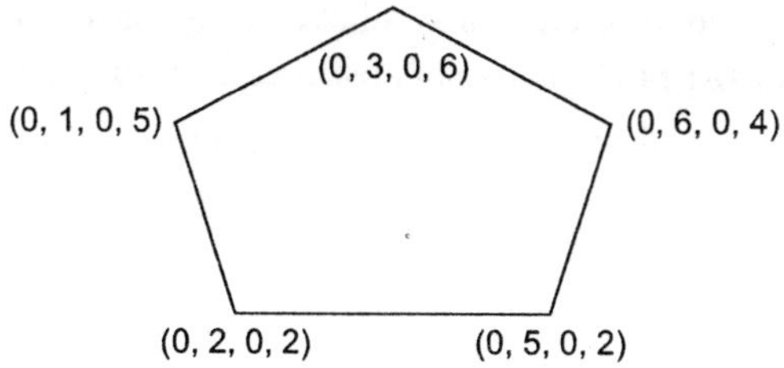

Fig. 1.9

The display file for the given polygon is

DF-OP	*DF-X*	*DF-Y*
5	0.2	0.2
2	0.5	0.2
2	0.6	0.4
2	0.3	0.6
2	0.1	0.5
2	0.2	0.2

ENTERING POLYGON IN DISPLAY FILE

When we say entering polygons we mean algorithms for entering polygons into display file. Information required to be specified in polygon case is number of sides and the co-ordinates of vertex points of a polygon to be drawn. Arrays are used to pass the co-ordinates of all vertices to the routine.

Following is the algorithm for entering the polygon into the display file using absolute commands.

ALGORITHM

Algorithm PolyAbs for entry of an absolute polygon into the display file Variables AB, AC are arrays containing vertices.

```
Global variables penX, penY the current pen position.
Local variable I for stepping through the polygon sides.
Start
{
if N < 3 then give error 'Polygon size error'
//*Enter polygon instructions
penX = AB[N] ;
penY = AC[N] ;
//*Enter information in display file
Display-file-enter(N);
//*Enter the instructions for the sides
For I = 1 to N do Lineabs(AB[I],AC[I]) ;
Return,
End;
}
```

Similarly programs can be developed using relative line commands to represent polygons. C language has got functions to support the use of absolute and relative line commands.

CORE and **GKS** Graphics Systems are some of the market prevalent products and support these primitives operations.

Graphics Kernel

The **Graphical Kernel System (GKS)** was the first ISO standard for low level computer graphics, introduced in 1977. GKS provides a set of low-level drawing features for two-dimensional line and vector graphics. The calls are designed to be portable across different programming languages, graphics devices and uses, so that applications written to use GKS will be readily portable to many platforms and devices.

A main developer and promoter of the GKS was professor José Luis Encarnação, formerly director of the Fraunhofer Institute for Computer Graphics (IGD) in Darmstadt, Germany.

GRAPHICAL INPUT/OUTPUT DEVICE

Graphical Interactve Input Devices

Data has to be passed on to the computer system so that it can be processed and presented to the user in some format. Same is the case with Computer graphics. Data has to be entered into the system via some input device (Keyboard, mouse, light pen etc) so that it can be manipulated by the programs and images presented to the user on some output device (Monitor or printer).

Any device that allows information from outside the computer to be communicated to the computer is considered an input device. Some common graphical input devices are:

Alphanumeric Keyboards : This is an input device. A standard known as ASCII has been developed to allow computer to encode keyboard characters. Whatever we key in is translated by the keyboard translation program in a machine readable form so that it can be understood by the system.

Track Balls : A track ball uses a hard sphere to control cursor movement. The ball can be rotated by hand in any direction. The trackball translates the sphere's direction and speed of rotation into a digital signal used to control the cursor.

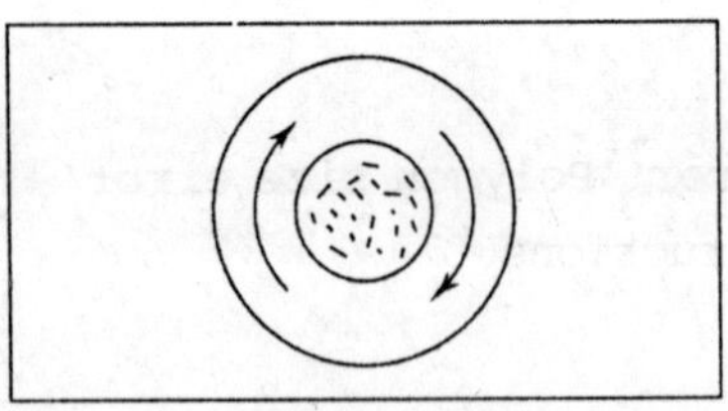

Fig. 1.10

Joystick : It is the most important input device used to play video games. A joystick uses a lever to control the position and speed with which the joystick is moved. This gets translated into digital signals that are sent to the computer to control the cursor movement.

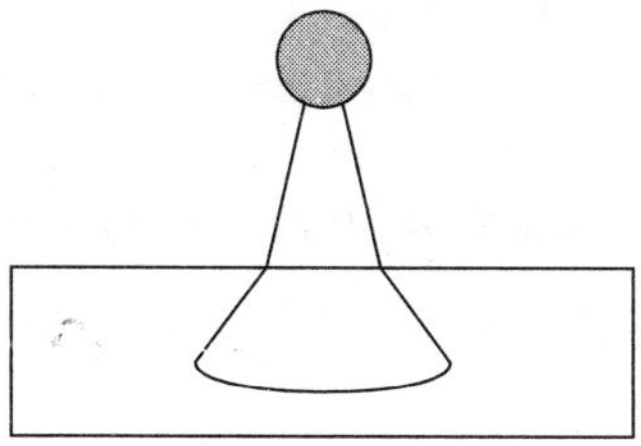

Fig. 1.11

Mouse : DOUG ENGELBART developed mouse as an alternative to keyboard in 1960's. Mouse has three buttons. When user presses one of the buttons, the mouse marks the place on the screen. It has a ball that is pressed against he mouse pad.

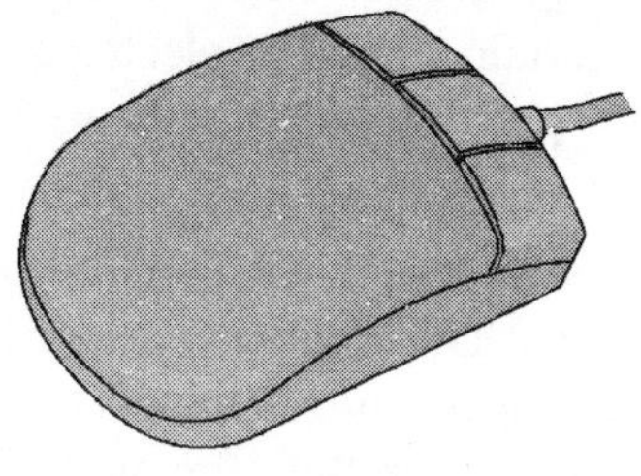

Fig. 1.12

The joystick, trackball, mouse etc are transducers that convert a graphic system user's movements into changes in voltage. **Transducer** is a device that converts energy from one form to other.

Light Pen : It is a pointing device that can be used to choose a displayed menu option. The pen consists of a photocell placed in a small tube. Light pen is very useful in graphics. The user at a CAD terminal can draw directly on the screen with the light pen.

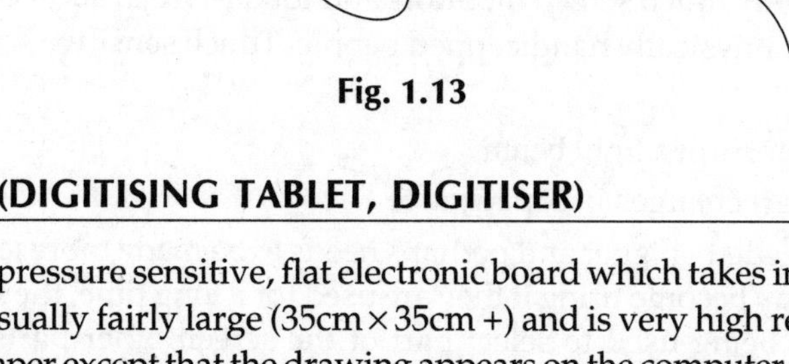

Fig. 1.13

GRAPHICS TABLET (DIGITISING TABLET, DIGITISER)

The graphics tablet is a pressure sensitive, flat electronic board which takes input from a pen or puck. The board or tablet is usually fairly large (35cm × 35cm +) and is very high resolution. It is much like drawing on a piece of paper except that the drawing appears on the computer screen rather than on the tablet. The position of the pen or puck is detected by the computer and the x-y coordinates transmitted to the screen. Some models are capable of making wider or narrower lines depending on whether greater or lesser force is applied to the pen. More advanced models also often have macro buttons and other buttons that duplicate menu bar commands.

This device is useful for people who don't know how to type or for artists etc who want to draw as they would on paper. Drawings can be placed on the tablet and then traced onto the screen. Digitizers, are based on the principle of an electric or magnetic field that is generated through one component (the pen) and detected through the other component (the tablet). There are several types:

1. Touch-sensitive – consists of a pen and a touch sensitive surface using a matrix of wires in the tablet.
2. Sonic digitizers – sound impulses detected by two microphone sensors on the tablet.
3. Light-detector digitizer – detects interruptions in a matrix of light beams.
4. Magnetic-field sensors – detects changes in the magnetic field.

Digitizer or digitizing tablets are flat boards that have a grid of interconnecting wires just below the surface. They also have either an electronic 'pen' or 'puck' that can be moved round the surface. The pen stylus is more natural, but the puck offer the advantage of having upto four or more buttons that can be programmed to perform certain tasks. The electronic circuitry of the digitizing tablet can tell exactly where you are holding the pen in relation to the rest of the board by transmitting pulses between the pen and the wired grid.

The computer then translates the location of the pen on the board into numerical coordinates that represents x and y values on the screen. The x value represents the horizontal position and the y value represents the vertical position. The resolution tablets range from 1000 to 10000 lines per inch, giving very accurate position to the computer. Both the puck or pen stylus has buttons that can be pressed to indicate a particular command to the computer.

What makes tablets popular as pointing devices is the absolute positioning of the cursor. With a tablet, there is a direct relationship to the movement on screen, so we can place the puck or pen on the lower right corner of the tablet, the cursor appears on the lower right corner of the screen. The only disadvantage to digitizing tablets is the desktop space they require. Also they can not be used to tracing natural pictures into the computers.

Touch Screen/panels : These are devices which allow the user to directly activate data by touching the screen. Touch is a more intuitive interface for users who are not familiar with computers. In public applications, users have little training in the technology and are simply instructed to 'touch your selection.' This has wide user appeal. They have many applications in museums, shops, restaurants, street maps etc. as touch systems are best used for selection of pre-programmed information.

It is also possible to buy touch screen monitors and touch-screen add-on kits for PCs – useful for young children and the physically handicapped people. Touch sensitive screen can work in several ways:

1. The finger can interrupt a light beam
2. The pad can detect changes in capacitance

A different GUI is needed - bigger and perhaps needs to be made more iconic. The drawbacks are that moving the arm may become tiring if they are used for a long time, the screen may become dirty and when the hand is being used to select part of the screen other parts may be obscured. The advantages are an intuitive interface, flexibility in the information provided, an ability to include graphics, signs and symbols and usually a rugged and reliable interface.

As the name implies, touch panels allow displayed objects or screen positions to be selected with the touch of a finger. A typical application of touch panels is for the selection of processing options that are implemented with graphical icons. Some systems, such as the plasma panels are designed with touch screens. Other systems can be adapted for touch input by fitting a transparent device with a touch sensing mechanism over the video monitor screen. Touch input can be recorded using optical, electrical, or acoustical methods. Optical touch panels employ a line of infrared light-emitting diodes **(LEDs)** along one vertical edge and along one horizontal edge of the frame. The opposite vertical and horizontal edges contain light detectors. These detectors are used to record which beams are interrupted when the panel is touched. The two crossing beams that are interrupted identify the horizontal and vertical coordinates of the screen position selected.

Positions can be selected with an accuracy of about ¼ inch. With closely spaced **LEDs**, it is possible to draw two horizontal or two vertical beams simultaneously. In this case, an average position between the two interrupted beams is recorded. The LEDs operate at infrared frequencies, so that the light is not visible to a user.

An electrical touch panel is constructed with two transparent plates separated by a small distance. One of the plates is coated with a conducting material, and the other plate is coated with a resistive material. When the outer plate is touched, it is fed into contact with the inner plate. This contact cracks a voltage drop across the massive plate that is converted to the coordinate values of the selected *screen* position. In acoustical touch panels, high-frequency sound waves are generated in the horizontal and vertical directions across a glass plate. Touching the screen causes part of each wave to be reflected from the finger to the emitters. The screen position at the point of contact is calculated from a measurement of the time interval between the transmission of each wave and its reflection to the emitter.

IMAGE SCANNER

The most common device used to input images into a computer is a scanner. Scanners are similar to copy machines, except they store the image electronically instead of transferring it into another piece of paper. There are many different type of scanners from hand held units that look like a mouse to drum scanners that can fill a entire room.

Most scanners expose the image to a bright light. Then electronic receptors called charged coupled device (CCD)sensors pick up that light and convert it to electronic pulses. Those pulses get translated to the numbers. There are black and white as well as color scanners. The resolution of scanners ranges from 100 dpi to 2000 dpi and beyond.

Voice Systems

Speech recognizers are used in some graphics workstations as input devices to accept voice commands. The voice-system input can be used to initiate graphics operations or to enter data. These systems operate by matching an input against a predefined dictionary of words and phrase called the vocabulary of the system.

A dictionary (vocabulary) is set up for a particular operator by having the operator speak the command words to be used into the system. Each word is spoken several times and the system analyzes the word and establishes a frequency pattern for that word in the dictionary along with the corresponding function to be performed.

Later, when a voice command is given, the system searches the dictionary for a frequency-pattern match. Voice input is typically spoken into a microphone mounted on a headset. The microphone is designed to minimize input of other background sounds. If a different operator is to use the system, the dictionary must be reestablished with that operator's voice patterns. Voice systems have some advantage over other input devices, since the attention of the operator does not have to be switched from one device to another to enter a command.

The biggest disadvantage is that voice systems are user-dependent while the need is for systems that are not user-dependent. For example, if one of the employee working on the voice system leaves the company then that system will have to be either bought again or programmed again which is a big bottleneck in the way.

GRAPHIC OUTPUT/DISPLAY DEVICES

Cathode Ray Tube(CRT)

The quality of displayed image is very important in most applications of computer graphics. CRT was the only available device which was capable of converting computer's electrical signals into variable images at high speeds.

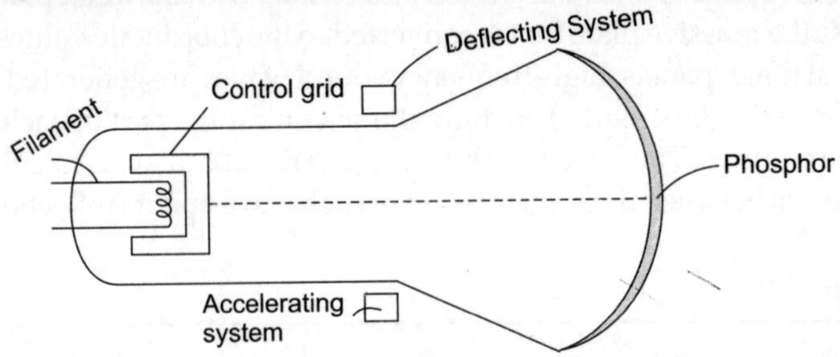

Fig. 1.14

The face of the CRT is more or less flat and is coated on the inside with phosphor which glows when electron beam strikes it.

A beam of electrons *i.e.*, cathode rays is emitted by electron gun and passes through focusing and deflection system that directs the beam on a specified point on the phosphor coated screen.

CRT is best suited for interactive computer graphics.

WHY PHOSPHORS ARE USED

The phosphors used in a graphic display are normally chosen for color characteristics and persistence. Generally, persistence measured as the time for the brightness to drop to 1/10 of it initial values, should last about 100 msec or less, allowing refresh at 30 hertz rates.

The phosphors should also possess a no. of other attributes: Small grain size for added resolution, high efficiency in terms of electric energy converted to light and resistance to burning under prolonged excitation. There are many different phosphors which have been produced to improve performance using various compounds of Zinc, Cadmium & Calcium.

DIRECT VIEW STORAGE TUBE

Some devices were developed where refreshing is not important. DVST is CRT with some modifications *i.e.*, storage capability. Whatever picture or image displayed is stored on the tube.

Bad points: Slow & difficult
Quality deteriorates with time

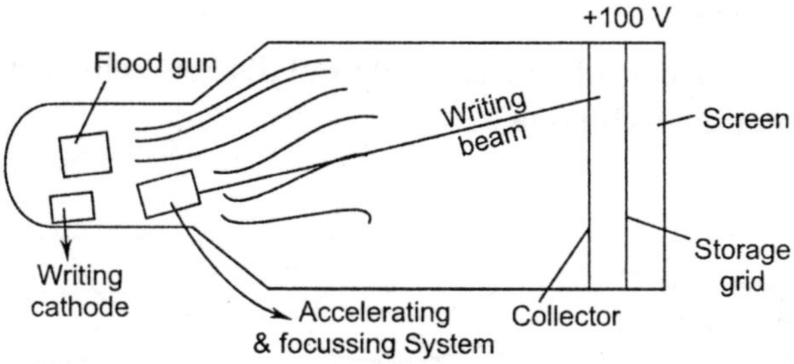

Fig. 1.15

DVST behaves like CRT with extremely long persistence. A line written on the screen will remain visible for up to an hour before it fades away from sight.

It has a similar focussing & accelerating system but difference is that beam doesn't white directly on the screen but on the storage grid as positive charged pattern. Storage grid is wire mesh grid coated with dielectric material (thin Al coating).

Function of collector is for smoothing purposes (unwanted electrons are removed).

RASTER AND RANDOM DISPLAY (MONITORS)

Raster Monitors/Displays

Depending on different types of display devices, there are different displays possible like Raster scan and Random scan. Earlier display devices use to support random scan as it took less memory because we were not interested in all the pixels of the image. But with cost of systems and memory going down, raster scan is used now-a-days. We will be referring to Raster scan in our book.

Computer graphics images are composed of a finite number of pixels. A display with good resolution might have 1000 divisions in X and Y directions. The screen would then have 1000 X 1000 or 1 million pixels. Each pixel requires at least one bit of intensity information, light or dark and further bits are need if shades of gray or different colors are desired. Thus if we actually store the information for each pixel in computer memory, a lot of memory would be required. This is in fact, what is done in some RASTER GRAPHIC DISPLAYS. The portion of memory used to hold pixels is called frame buffer. The memory is usually scanned and displayed by DMA *i.e.*, special hardware independent of central processor (leaving the processor free for generation of images).

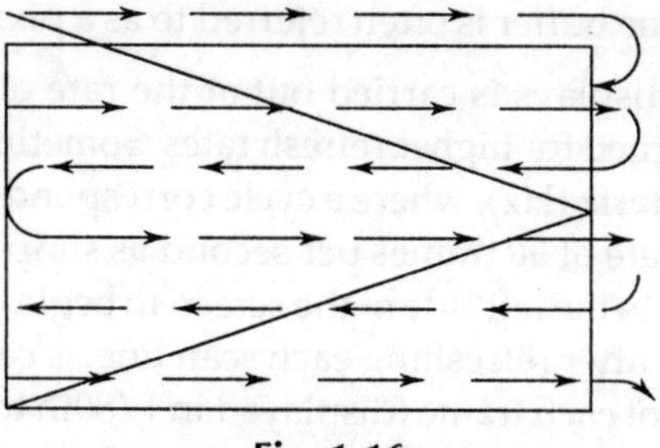

Fig. 1.16

The term RASTER is a synonym for "matrix" therefore a raster scan CRT scans a matrix with electron beam. The rate at which electron beam scans the surface of CRT is often directly related to the frequency of local line voltage.

A raster CRT device can be considered as a matrix of discrete cells each of which can be made bright thus it is a point plotting technique.

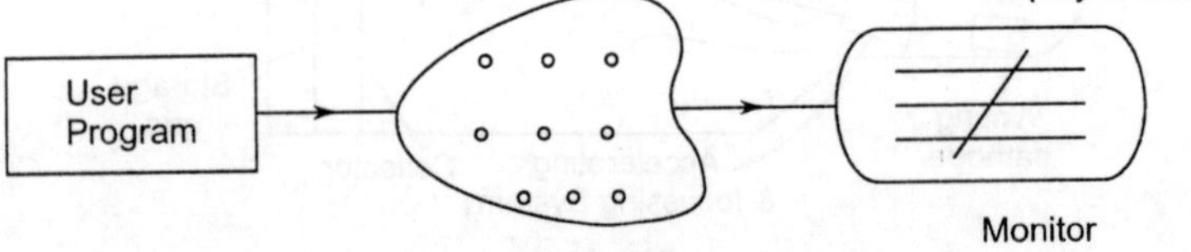

Fig. 1.17

In the raster display, Frame buffer may be examined to determine what is currently being displayed. Surfaces as well as lines may be displayed on raster scan display devices. The raster display can also display color images.

The most common type of graphics monitor employing a CRT is the **raster-scan** display, based on television technology. In a raster-scan system, the electron beam is swept across the screen, one row at a time from top to bottom. As the electron beam moves across each row, the beam intensity is turned on and off to create a pattern of illuminated spots. Picture definition is stored in a memory area called the refresh buffer or frame buffer.

This memory area holds the set of intensity values for all the screen points. Stored intensity values are then retrieved from the refresh buffer and "painted" on the screen one row (scan line) at a time. Each screen point is referred to as a pixel (shortened form of picture element). The capability of a raster-scan system to store intensity information for each screen point makes it well suited for the realistic display of scenes containing subtle shading and color patterns. Home television sets and printers are examples of other systems using raster-scan methods. Intensity range for pixel positions depends on the capability of the raster system. In a simple black-and-white system, each screen point is either on or off, so only one bit per pixel is needed to control the intensity of screen positions. For a bi-level system, a bit value of 1 indicates that the electron beam is to be turn on at that position, and a value of **0** indicates that the beam intensity is to be off.

Additional bits are needed when color and intensity variations can be displayed. Up to **24** bits per pixel are included in high-quality systems, which can require several megabytes of storage for the frame buffer, depending on the resolution of the system. **A** system with **24** bits per pixel and a screen resolution of **1024 X 1024** requires 3 megabytes of storage for the frame buffer. On a black-and-white system with one bit per pixel, the frame buffer is commonly called a bitmap. For Systems with multiple bits per pixel, the frame buffer is often referred to as a pixmap.

Refreshing on raster-scan displays is carried out at the rate of 60 to 80 frames per second, although some systems are designed for higher refresh rates. Sometimes, refresh rates are described in units of cycles per second, or Hertz (Hz), where a cycle corresponds to one frame. Using these units, we would describe a refresh rate of ***60*** frames per second as simply 60 Hz. At the end of each scan line, the electron beam returns to the left side of the screen to begin displaying the next scan line. The return to the left of the screen, after refreshing each scan line, is called the horizontal retrace of the electron beam. And at the end of each frame (displayed in 1/80th to 1/60th of a second), the electron beam returns (vertical retrace) to the top left comer of the screen to begin the next frame.

On some raster-scan systems (and in **TV** sets), each frame is displayed in two passes using an **interlaced** refresh procedure. In the first pass, the beam sweeps across every other scan line from top to bottom. Then after the vertical retrace, the beam sweeps out the remaining scan lines. Interlacing of the scan lines in this way allows us to see the entire scene displayed in one-half the time it would have taken to sweep across all the lines at once from top to bottom.

Interlacing is primarily used with slower refreshing rates. On an older, **30** frame per-second, non interlaced display, for instance, some flicker is noticeable. But with interlacing, each of the two passes can be accomplished in 1/60th of a second, which brings the refresh rate nearer to **60** frames per second. This is an effective technique for avoiding flicker, providing that adjacent scan lines contain similar display information.

Random Monitors/Displays

When operated as a random-scan display unit, a CRT has the electron beam directed only to the parts of the screen where a picture is to be drawn. Random scan monitors draw a picture one line at a time and for this reason are also referred to as vector displays (or stroke-writing or calligraphic displays). The component lines of a picture can be drawn and refreshed by a random-scan system in any specified order.

A pen plotter operates in a similar way and is an example of a random-scan, hard-copy device. Refresh rate on a random-scan system depends on the number of lines to be displayed. **Picture** definition is now stored as a **set of line drawing commands** in an area of memory referred to as the **refresh display file.** Sometimes the refresh display file is called the display list, display program, or simply the **refresh buffer.**

To display a specified picture, the system cycles through the set of commands in the display file, drawing each component line in turn. After all line drawing commands have been processed, the system cycles back to the first line command in the list. Random-scan displays are designed to draw all the component lines of a picture **30 to 60 times** each second. High quality vector systems are capable of handling approximately 100,000 "short" lines at this refresh rate. When a small set of lines is to be displayed, each refresh cycle is delayed to avoid refresh rates greater than 60 frames per second. Otherwise, faster refreshing could bum out the phosphor.

Random-scan systems are designed for line drawing applications and cannot display realistic shaded scenes. Devices such as DVST, plasma panel etc support only line drawing. They don't support for solid areas which can be constructed on raster displays. Such line drawing devices are calligraphic displays.

Since picture definition is stored as a set of line drawing instructions and not as a set of intensity values for all screen points, vector (random) displays generally have higher resolution than raster systems. Also, vector displays produce smooth line drawings because the CRT beam directly follows the line path. **A raster system, in contrast,** produces **jagged** lines that are plotted as the point sets.

Difference between Raster and Random displays : The difference between raster and random display is that raster display gives a realistic image and is not confined to just line or calligraphic drawings. Any kind of graphics can be designed using raster displays. Vector (random) displays generally have higher resolution than raster systems as we can pass primitive commands directly. For example if we have to draw a line, raster would print the pixels of the line row by row on each scan line but in random display line is directly drawn from the current pen position to the final co-ordinates passed. Also, vector displays produce smooth line drawings because the CRT beam directly follows the line path. **A raster system, in contrast,** produces **jagged** lines that are plotted as the point sets.

Random	*Raster*
Restricted to engineering, line drawing applications	Stores intensity information for each screen point so well suited for real life applications which include shading and coloring
Doesn't use interlacing	Uses interlacing
Higher resolution	Lower resolution
More expensive	Less expensive
Uses monochrome or beam penetration type	Uses monochrome or shadow mask type
Image is displayed by steering the beam along the vectors	Image is displayed by scanning the whole display area
Editing is easy	Editing is difficult
Refresh rate depends directly on picture complexity	Refresh rate independent of picture complexity

COLORED DISPLAYS

The world would look so dull if there were no colors or if the quality of colors is not good. Earlier graphics applications were developed in black and white but with the development in technology and colored monitors becoming popular, graphics applications are now being developed using colored displays.

A CRT monitor displays color pictures by using a combination of phosphors that emit different-colored light. By combining the emitted light from the different phosphors, a range of colors can be generated. The two basic techniques for producing color displays with a CRT are the **beam-penetration method and the shadow-mask method.**

There are two ways of getting colored displays:

1. Beam penetration color display
2. Shadow mask color display

The normal CRT can create image of a single color (black and white) due to limitation of its phosphor.

A colored CRT for line drawing displays has been developed and it uses a multi layer (RBG) phosphor and achieves color display.

1. Beam Penetration Colored Display

The beam-penetration method for displaying color pictures has been used with random-scan monitors. Beam penetration colored display makes use of CRT but with multi layer phosphor. The normal CRT can create images of single color due to limitation of phosphor. A color CRT device for live drawing display has been developed and it uses a multi layer phosphor and achieves color control by modulating a normally constant parameter, namely the **"beam accelerating potential"**.

The beam penetration CRT is similar to normal CRT's, the only unusual component is the multi layer phosphor in which a layer of red phosphor is deposited behind the initial layer of green phosphor. If the accelerating potential is increased, the velocity of the beam striking the phosphor is greater and as a result the beam penetrates into green phosphor, increasing the green component or the light output. When a fairly low potential electron beam strikes the tube face, it excites only the red phosphor and the therefore produces a red trace.

Two layers of phosphor, usually red and green, are coated onto the inside of the CRT screen, and the displayed color depends on how far the electron beam penetrates into the phosphor layers. A beam of slow electrons excites only the outer **red** layer. A beam of very fast electrons penetrates through the **red** layer and excites the inner green layer. At intermediate beam speeds, combinations of red and green light are emitted to show two additional colors, orange and yellow. The speed of the electrons, and hence the screen color at any point, is controlled by the beam-acceleration voltage. Beam penetration has been an inexpensive way to produce color in random-scan monitors, but only four colors are possible, and the quality of pictures is not as good as with other methods.

In this way a limited range of colors *i.e.*, red, orange, yellow and green can be generated.

Advantages : The biggest advantage is that it is at half cost of shadow mask and its resolution is better.

Disadvantage : Biggest disadvantage is that change of color takes time which doesn't suit interactive graphics at all.

2. Shadow Mask Colour Display

In this display, there are three electron guns, one for each of three primary colors *i.e.*, red, green and blue. The electron guns are frequently arranged in a triangular pattern called delta corresponding to a similar triangular pattern of red, green and blue phosphor dots on the face of the CRT.

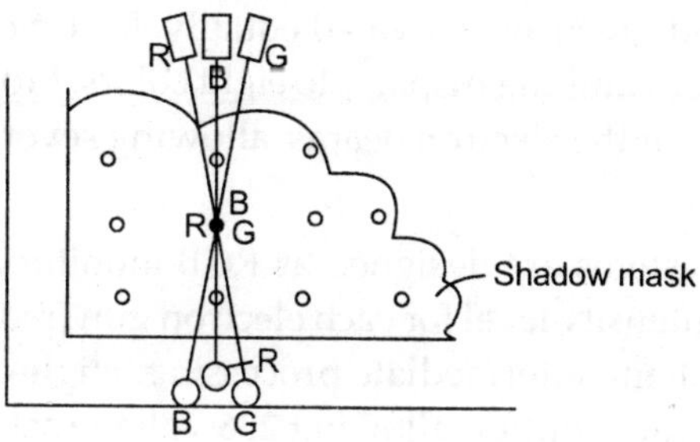

Fig. 1.18

To ensure that individual electron guns excite the correct phosphor dots (*e.g.*, red gun excites only red phosphor dot), a perforated metal grid is placed between the electron guns and the face of the CRT. This is the shadow mask (the perforations in the shadow mask are arranged in the same triangular pattern as phosphor dots).

Note : Distance between perforations is called pitch.

The color guns are arranged so that the individual beams converge and intersect at the shadow mask. Upon passing through the hole in the shadow mask the red beam, for *e.g.*, is prevented or masked from intersecting either the green or blue phosphor dot. It can only intersect the red phosphor dot.

By varying the strength of electron beam for each individual primary color, different shades can be combined into a large number of colors for each pixel. Uses much wider range of colors.

It is used in colored TVs and gives us a large number of colors as compared to beam penetration method. Shadow-mask methods are commonly used in raster scan systems (including color TV) because they produce a much wider range of colors than the beam penetration method. A shadow-mask CRT has three phosphor color dots at each pixel position. One phosphor dot emits a red light, another emits a green light, and the third emits a blue light. This type of CRT has three electron guns, one for each color dot, and a shadow-mask grid just behind the phosphor-coated screen. Figure illustrates the delta shadow-mask method, commonly used in color CRT systems. The three electron beams are deflected and focused as a group onto the shadow mask, which contains a series of holes aligned with the phosphor-dot patterns. When the three beams pass through a hole in the shadow mask, they activate a dot triangle, which appears as a small color spot on the screen. The phosphor dots in the triangles are arranged so that each electron beam can activate only its corresponding color dot when it passes through the Shadow mask.

Another configuration for the three electron guns is an in-line arrangement in which the three electron guns, and the corresponding red-green-blue color dots on the screen, are aligned along one scan line instead of in a triangular pattern. This in-line arrangement of electron guns is easier to keep in alignment and is commonly used in high-resolution color CRTs.

We obtain color variations in a shadow-mask CRT by varying the intensity levels of the three electron beams. By turning off the red and green guns, we get only the color coming from the blue phosphor. Other combinations of beam intensities produce a small light spot for each pixel position, since our eyes tend to merge the three colors into one composite. The color we see depends on the amount of excitation of the red, green, and blue phosphors.

A white (or gray) area is the result of activating all three dots with equal intensity. Yellow is produced with the green and red dots only, magenta is produced with the blue and red dots, and cyan shows up when blue and green are activated equally. In some low-cost systems, the electron beam can only be set to on or off, limiting displays to eight colors. More sophisticated systems can set intermediate intensity levels for the electron beams, allowing several million different colors to be generated.

Color CRTs in graphics systems are designed as RGB monitors. These monitors use shadow-mask methods and take the intensity level for each electron gun (red, green, and blue) directly from the computer system without any intermediate processing. High-quality raster-graphics systems have 24 bits per pixel in the frame buffer, allowing **256** voltage settings for each electron gun and nearly 17 million color choices for each pixel. An **RGB color system** with **24 bits** of storage per pixel is generally referred to as a full-color system or a **true-color** system.

Plasma Panel

Plasma panels, also called gas-discharge displays, are constructed by filling the region between two glass plates with a mixture of gases that usually uses neon. A series of vertical conducting ribbons is placed on one glass panel, and a set of horizontal ribbons is built into the other glass panel. Firing voltages applied to a pair of horizontal and vertical conductors cause the gas at the intersection of the two conductors to break down into glowing plasma of electrons and ions. Picture definition is stored in a refresh buffer, and the firing voltages are applied to refresh the pixel positions (at the intersections of the conductors) 60 times per second.

It is an alternative to CRT as there was a search for a device which

- Can retain display indefinitely
- No compromise on quality of display
- Small space requirement
- Low voltage power supply

The term plasma is the name of the device which refers to the neon gas that is sandwiched & sealed between two glass panels. It is a panel of very tiny neon gas bulbs which can selectively be made to glow. By apply firing voltage, glow starts. Once the glow starts, the voltage can be decreased up to which glow continues (sustaining voltage). Below this voltage, glow dies (cut of voltage). Plasma Panel need not be refreshed. Cost is high and resolution low. It is an array of neon gas where on means bright glow and off means no glow.

Alternating methods are used to provide faster application of the firing voltages, and thus brighter displays. Separation between pixels is provided by the electric field of the conductors. One disadvantage of plasma panels has been that they were strictly monochromatic devices, but systems have been developed that are now capable of displaying color and grayscale.

Thin-film electroluminescent displays are similar in construction to a plasma panel. The difference is that the region between the glass plates is filled with a phosphor, such as zinc sulfide doped with manganese, instead of a gas. When a sufficiently high voltage is applied to a pair of crossing electrodes, the phosphor becomes a conductor in the area of the intersection of the two electrodes. Electrical energy is then absorbed by the manganese atoms, which then release the energy as a spot of light similar to the glowing plasma effect in a plasma panel. Electroluminescent displays require more power than plasma panels, and good color and gray scale displays are hard to achieve.

LCD AND LED

Liquid Crystal displays are commonly used in small systems, such as calculators and portable, laptop computers. These non emissive devices produce a picture by passing polarized light from the surroundings or from an internal light through a liquid-crystal material that can be aligned to either block or transmit the light. The term **liquid crystal** refers to the fact that these compounds have a crystalline arrangement of molecules, yet they flow like a liquid. Flat-panel displays commonly use nematic (threadlike) liquid-crystal compounds that tend to keep the long axes of the rod-shaped molecules aligned. A flat-panel display can then be constructed with a nematic liquid crystal. Two glass plates, each containing a light polarizer at right angles to the other plate, sandwich the liquid-crystal material. Rows of horizontal transparent conductors are built into one glass plate, and columns of vertical conductors are put into the other plate. The intersection of two conductors defines a pixel position. Polarized light passing through the material is twisted so that it will pass through the opposite polarizer. The light is then reflected back to the viewer. To turn off the pixel, we apply a voltage to the two intersecting conductors to align the molecules so that the light is not twisted. This type of flat-panel device is referred to as a passive-matrix LCD.

Picture definitions are stored in a refresh buffer, and screen is refreshed at the rate of 60 frames per second, as in the emissive devices. A hand calculator with Back lighting is also commonly applied using solid-state electronic devices. Colors can be displayed by using different materials or dyes and by placing a triad of color pixels at each screen location.

Another method is to place a transistor at each pixel location, using thin-film transistor technology. The transistors are used to control the voltage at pixel locations and to prevent charge from gradually leaking out of the liquid-crystal cells. These devices are called active-matrix displays.

LED

A type of emissive device is the light-emitting diode **(LED). A** matrix of diodes is arranged to form the pixel positions in the display, and picture definition is stored in a refresh buffer. As in scan-line refreshing of a **CRT,** information is read from the refresh buffer and converted to voltage levels that are applied to diodes to produce the light patterns in the display.

VGA AND SVGA MONITORS

VGA Monitors

Abbreviation of *video graphics array*, a graphics display system for PCs developed by IBM. VGA has become one of the de facto standards for PCs. In text mode, VGA systems provide a resolution of 720 by 400 pixels. In graphics mode, the resolution is either 640 by 480 (with 16 colors) or 320 by 200 (with 256 colors). The total palette of colors is 262,144.

Unlike earlier graphics standards for PCs -- MDA, CGA, and EGA -- VGA uses analog signals rather than digital signals. Consequently, a monitor designed for one of the older standards will not be able to use VGA.

Since its introduction in 1987, several other standards have been developed that offer greater resolution and more colors (SVGA, 8514/A graphics standard, and XGA), but VGA remains the lowest common denominator. All PCs made today support VGA, and possibly some other more advanced standard.

It has been technologically outdated in the PC market for some time. VGA was the most recent graphical standard that the majority of manufacturers conformed to, making it the lowest common denominator that all PC graphics hardware supports before a device-specific driver is loaded into the computer. For example, the Microsoft Windows splash screen appears while the machine is still operating in VGA mode, which is the reason that this screen always appears in reduced resolution and color depth.

VGA was officially superseded by IBM's XGA standard, but in reality it was superseded by numerous extensions to VGA made by clone manufacturers that came to be known as "Super VGA".

SVGA Monitors

Super Video Graphics Array, almost always abbreviated to **Super VGA** or just **SVGA** is a broad term that covers a wide range of computer display standards.

Originally, it was an extension to the VGA standard first released by IBM in 1987. Unlike VGA—a purely IBM-defined standard—Super VGA was defined by the Video Electronics Standards Association (VESA), an open consortium set up to promote interoperability and define standards. When used as a resolution specification, in contrast to VGA or XGA for example, the term *SVGA* normally refers to a resolution of 800 × 600 pixels.

Super VGA was first defined in 1989. In that first version, it called for a resolution of 800 × 600 4-bit pixels. Each pixel could therefore be any of 16 different colors. It was quickly extended to 1024 × 768 8-bit pixels, and well beyond that in the following years.

Although the number of colors was defined in the original specification, this soon became irrelevant as (in contrast to the old CGA and EGA standards) the interface between the video card and the VGA or Super VGA monitor uses simple analog voltages to indicate the desired color depth. In consequence, so far as the monitor is concerned, there is no theoretical limit to the number of different colors that can be displayed. Note that this applies to *any* VGA or Super VGA monitor.

While the output of a VGA or Super VGA video card is analog, the internal calculations the card performs in order to arrive at these output voltages are entirely digital. To increase the number of colors a Super VGA display system can reproduce, no change at all is needed for the monitor, but the video card needs to handle much larger numbers and may well need to be redesigned from scratch. Even so, the leading graphics chip vendors were producing parts for high-colour video cards within just a few months of Super VGA's introduction.

On paper, the original Super VGA was to be succeeded by Super XGA, but in practice the industry soon abandoned the attempt to provide a unique name for each higher display standard, and almost all display systems made between the late 1990s and the early 2000s are classed as Super VGA.

Monitor manufacturers sometimes advertise their products as *XGA* or *Super XGA*. In practice this means little, since *all* Super VGA monitors manufactured since the later 1990s have been capable of at least XGA and usually considerably higher performance.

SUMMARY

Computer graphics has been defined as the collection of data structure, graphic algorithms and any higher level language. Passive Computer Graphics is called Off-line graphics while Interactive Computer Graphics is called On-line graphics. Application areas include Flight simulators, CAD, video games and many more. The survey of computer graphics takes us into the start of computer graphics (black era) till the present day graphics (Colored era).

Components of Computer graphics include Frame buffer, monitor and display controller. Input devices include keyboards, mouse, light pen, joystick, digitizer, touch panel, image scanners, voice systems etc while output devices include monitors (CRT) and printers/plotters.

VGA is a graphics display system for PCs developed by IBM. VGA has become one of the de facto standards for PCs. In text mode, VGA systems provide a resolution of 720 by 400 pixels. In graphics mode, the resolution is either 640 by 480 (with 16 colors) or 320 by 200 (with 256 colors). The total palette of colors is 262,144.

Super Video Graphics Array, almost always abbreviated to **Super VGA** or just **SVGA** is a broad term that covers a wide range of computer display standards. Originally, it was an extension to the VGA standard first released by IBM in 1987. Super VGA was first defined in 1989. In that first version, it called for a resolution of 800 × 600 4-bit pixels. Each pixel could therefore be any of 16 different colors. It was quickly extended to 1024 × 768 8-bit pixels, and well beyond that in the following years.

Analog to digital conversion and vice versa is done by A/D converter. Raster scan scans the screen line by line while random scan plots the image directly through the use of primitive commands. Raster scan is being used now-a-days in graphics applications. Even the home TV uses raster scan technology for rendering real images.

Graphics primitives are primitive commands used by earlier graphics systems. Random scan uses graphics primitives to plot the line or surfaces. GKS and CORE are some names associated with graphics primitives.

EXERCISE

1. What do you understand by Computer Graphics? Give application areas of Interactive Computer Graphics.
2. Explain briefly the concept of Graphics primitives.
3. Why do Computer Graphics systems often use more than one processor?
4. What is display memory called in a system which has portion of memory reserved for graphics use only?
5. Good graphic programmers avoid the use of floating point operation whenever possible. Why?

6. Explain the following terms
   (*i*) Persistence (*ii*) Phosphorence
   (*iii*) Raster scan (*iv*) Pixels & frame buffer.
7. What do you understand by V-RAM and how much V-RAM do you recommend for your system?
8. What do you understand by Input/ Output devices? Explain the working of CRT.
9. What is the difference between Raster and Random scan? Highlight the advantages of using Raster scan.
10. Fill in the blanks:
    (*a*) CAD stands for ....
    (*b*) CAM stands for ....
    (*c*) DMA stands for ....
    (*d*) Pixel stands for ....
    (*e*) CRT is coated with .... to avoid burning under prolonged excitation.

ANSWERS

10. (*a*) Computer Aided Designing (*b*) Computer Aided Manufacturing
    (*c*) Direct memory Access (*d*) Picture element
    (*e*) Phosphor.

2

DRAWING GEOMETRY–LINE & CIRCLE DRAWING ALGORITHMS

ELEMENTS OF 2D GEOMETRY FOR GRAPHICS

2D geometry is used extensively in graphics and so we must be familiar with geometry. We must know the equations related to lines, circles, ellipses etc in order to generate or scan convert them on the system. These equations can be used directly in our programs so derivations are skipped in this book considering them out of scope.

We can use built-in functions of C language to draw lines, circles, ellipses, arcs and polygons but we are interested in drawing them through our own algorithms as they are more flexible.

First let us define what lines are and it can easily be said that any line can be drawn using two endpoints (x_1, y_1) and (x_2, y_2)

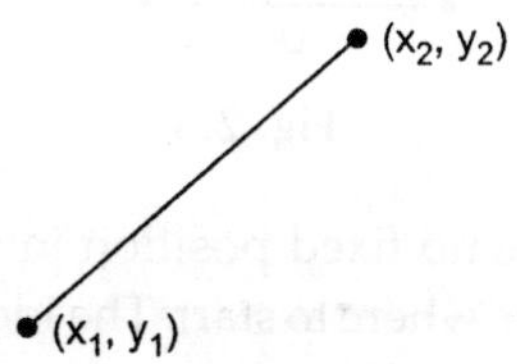

Fig. 2.1

The line equation is $y = mx + b$

Slope $m = (y_2 - y_1)/(x_2 - x_1)$

where (x_1, y_1) and (x_2, y_2) are end point co-ordinates provided by the user

and $b = y_1 - mx_1$

Slope m is the change in height divided by change in width for two points on the line.

The intercept b is the height at which line crosses the Y axis.

LINE SEGMENT

Let us consider only those points on a line that lie between two end points A_1 & A_2. This is called a line segment.

Length of a line segment is very important to evaluate because our algorithm will focus on that. So the question is how long is a line segment?

Given two endpoints A_1 and A_2, we can determine its length L using Pythagoras theorem.

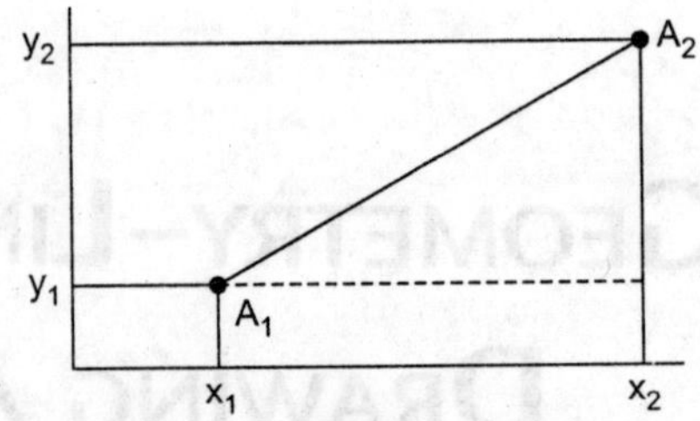

Fig. 2.2 *Pythagoras theorem*

$$L_2 = (x_2 - x_1)^2 + (y_2 - y_1)^2$$

or

$$L = ((x_2 - x_1)^2 + (y_2 - y_1)^2)^{1/2}$$

VECTORS

A vector has a single direction and a length. A vector may be denoted $[D_x, D_y]$ where D_x indicates how far to move along x-axis direction and D_y indicates how far to move along the y-axis.

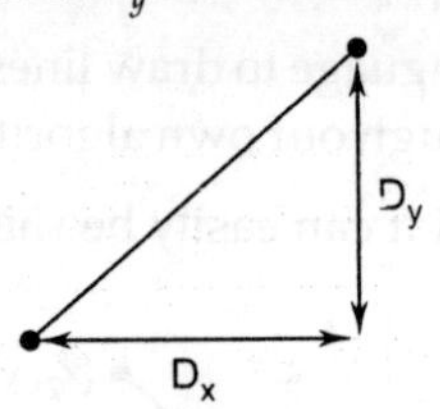

Fig. 2.3

Unlike line segments, vectors have no fixed position in space. They tell us how far and what direction to move but they do not tell us where to start. The idea of a vector is useful because it closely parallels the manner in which a pen draws lines on paper or an electron beam draws lines.

SCAN CONVERSION

Scan Conversion is the process of representing continuous objects as a collection of discrete pixels. Displaying discrete pixels of the object is called SCAN CONVERSION (Students may be asked to scan convert a point, line, circle or an ellipse in examinations).

The video output circuitry is capable of converting binary values stored in its display memory into pixel on, pixel off information. This information is used by raster output device to display a point. This helps the graphics programmers to display or create models composed of discrete dots.

Any thing in the world can be produced with a dense matrix of dots but we think in terms of graphic objects such as points, lines, circles and ellipses.

Computer graphics has come a long way since the start of graphics. Many algorithms have been developed to scan convert the above mentioned shapes. However regardless of the method used, computer can produce images on raster devices only by turning appropriate pixels on or off.

Scan conversion algorithm can be implemented in computer hardware or firmware (programs written in ROM). However scan conversion algorithms can be implemented in software as per our requirements.

HOW TO HANDLE SCREEN COORDINATES & HOW "C" PROGRAM WORKS

The point plotting/ scan conversion techniques are based on the use of a Cartesian co-ordinate system. Points are represented by x and y co-ordinates, the value of x increases from L – R and y from top to bottom (Check out the coordinates of your screen by writing simple programs using C language).

Let us start by writing simple programs in C programming language for graphics and see how the screen behaves. When we start drawing any graphics on the screen, we need a header file **graphics.h** and a library file called **graphics.lib.** The header file contains the information and explanations of all functions and constants we need. Both these files are provided as part of **TURBO C**.

To move from the text mode to the graphics mode that offers the best resolution, the system puts the number corresponding to that mode in variable **gm**. The **gm** number tells us which monitor we are using and its resolution.

The programs given in the book are developed using VGA adapter with the resolution 640×480

To understand **gd**, we've to understand the concept of device drivers. Turbo C offers some graphics drivers. These are the file with **BGI(*.bgi)** extension. Throughout our programs, **gd** has been assigned the value DETECT thereby asking initgraph( ) function to figure out which BGI file is needed.

The basic tools or built in functions used for drawing shapes are function like putpixel( ), line( ), circle( ), ellipse( ), arc( ) and drawpoly( ).

putpixel (x_1, y_1) illuminates or lights the pixel at position (x_1, y_1) on the screen.

line (x_1, y_1, x_2, y_2) draws a line from point (x_1, y_1) to point (x_2, y_2)

LINE DRAWING ALGORITHMS

Straight line segments are used in almost every graphics application such as generating sceneries, bar charts, block diagram, graph, engineering drawing, architectural plan etc. Since the straight line drawing is very important and so useful it is worth taking care that they are well drawn.

Criteria for good computer generated lines

1. Lines should appear straight and not zigzag. Point Plotting techniques are admirably suited to the generation of vertical, horizontal or lines at 45 degree to x and y axis.
2. Line should terminate accurately
3. Lines should have constant density *i.e.*, point should be evenly distributed on the line.

Scan converting algorithms compute the points for us and corresponding to these points, signals are generated. Algorithms should be such that they require minimum computations.

There are two lines drawing algorithm which are employed by graphics designers/developers:

1. DDA (Digital differential analyzer) method
2. Bresenham's line drawing algorithm

DDA LINE DRAWING ALGORITHM

One technique for obtaining a rasterized straight line is to solve the differential equation for a straight line

$$D_Y/D_Y = \text{constant} \quad \text{or} \quad \Delta_y/\Delta_x = y_2 - y_1/x_2 - x_1$$

The solution is for the above differential equation is

$$Y_{i+1} = Y_i + \Delta_y$$

$$Y_{i+1} = Y_i + (y_2 - y_1/x_2 - x_1)\,\Delta x \quad \text{...(1)}$$

where (x_1, y_1) and (x_2, y_2) are the end points of the required straight line and Y_i is the initial value for any given step along the line.

In fact, equation 1 represents a recursive relation for successive values of y along the required line and is usually used to rasterize a line. This method is called digital differential analyzer (DDA) method.

Now we can use the above recursive relation in our computer program. Following is a simple DDA algorithm which will work in all quadrants and would rasterize a line. The line end points are (x_1, y_1) and (x_2, y_2) and are not equal. The line end points are provided by the user through input commands of the program.

DDA Algorithm

Integer is integer floor function

Sign returns – 1, 0, 1 as its arguments is < 0, = 0, > 0.

/*Appropriate the line length so that we can move along either of X or Y axis*/

If $abs(x_2 - x_1) >= abs(y_2 - y_1)$ then

$\text{len} = abs(x_2 - x_1)$

Else

$\text{len} = abs(y_2 - y_1)$

End if

/* Evaluating Δx and Δy to be used in our program*/

$$\Delta x = (x_2 - x_1)/\text{len}$$

$$\Delta y = (y_2 - y_1)/\text{len}$$

/* To round the values we use multiplication by 0.5 and using sign function makes algorithm work in all quadrants*/

$$x = x_1 + 0.5 * \text{sign}(\Delta x)$$

$$y = y_1 + 0.5 * \text{sign}(\Delta y)$$

/*Begin the loop*/

$$I = 1$$

As long as $(I \le len)$

Putpixel (integer (x)), integer (y))

$$x = x + \Delta x$$
$$y = y + \Delta y$$
$$I = I + 1$$

End loop

Lets take an example to illustrate the algorithm. We will solve a numerical and plot the line and then scan convert it on the system through a C program.

Example : Consider the line from (0, 0) to (6, 6), use DDA to rasterize the line.

Let us perform some initial calculations

Initially $X_1 = 0$ $Y_1 = 0$ $X_2 = 6$ $Y_2 = 6$

So our first step would be to evaluate the length

Length $= abs(x_2 - x_1) = 6 - 0 = 6$

Length $= abs(y_2 - y_1) = 6 - 0 = 6$

So length = 6 (in any X or Y direction)

Had $(x_2 - x_1)$ been larger then X direction would have been chosen otherwise Y direction.

So our next step would be to evaluate Δx and Δy as in our algorithm

$$\Delta x = x_2 - x_1/\text{length} = 6 - 0/6 = 1$$
$$\Delta y = y_2 - y_1/\text{length} = 6 - 0/6 = 1$$
$$x = x_1 + 0.5 * \text{sign}(\Delta x)$$
$$= 0 + 0.5 * \text{sign}(1)$$ **/* since sign(1) returns 1*/**
$$x = 0.5$$

Similarly, $y = 0.5$

Evaluating through main loop gives us

i	plot	x	y
1		0.5	0.5
2	(0, 0)	1.5	1.5
3	(1, 1)	2.5	2.5
4	(2, 2)	3.5	3.5
5	(3, 3)	4.5	4.5
6	(4, 4)	5.5	5.5
7	(5, 5)	6.5	6.5
8	(6, 6)	7.5	7.5

So we can see from the above table how DDA method evaluates and plot new points (0.5 is taken as 0 in above table because we are considering floor value).

Exercise : Draw a line from (0, 0) to (– 8, – 4) in third quadrant and develop a C program to draw a line using DDA algorithm.

Layout of DDA algorithm using "C"

Sign (int *x*)

```
{
        if (k > 0) return 1;
        if (k < 0) return -1;
        if (k = 0) return 0;
}
        dx = x2 - x1;
        dy = y2 - y1;
  if  (abs(dx) > = abs(dy))
        len = abs(dx);
  else
        len = abs(dy);
        xinc = dx / len;
        yinc = dy / len;
        x = x1 + 0.5 * sign (dx);    /* to round off
        y = y1 + 0.5 * sign (dy);
      while (i < = len)
 {
        putpixel(floor x, floor y);
        x+ = xinc;
        y+ = yinc;
        i ++;
 }
```

For the sake of students we have given a program for DDA method in C language. Students can modify it according to their need and requirement. You can make it more interactive and user friendly.

```
#include<stdio.h>
#include<conio.h>
#include<graphics.h>
#include<math.h>
void dda(int,int,int,int);
int sig(int);
int f1=0,p[8],x,y;
main()
{
int gd=DETECT,gm,i,j=0;
int xa[1]={400};
int ya[1]={100};
int xb[1]={800};
int yb[1]={400};
```

```
clrscr();
printf("line drawing using dda method");
initgraph(&gd,&gm," ");
while(j<1)
{
dda(xa[j],ya[j],xb[j],yb[j]);
j++;
}
getch();
closegraph();
return(0);
}
void dda(int xa,int ya,int xb,int yb)
{
int dx,dy,l,x1,y1,f,c;
dx=xb-xa;
dy=yb-ya;
if(abs(dx)>=abs(dy))
l=abs(dx);
else
l=abs(dy);
x1=(dx)/l;
y1=(dy)/l;
x=x1+(0.5*sig(dx));
y=y1+(0.5*sig(dy));
while(f1<=l)
{
f=floor(x);
c=floor(y);
putpixel(f,c,WHITE);
x+=x1;
y+=y1;
f1++;
}
}
int sig(int k)
{
if (k>0)
return(1);
if (k<0)
return(-1);
```

```
if (k==0)
return(0);
}
```

Bresenham's Line Algorithm

Bresenham's line algorithm is an efficient method for scan converting straight lines in that it uses only integer addition, subtraction and multiplication by 2 and floating point operations are avoided in Bresenham's algorithm. The computer can perform the operations of integer addition and subtraction very rapidly. The lines drawn are of superior quality as compared to DDA method.

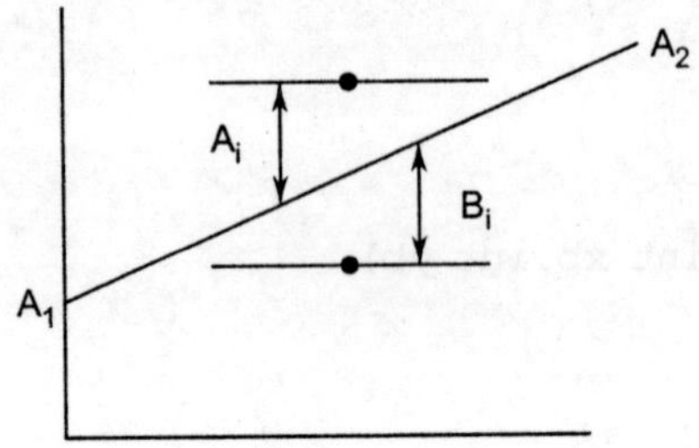

Fig. 2.4

In this algorithm we talk about a true line as shown in the above figure. Call the distance to those pixels lying immediately above the true line A_i and the distance to those directly below it B_i.

We will keep on talking about A_i and B_i throughout the algorithm. Bresenham's algorithm identifies the decision or test variable

$$d_i = B_i - A_i$$

when $d_i < 0$, the closet pixel in the raster will be the pixel below the true line.

Conversely, when $d_i >= 0$ the pixel immediately above the true line is closest.

To implement the algorithm all that remains is to calculate and update the various values of d_i.

Initially set

$$d_1 = 2d_y - d_x$$

where

$$d_x = X_2 - X_1$$

$$d_y = Y_2 - Y_1$$

Thereafter if $d_i >= 0$ the x and y are incremented

$$X_{i+1} = X_i + 1$$

$$Y_{i+1} = Y_i + 1$$

and

$$d_{i+1} = d_i + 2(d_y - d_x)$$

If $d_i < 0$ then only x is incremented

$$X_{i+1} = X_i + 1$$

$$d_{i+1} = d_i + 2d_y$$

Example : Indicate which raster locations would be chosen by Bresenham's algorithm when scan converting a line from screen co-ordinates (1, 1) to (8,5).

Solution : First the starting values (Initial values) must be found

$$d_x = x_2 - x_1$$
$$= 8 - 1$$
$$= 7$$
$$d_y = d_y - y_1$$
$$= 5 - 1$$
$$= 4$$

Therefore
$$d = 2d_y - d_x$$
$$= 2 * 4 - 7$$
$$= 1 \text{ Initial value}$$

Applying the above procedure again and again would get us the required solution.

Ultimately we would get a table of x and y that can be plotted to give a line segment.

x	y	d
1	1	1
2	2	– 5
3	2	3
4	3	– 3
5	3	5
6	4	– 1
7	4	7
And so on	And so on	1

Following is the C implementation of Bresenham's algorithm.

Bresenham's Line Program

```
//TO DRAW A LINE (BRESENHAM'S LINE DRAWING ALGORITHM)...
#include<conio.h>
#include<stdio.h>
#include<graphics.h>
#include<math.h>
#include<dos.h>
void line1 (int x1, int y1, int x2, int y2)
{
int dx, dy, 1, x, y, p, xend;
dx = (x2-x1) ;
dy = (y2-y1) ;
p = 2*dy-dx  ;
if (x2 > x1)    //checks which x(x1 or x2) to use as starting point
{                   //and which x(x1 or x2) to use as end point
```

```
        x=x1 ;
        y=y1 ;
        xend=x2;
}
else
{
x = x2 ;
y = y2 ;
xend = x1 ;
}
while (x<xend)
{
putpixel (x, y, RED);
x++ ;
if (p < 0)
p = p + 2*dy
else
{
y++ ;
p = p + 2* (dy-dx) ;
}
}
}
void main (void)
{
int gd=DETECT,gm;
clrscr() ;
initgraph (& gd, & gm," ");
setbkcolor (GREEN) ;
line1 (200, 0, 300, 300) ;
getch ( );
}
```

BRESENHAM'S CIRCLE GENERATION

If a circle is to be scan-converted nicely, the use of trigonometric and power functions must be avoided. It is therefore desirable to perform the calculations necessary to find the scan converted points with only integer addition, subtraction, multiplication by powers of 2. Bresenham's circle algorithm allows these goals to be met with limited number of steps.

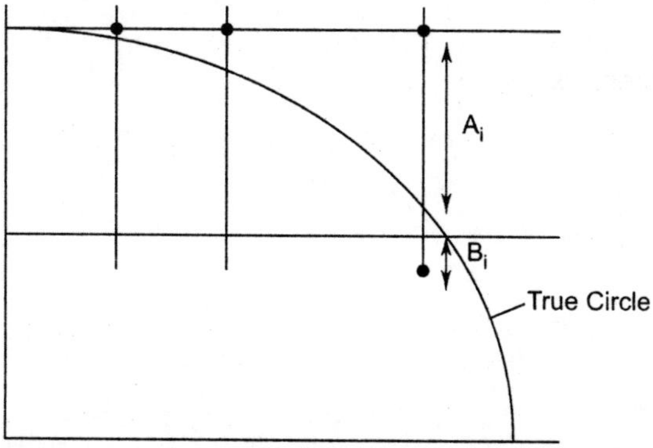

Fig. 2.5

As in the case of straight line, the best approximation of a circle will be defined by those pixels in the raster that fall the least distance from the true circle.

Decision variable d_i value is derived as (derivation is beyond the scope of this book).

$$d_i = 3 - 2r$$

Thereafter if $d_i < 0$ then only x is incremented

$$x_{i+1} = x_i + 1$$

and decision variable changes to

$$d_{i+1} = d_i + 4x_i + 6$$

and if $d_i >= 0$ then x & y are incremented

$$x_{i+1} = x_i + 1$$

$$y_{i+1} = y_i - 1$$

$$d_{i+1} = d_i + 4(x_i - y_i) + 10$$

We are giving Bresenham's Program for circle generation in C:

Bresenham's Circle C Program

```
# include<stdio.h>
# include<conio.h>
# include<math.h>
# include<dos. h>
# include<graphics. h>
void circlemid (int, int, int, int);
void plotpoints (int xcen, int ycen, int r)
{
int p, x, y;
x = 0;
y = r;
p = 3-2*r;
while (x<y)
```

```
{
circlemid (xcen, ycen, x, y) ;
x++ ;
if (p<0)
p = p+4*x+6;
else
{
y--;
p = p+4* (x-y)+10;
}
}
}
void circlemid (int xcen, int ycen, int x, int y)
{
static int i = 0;
putpixel (xcen+x, ycen+y, i++) ;
putpixel (xcen-x, ycen+y, i++) ;
putpixel (xcen+x, ycen-y, i++) ;
putpixel (xcen-x, ycen-y, i++) ;
putpixel (xcen+y, ycen+x, i++) ;
putpixel (xcen-y, ycen+x, i++) ;
putpixel (xcen+y, ycen-x, i++) ;
putpixel (xcen-y, ycen-x, i++) ;
delay (10);
}
void main ( )
{
int gd==DETECT, gm;
int i ;
clrscr () ;
initgraph(&gd, &gm," ");
for (i=0; i<=15; i++)
{
setbkcolor (i);
plotpoints (300, 230, i+i*3) ;
}
setcolor (4);
outtextxy (282, 227, "Ehtiram") ;
getch ( ) ;
}
```

MIDPOINT CIRCLE GENERATION

As in the case of straight line, the best approximation of a circle will be defined by those pixels in the raster that fall the least distance from the true circle.

Decision variable d_i value is derived as (derivation is beyond the scope of this book).

$$d_i = 1 - r$$

Thereafter if $d_i < 0$ then only x is incremented

$$x_{i+1} = x_i + 1$$

and decision variable changes to

$$d_{i+1} = d_i + 2x_i + 3$$

and if $d_i >= 0$ then x & y are incremented

$$x_{i+1} = x_i + 1$$

$$y_{i+1} = y_i - 1$$

$$d_{i+1} = d_i + 2(x_i - y_i) + 5$$

This algorithm is quite similar to Bresenham's algorithm except that initial estimate and decision variable equations are changing by half.

ELLIPSE GENERATION ALGORITHMS

Ellipse has two axes-major and minor axis. It is quite similar to circle.

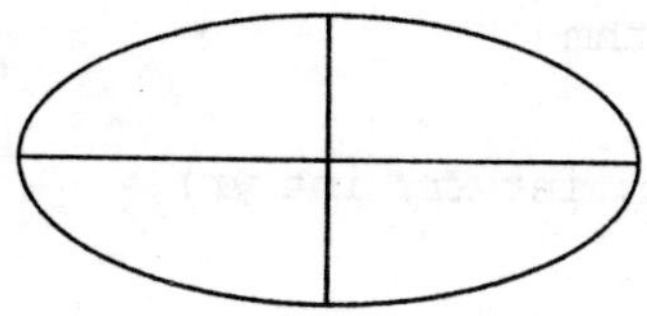

```
//Ellipse Generating Algorithm
//Simple Cartesian-Coordinate
void ellipse(int xc, int yc, int xr, int yr)
{
int len;
  if (xr > yr)
  {
  int y12, y22;
  int y11 = yc, y21 = yc;
    for (int x=xc-xr+1; x<=xc+xr; ++x)
    {
      len = yr * sqrt(1 - SQR((x - xc) / double(xr)));
      y12 = yc + len;
      y22 = yc - len;
      line(x-1, y11, x, y12);
```

```
      line(x-1, y21, x, y22);
      y11 = y12;
      y21 = y22;
    }
  }
  else
  {
  int x12, x22;
  int x11 = xc, x21 = xc;
    for (int y=yc-yr+1; y<=yc+yr; ++y)
    {
      len = xr * sqrt(1 - SQR((y - yc) / double(yr)));
      x12 = xc + len;
      x22 = xc - len;
      line(x11, y-1, x12, y);
      line(x21, y-1, x22, y);
      x11 = x12;
      x21 = x22;
    }
  }
}
//Ellipse Generating Algorithm
//Simple Polar-Coordinate
void ellipse(int xc, int yc, int xr, int yr)
{
const int ITERATIONS = 1000;
double theta;
 moveto(xc + xr, yc);
 for (int i=1; i<=ITERATIONS; ++i)
 {
   theta = 2 * PI * i / ITERATIONS;
   lineto(ROUND(xc+xr*cos(theta)), ROUND(yc+yr*sin(theta)));
 }
}
```

CHARACTER GENERATION

What would graphics be without the use of text? Text has always been an integral part of computer graphics.

Graphics is made up of points, lines, curves and polygons. Along with these, string of characters are often displayed which give instructions and information to the user. Characters can be created in graphics through software and hardware.

There are two methods for character generation. One is called the **STROKE METHOD**. This method creates character out of a series of line segments. We can build our own stroke method character generation by calls to our DDA algorithm. Any character is possible through DDA algorithm.

In actual graphic displays, the commands for drawing the character line segments may be in either hardware or software. In the stroke method change of scale is possible *i.e.*, the characters may be made twice as large by simply doubling the length of each segment.

The second method of character generation is **DOT MATRIX** or **BIT MAP METHOD**.

In this scheme, characters are generally represented by an array of dots. An array of 5 dots wide and 7 dots high is often used but 7×9 and 9×13 arrays are also found. High resolution devices such as inkjet or laser printers may use character array that are over 100 pixels on a side.

This array is like a small frame buffer just big enough to hold a character. The dots are the pixels for this small array. Placing the character on the screen then becomes a matter of copying pixel values from the small character array into some portion of screen's frame buffer. The memory containing the character dot matrix array is often a hardware device called **"a character generation chip"** but RAM may also be used when many fonts are desired. The size of the dot is fixed so dot matrix method does not lend itself to variable size characters.

SUMMARY

We looked at geometry involved in drawing lines. We derived equations and these equations can be used by computer programs to generate lines.

There are two lines drawing algorithm which are employed by graphics designers/developers:

1. DDA (Digital differential analyzer) method
2. Bresenham's line drawing algorithm

Bresenham's method is a better method since it avoids the use of floating point operations.

DDA technique for obtaining a rasterized straight line is to solve the differential equation for a straight line

$$D_Y/D_Y = \text{constant} \quad \text{or} \quad \Delta y/\Delta x = y_2 - y_1/x_2 - x_1$$

The solution is for the above differential equation is

$$Y_{i+1} = Y_i + \Delta y$$
$$Y_{i+1} = Y_i + (y_2 - y_1/x_2 - x_1)\,\Delta x$$

where (x_1, y_1) and (x_2, y_2) are the end points of the required straight line and Y_i is the initial value for any given step along the line.

Bresenham's line algorithm is an efficient method for scan converting straight lines in that it uses only integer addition, subtraction and multiplication by 2 and floating point operations are avoided in Bresenham's algorithm. The computer can perform the operations of integer addition and subtraction very rapidly. The lines drawn are of superior quality as compared to DDA method.

Screen coordinates increase from left to right and from top to bottom. The resolution of the system used to write programs in this book was 640 × 480 (VGA resolution)

Circle has eight-point symmetry so it is very easy to plot the circle. Bresenham's circle algorithm uses this symmetry to draw the circle. Circle mid-point and ellipse generation algorithm is also given in the book.

Characters are always required in Graphics. Two methods of character generation stroke and bit map method have been discussed.

EXERCISE

1. How are characters generated? Explain different methods of character generation.
2. Write a program to draw a circle using Bresenham's algorithm.
3. The endpoints of a given line are (0,0) and (6,18). Compute each value of y as x steps from 0 to 6 and plot the result using DDA method.
4. What are the steps required to plot a line whose slope is between 0 & 45 degrees using Bresenham's method?
5. Indicate which raster locations would be chosen by Bresenham's algorithm when scan converting a line from pixel coordinate (1, 1) to pixel coordinate (8, 5).
6. Which one is better line algorithm: DDA or Bresenham's algorithm? Explain your answer.
7. Modify Bresenham's circle algorithm to circle mid-point algorithm and develop a C program for the same.
8. How will you scan convert an ellipse using Bresenham's algorithm? Explain the steps involved.

3

2-D TRANSFORMATIONS & GRAPHICS OPERATIONS

(Covers 2-D transformations like Scaling, translation, rotation, reflection and shearing and graphics operations like windowing, clipping and Filling).

2-D TRANSFORMATION

There are situations where the picture displayed on the screen has to be doubled to its size, shrunk to half of its size, rotated by some angle or positioned at another position on the screen. One good thing about computer graphics is the flexibility and ease with which certain changes in the picture can be done. These changes are possible because the graphic image has been coded as numbers and stored in computer's memory. These coded numbers can be modified by certain operations called TRANSFORMATIONS. These operations are possible through software or hardware. Transformations allow us to uniformly change the dimension and size of the picture.

Now let's have a look at geometric transformations of scaling, translation and rotation, though co-ordinate transformations are also possible.

Matrices are an integral part of mathematics and it is the matrix concept that makes it possible to develop programs for scaling, rotation and translation. Our computer graphic images are made up of a series of line segments which are represented by the co-ordinates of their end points and changes in an image can be easily made by performing mathematical operations on these co-ordinates.

Let us recall that matrices consist of rows and columns and they can be multiplied and added together to form a new matrix.

Suppose we want to define matrix on the computer system using any programming language such as C then loops can be used to create a matrix. Matrix of any order can be created by giving the user the option of selecting the order in an interactive manner.

The matrix operation of prime importance to us is that of multiplication. We can multiply two matrices together if the number of columns in the first matrix is the same as the number of rows in the second matrix.

Multiplication of matrices is not commutative *i.e.*,

$$A*B = B*A$$

The multiplication of two matrices gives a resultant matrix which has the same number of rows as the first matrix and same number of columns as the second matrix.

The resultant matrix C is given in terms of the elements of matrices A & B by the formula.

$$C(i,k) = A(i,j) \times B(j,k)$$

And of course, multiplication is associative

i.e., $A(BC) = (AB)C$

Similarly we have the concept of Identity matrix which when multiplied with any other matrix A gives the original matrix

$$A = AI$$

where I is the Identity matrix

There are five (5) types of graphics transformations namely Scaling, Rotation, Translation, Reflection and Shearing. We will be dealing with them separately. Let's first discover Scaling transformation.

SCALING TRANSFORMATION

This is a transformation that we see in so many graphics and graphic systems. The change of size and that too in interactive manner (if required) gives graphics a new dimension in computing. There are times when we require a change of scale to suit our requirements.

Transformation matrix of the form

$$\begin{vmatrix} S_X & O \\ O & S_Y \end{vmatrix}$$

change the size & properties of the displayed image. This type of transformation is called scaling transformation. S_X is the scale factor for X axis and S_Y for the Y axis. When we scale the object (enlargement or reduction), every point except the origin changes.

Please note: We are using matrices notation with | | and users should not mix it up with determinant symbol.

Scaling transformation can be depicted in equation form also.

$$X' = S_X * X$$

$$Y' = S_Y * Y$$

This means that X′ is the transformed point after scaling transformation has been made. The same holds for Y′.

Let us begin with the smallest thing in the universe, a point Q with coordinates $[x, y]$.

Suppose a point Q_1 has coordinates $[X_1 \ Y_1]$. As can be seen, $[X_1 \ Y_1]$ is represented by 1×2 matrix and when multiplied by 2×2 scaling matrix S, a resultant matrix of order 1×2 is obtained which can be interpreted as another point Q_2 with coordinates $[X_2 \ Y_2]$ after scaling.

i.e., Q_2 is represented as

$$[X_2\ Y_2] = [X_1\ Y_1] * \begin{vmatrix} S_X & O \\ O & S_Y \end{vmatrix}$$

Thus, the matrix S has done wonders for us by giving a new point Q_2 against the original point Q_1. If the scaling operation was performed using $S_X = 2$ and $S_Y = 2$ then the original point $[X_1\ Y_1]$ is multiplied by 2 in both X and Y direction giving a new point with double value *i.e.*, $[X_2\ Y_2]$. In the same way other points of the image are scaled until the entire image has undergone scaling.

As can be seen in the figure, a small object (circle) has been scaled to double its size

Fig. 3.1

While developing simple programs for scaling, the above concept can be used. All points on the plane are scaled one by one and can be joined with the help of line segments. Try out the approach on a triangle or a rectangle.

The program has been given on the above approach.

The contents of matrix S do matter when we are multiplying our points on the plane with it. Suppose the scaling matrix S were identity matrix as shown below

$$\begin{vmatrix} 1 & 0 \\ 0 & 1 \end{vmatrix}$$

Then the image would not change as anything multiplied by identity matrix would remain the same after applying the scaling transformation.

Fig. 3.2

In general terms, 2D Transformation of the form

$$\begin{vmatrix} S_X & 0 \\ S_Y & 0 \end{vmatrix}$$

changes the size & properties of the image. This is called scaling transformation. S_X is the scale factor for X co-ordinates and S_Y for the Y co-ordinate. Note that when we scale the image, every point except the origin changes.

The Scaling transformation matrix can be expanded in homogeneous notation where an additional row and column adds up and the homogeneous concept would be covered up later in the chapter.

So homogenous scaling matrix is given below which is a 3×3 matrix

$$\begin{vmatrix} S_X & 0 & 0 \\ 0 & S_Y & 0 \\ 0 & 0 & 1 \end{vmatrix}$$

Try Scaling operation on a rectangle to double it and the rectangle has vertices (10, 0), (60, 0), (10, 80) & (60, 80).

We choose $S_x = S_y = 2$, the vertices become (20, 0), (120, 0), (20, 160) & (120, 160).

Program can be developed in C for scaling a triangle and rectangle according to our parameters and one program has been attached here in the book.

Program attached

```
//TO SCALE A POLYGON BY MATRIX TRANSFORMATION....
#include<conio.h>
#include<stdio.h>
#include<graphics.h>
#include<math.h>
#include<dos.h>
#include<process.h>
float x[10], y[10], sx, sy;
int n;
void scale (float a[10] [10])
{
printf ("\n enter scaling factor x and y;");
scanf ("%f %f", &sx, & sy);
a [0] [0]=sx;
a [1][1]=sy;
a [2] [2]=1.0;
a [0] [1]=a[0] [2]=a[1] [0]=a[1] [2]=a[2] [0]=a[2] [1]=0.0;
}
void matrix2 (float c[10] [10])
{
int i, k;
for (i=0;i<=n;i++)
{
x [i]=c[i][0];
y [i]=c[i] [1];
}
for (i=0;i<n-1;i++)
{
line (x[i] ,y[i],x[i+1],y[i+1] );
}
line (x[i],y[i],x[0] ,y[0] ) ;
}
void matrix (float b[10] [10])
{
int i, j, k;
for (i=0;i<=n;i++)
```

```
for (j=0;j<=1;j++)
{
if (j==0)
b [i][j]=x[i];
else
b [i] [j]=y[i];
}
for (k=0;k<n;k++)
{
b[k][2]=1.0;
}
}
void mult (float a[10] [10],float b[10] [10],float c[10] [10]
{
int i, j, k;
matrix (b);
for (i=0;i<=n;i++)
for(j = 0; j <= 2; j++)
{
c[i][j]=0;
for(k=0;k<=2;k++)
{
c[i] [j] = c[i] [j] + b[i] [k]* a[k] [j];
}
matrix2 (c) ;
}
void main ()
{
float a[10] [10],c[10] [10];
float b[10] [10], i;
int gd=DETECT, gm;
char str[40] = "after scaling x and y by";
char strl[40] = "we get";
int t;
clrscr ( );
initgraph (&gd,&gm," ");
setbkcolor (RED);
printf ("enter number of vertics of polygen");
scanf ("%d", & n);
if (n>10)
{
```

```
exit (0);
}
printf ("enter coordinates of vertics of polygon");
for (i=0;i<n;i++)
scanf ("%f %f",&x[i], & y[i]);
setcolor (1);
for (i=0;i<n-1;i++)
{
line(x[i], y[i], x[i+1] ,y[i+1] );
}
line(x[i] ,y[i],x[0],y[0]) ;
scale (a);
gotoxy (14 ,14);
for (t=0;str[t] ! = ' \0'; t++)
{
delay(100);
printf ("% c", str [t] ) ;
}
delay (100) ;
printf (%2.2f and %2.2f", sx, sy);
for (t=0; strl[t] ! = '\0' ; t++)
{
delay (100) ;
printf ("%c", strl [t])) ;
}
delay (100) ;
setlinestyle (DOTTED_LINE, 1, 1) ;
setcolor (GREEN) ;
mult (a, b, c) ;
getch () ;
}
```

Try out the above program in C and see a scaled image on the screen. When scaling factors S_x and S_y are greater than 1 *i.e.*, $S_x > 1$ and $S_y > 1$ then it is called enlargement in size(Positive scaling) and when the reverse case arises *i.e.*, $S_x < 1$ and $S_y < 1$ then it is called reduction in size(Negative scaling).

The scaling matrix that we have just used is with respect to the origin. Things would change if we would be scaling with reference to any other arbitrary point. We will be dealing with this concept at the end of the chapter once all transformations are covered. We shall be solving some problems too in this regard.

ROTATION TRANSFORMATION

We need to transform our image as and when required. There are situations when we need to rotate (tilt) our image by certain angle to conform to our graphic requirements. Next transformation we would like to consider is that for rotation.

Suppose we have a point $Q_1 = [X_1, Y_1]$ and we rotate it about the origin by an angle θ to get a new position $Q_2 = [X_2, Y_2]$. Now these rotations can be anti-clockwise or clockwise. Anti-clockwise rotation is also referred to as counter-clockwise rotation and it is this type of rotation that we are interested in.

Rotation transformation is given by the matrix of the form

$$\begin{vmatrix} \text{Cos}\,\theta & \text{Sin}\,\theta \\ -\text{Sin}\,\theta & \text{Cos}\,\theta \end{vmatrix}$$

in counter-clockwise (Anti-clockwise) direction.

Whenever we have to rotate an image by some angle, we provide the angle to the computer program that performs the rotation and displays the image in new form. For example if we have to perform the rotation of 30 degrees with respect to the origin then the rotation matrix becomes

$$\begin{vmatrix} \text{Cos } 30 & \text{Sin } 30 \\ -\text{Sin } 30 & \text{Cos } 30 \end{vmatrix}$$

Now it can be applied to any point, let us say Q (4 ,5) then new point Q′ would be given by

$$= \begin{vmatrix} 4 & 5 \end{vmatrix} * \begin{vmatrix} \text{Cos } 30 & \text{Sin } 30 \\ -\text{Sin } 30 & \text{Cos } 30 \end{vmatrix}$$

$$= \begin{vmatrix} 4 & 5 \end{vmatrix} * \begin{vmatrix} 0.866 & 0.5 \\ -0.5 & 0.866 \end{vmatrix}$$

$$Q, = \begin{vmatrix} 0.964, 6.330 \end{vmatrix}$$

So new point Q, = (0.964, 6.330) after a rotation by 30 degrees in counter clockwise pen motion.

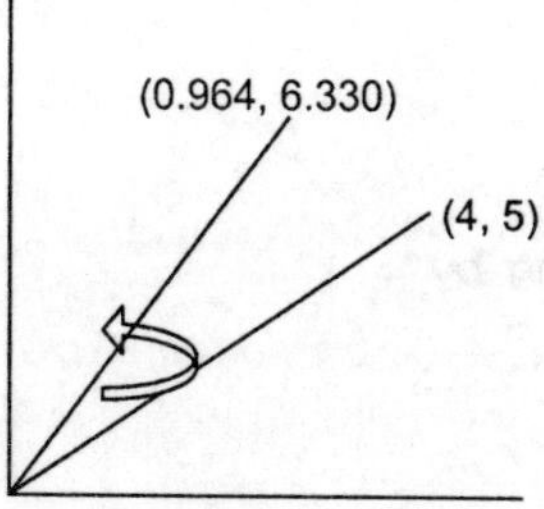

Fig. 3.3

We can also rotate the object or image in clockwise direction. In order to rotate in clockwise direction, we use a negative angle so that rotation matrix for an angle θ clockwise would be

$$\begin{vmatrix} \text{Cos}\,(-\theta) & \text{Sin}\,(-\theta) \\ -\text{Sin}\,(-\theta) & \text{Cos}\,(-\theta) \end{vmatrix}$$

So our transformation matrix for clockwise rotation is

$$\begin{vmatrix} \text{Cos}\,\theta & -\text{Sin}\,\theta \\ \text{Sin}\,\theta & \text{Cos}\,\theta \end{vmatrix}$$

In homogenous notation, the rotation matrix in counter clockwise direction is

$$\begin{vmatrix} \text{Cos}\,\theta & \text{Sin}\,\theta & 0 \\ -\text{Sin}\,\theta & \text{Cos}\,\theta & 0 \\ 0 & 0 & 1 \end{vmatrix}$$

The rotation transformation matrix has been developed with respect to the origin and if rotation has to be performed about any other point or some arbitrary axis then transformation matrix will have to be modified.

C PROGRAM TO ROTATE A POLYGON ABOUT AN ARBITRARY POINT BY MATRIX TRANSFORMATION....

```
#include<conio.h>
#include<stdio.h>
#include<graphics.h>
#include<math.h>
#include<dos.h>
float x[10],y[10],xc,yc;
int n;
void identity(float d[10][10], int xc, int yc)
{
d[0] [1]=d[0] [2]=d[1] [0]=d(1] [2]=0;
d[1][1]=d[2][2]=d[0][0]=1;
d[2] [0]=-xc;
d[2] [1]=-yc;
}
void rotat(float a[10] [10])
{
float x, y,b, angle;
char str[20]=="after rotating by";
char strl[40]="we get";
int t;
printf("\n enter angle:");
scanf("%f", & angle);
gotoxy (14,14);
for(t=0; sr[t]!='\0';t++)
{
delay (100) ;
printf( "%c", Str [t] ) ;
```

```
}
delay (100)
printf("2.2f degrees", angle);
for (t=0;strl[t] !='\0';t++)
{
delay (100) ;
printf("%c",strl[t] ) ;
}
delay (100);
b=angle*22/(7*180) ;
a[0] [0]=a[1] [1]=cos(b) ;
a[0] [1]=sin(b) ;
a[1][0]=-
sin (b);
a[0] [2]=a[1] [2]=a[2] [0]=a[2] [1]=0.0;
a[2][2]=1.0;
}
void matrix2 (float p[10] [10])
{
int i, k;
for (i=0;i<=n;i++)
{
x [i] = p[i][0];
y [i] = p[i][1];
}
for (i=0;i<n-1;i++)
{
delay(400);
line(x[i] ,y[i],x[i+1] ,y[i+1]);
}
delay(400) ;
line(x[i],y[i],x[0],y[0]) ;
}
void matrix (float b[10] [10])
{
int i, j, k;
for (i=0;i<=n;i++)
for(j=0;j<=1;j++)
{
if (j==0)
b[i] [j]=x[i];
```

```
else
b[i] [j]=y[i];
}
for (k=0; k<n;k++)
{
b[k] [2] =1 .0;
}
}
void mult (float f[10] [10], float b[10] [10] , float p[10] [10])
{
int i, j , k;
//matrix (b);
//rotat (a) ;
for(i=0;i<=n;i++)
for(j=0;j<=2;j++)
{
p[i] [j]=0;
for (k=0; k<=2; k++)
{
p[i] [j]+=b[i][k]*f[k] [j];
}}
// matrix2(c);
}
void mult2 (float a[10] [10] , float b[10] [10] , float c(10] [10]
{
int i, j, k;
//matrix (b) ;
//rotat(a) ;
for (i=0;i<=2;i++)
for (j=0;j<=2;j++)
{
c[i] [j]=0;
for (k=0; k<=2 ;k++)
{
c[i] [j]+=b[i][k]*a [k] [j];
}
}
// matrix2(c);
}
void main ( )
{
```

```
float a[10][10],c[10][10],e[10][10],f[10][10],p[10][10];
float b[10] [10],d[10] [10], i;
int gd=DETECT,gm;
clrscr ( ) ;
initgraph (&gd, &gm, " ");
setbkcolor (RED);
printf ("enter number of vertices of polygon")'
scantf ("%d", &n);
printf ("enter coordinates of vertices of polygon");
for (i=0; i<n; i++)
scanf ("%f %f",&x[i],&y[i]);
for(i=0;i<n-1;i++)
{
line (x [i] ,y[i],x[i+1],y[i+1]) ;
}
line (x[i],y[i],x[0],y[0]) ;
printf ("\n enter the x and y coordinates about which u want to rotate:");
scanf ("% f. %f", &xc, &yc);
identity (d, xc, yc) ;
rotat (a);
mult2 (a, d, c) ;
matrix2 (c) ;
identity (e, -xc, -yc);
mult2 (e, c, f) ;
// matrix2 (f);
matrix (b) ;
mult (f, b, p);
//matrix2 (p);
getch ( ) ;}
```

HOMOGENEOUS COORDINATES & TRANSLATION

Moving the image at some other position on the screen is called translation transformation. It is easily achieved by adding to each point the translation amount (T_x and T_y) by which we want the image to be shifted on the screen.

In general in order to translate the image to the right and up by (T_x, T_y), point [X_1 Y_1] is replaced by a new point [X_2 Y_2] such that

$$X_2 = X_1 + T_x$$

and

$$Y_2 = Y_1 + T_y$$

The homogeneous transformation matrix for a translation of T_x, T_y is

$$\begin{vmatrix} 1 & 0 & 0 \\ 0 & 1 & 0 \\ T_X & T_Y & 1 \end{vmatrix} 3 \times 3$$

Now Translation matrix is a 3×3 matrix while their counterparts (Scaling and Rotation) are 2×2 matrices which means we won't be able to multiply them together (Remember the rule, number of columns of one matrix should be equal to the number of rows of the other matrix). It is the need of many graphic applications to apply these transformations together in composite manner to give special effects and to give more versatility to the image.

One way of doing so is to use homogeneous coordinates. In homogeneous coordinates, we use 3×3 matrices instead of 2×2 matrices, introducing dummy row and column to our transformation matrices.

C PROGRAM TO TRANSLATE A POLYGON BY MATRIX TRANSFORMATION....

```
#include<conio.h>
#include<stdio.h>
#include<graphics.h>
#include<math.h>
#include<dos.h>
#include<process.h>
float x[10],y[10],tx,ty;
int n;
void scale(float a[10] [10])
{
printf("\n enter translation factor x and y;");
scanf (" %f %f", &tx, &ty);
a[0][0]=1.0;
a[1][1]=1.0;
a[2] [2]=1.0;
a[0] [1]=a[0] [2]=a[1] [0]=a[1] [2]=0.0;
a[2] [0] =tx;
a[2] [1]=ty;
}
void matrix2 (float c[10] [10])
{
int i, k;
for (i=0; i<=n; i++)
{
x[i]=c[i][0] ;
y[i]=c[i][1];
for (i=0;i<n-1;i++)
```

```
{
line(x[i],y[i],x[i+1] ,y[i+1] );
}
line(x[i],y[i],x[0],y[0]);
}
void matrix(float b[10] [10] )
{
int i, j, k;
for (i=0;i<=n; i++)
for (j=0;j<=1;j++)
{
if (j==0)
b[i][j]=x[i];
else
b[i][j]=y[i];
}
for(k=0;k<n;k++)
{
b[k] [2]=1.0;
]
}
void mult (float a[10][10], float b[10] [10], float c[10] [10])
{
int i, j, k;
matrix (b);
for (i=0;i<=n;i++)
for(j=0;j<=2;j++)
c[i][j]=0;
for(k=0;k<=2;k++)
{
c[i] [j]+=b[i] [k]*a[k] [j];
}
}
matrix2 (c);
}
void main ( )
{
float a[10] [10],c[10] [10];
float b[10] [10],i;
int gd=DETECT, gm;
```

```
char str[40]="after translating x and y by";
char strl[40]="we get";
int t;
clrscr ( ) ;
initgraph(&gd, &gm," ");
setbkcolor (RED) ;
printf ("enter number of vertics of polygen");
scant ("%d", &n) ;
if(n>10) .
{
exit (0) ;
}
printf ("enter coordinates of vertics of polygen");
for (i=0;i<n;i++)
scant ("%f %f",&x[i],&y[i]);
setcolor (1) ;
for (i=0;i<n-l;i++)
{
line(x[i] ,y[i],x[i+l],y[i+l] );
}
line(x[i],y[i],x[0],y[0]);
scale(a);
gotoxy (14,14) ;
for(t=0; srt[t]!='\0';t++)
{
delay(100);
printf ("%c",str [t] ) ;
}
delay (100) ;
printf (" %2.2f and %2.2f ",tx,ty);
for(t=0;strl[t]!=!\0';t++)
{
delay (100) ;
printf ("%c", srtl[t]);
}
delay(100) ;
setlinestyle (DOTTED_LINE, 1, 1) ;
setcolor (GREEN) ;
mult (a, b, c) ;
getch ();
```

}

In homogeneous notation, Scaling matrix would become

$$\begin{vmatrix} S_X & 0 & 0 \\ 0 & S_Y & 0 \\ 0 & 0 & 1 \end{vmatrix}$$

In homogeneous coordinates, our Rotation matrix would become compatible with other transformation matrices of scaling and translation.

$$\begin{vmatrix} \text{Cos } \theta & \text{Sin } \theta & 0 \\ -\text{Sin } \theta & \text{Cos } \theta & 0 \\ 0 & 0 & 1 \end{vmatrix}$$

CONCATENATION OF MATRIX TRANSFORMATIONS (COMPOSITE TRANSFORMATIONS)

Computer Graphics is an interesting field. It requires a lot of graphics operations to be performed one after the other to achieve reality in display. Consider the following sequence, we may be asked to do these steps in sequence

1. First scale a point with $S_x = S_y = 3$
2. Translate it with $T_x = 20$ $T_y = 20$ we have (X 'Y' 1) = (X Y 1) multiplied by (Scaling Matrix)

$$= (X\,Y\,1) * \begin{vmatrix} 3 & 0 & 0 \\ 0 & 3 & 0 \\ 0 & 0 & 1 \end{vmatrix}$$

Then next transformation would yield (X "Y" 1) = (X 'Y' 1) * multiplied by (Translation Matrix)

$$= (X'\,Y'\,1) * \begin{vmatrix} 1 & 0 & 0 \\ 0 & 1 & 0 \\ 20 & 20 & 1 \end{vmatrix}$$

This would yield (X "Y" 1) = (X Y 1) multiplied by (Scaling matrix)(Translation matrix)

$$= (X\,Y\,1) * \begin{vmatrix} 3 & 0 & 0 \\ 0 & 3 & 0 \\ 0 & 0 & 1 \end{vmatrix} * \begin{vmatrix} 1 & 0 & 0 \\ 0 & 1 & 0 \\ 20 & 20 & 1 \end{vmatrix}$$

$$= (X\,Y\,1) * \begin{vmatrix} 3 & 0 & 0 \\ 0 & 3 & 0 \\ 20 & 20 & 1 \end{vmatrix}$$

So if we started with a point Q[4 5], just place 4 and 5 in place of X and Y and get the values of X" and Y". The readers should practice more and more and should use the graph copy to see the real and exact changes in the co-ordinates. Solved examples at the end of the chapter will clear the doubts further.

Q. Perform translation for a rectangle with vertices (10, 0) (70, 0) (10, 100) (70, 100) to translate 100 units to the right & 20 units up as an exercise and plot the new rectangle on graph paper.

As we have seen transformation matrices have been developed with respect to origin. We are faced with the problem of transforming objects which do not lie on the origin and for that transformation about the arbitrary point have to be performed.

ROTATION ABOUT AN ARBITRARY POINT

Let's now determine the transformation matrix for counter-clockwise rotation about point Q (X_C, Y_C).

This form of rotation is performed in three transformation steps:

1. Translate the point (X_C, Y_C) to the origin
2. Rotate about the origin by the specified angle
3. Translate the centre of rotation back to where it belong *i.e.*, from where we started.

Translation matrix which moves (X_c, Y_c) to the origin is given by the matrix given below.

$$T_{one} = \begin{vmatrix} 1 & 1 & 0 \\ 1 & 1 & 0 \\ -X_c & -Y_c & 1 \end{vmatrix}$$

The minus (–) sign preceding X_c and Y_c is because of the fact that translation is performed in opposite direction and throughout this book we will be using this convention. This type of concept is called inverse of Scaling transformation (negative translation) and can be applied to Translation and Rotation transformations as well.

The rotation transformation is

$$R = \begin{vmatrix} \text{Cos}\,\theta & \text{Sin}\,\theta & 0 \\ -\text{Sin}\,\theta & \text{Cos}\,\theta & 0 \\ 0 & 0 & 1 \end{vmatrix}$$

and the translation matrix to move the point back to its correct position, this is positive translation

$$T_{two} = \begin{vmatrix} 1 & 1 & 0 \\ 0 & 1 & 0 \\ X_c & Y_c & 1 \end{vmatrix}$$

Now the required transformation is given by the concatenation of T_{one}, R and T_{two} matrices. They are left multiplied in the order Tone multiplied by R multiplied by Two gives us

$$= \mathbf{T_{one} * R * T_{two}}$$

This multiplication will give us the desired result of rotating an object with respect to an arbitrary point. The solved problems at the end of the chapter will elaborate this concept further.

We will be developing a matrix which will represent an object. That would be object matrix on which rotation transformation is to be performed. Now this object matrix is left multiplied with the transformation matrices that have been developed above.

The final solution would be

$$\text{Rotation}_{\text{arbitrarypt}} = [\text{Object matrix}]*[\mathbf{T_{one} * R * T_{two}}]$$

This equation rotates an object about an arbitrary point. Solved problems will show how the object matrix is made through data provided and how ultimately we get the desired results after transformations.

It is not as if we can only perform rotation about arbitrary point, we can perform other transformations too. Just wait for a while before all transformations are covered and we start solving the problems numerically.

Apart from the above basic transformations, some other types of transformations are useful in computer graphics applications. These are reflection and shearing.

REFLECTION TRANSFORMATION

Reflection is nothing but the mirror image of an original object. There are different types of reflections:

1. **Reflection about X-axis**

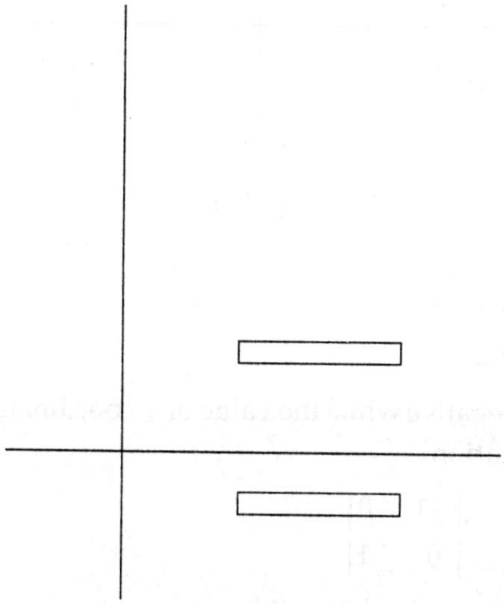

Fig. 3.4

From the figure, we know that

$$X' = X$$

$$Y' = -Y$$

i.e., the value of X remains unchanged while the value of Y coordinate becomes negative. This can be **shown in form** of matrix notation

$$\begin{vmatrix} 1 & 0 \\ 0 & -1 \end{vmatrix}$$

$$[X'Y'] = [X\,Y] * \begin{vmatrix} 1 & 0 \\ 0 & -1 \end{vmatrix}$$

2. Reflection about Y-axis

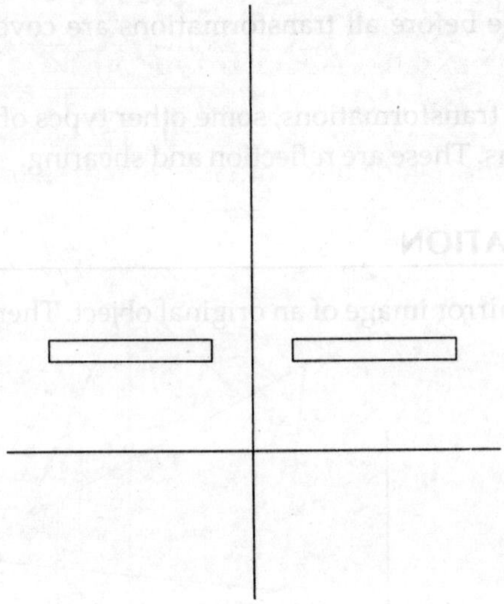

Fig. 3.5

From the figure, we know that

$$X' = -X$$

$$Y' = Y$$

i.e., the value of X becomes negative while the value of Y coordinate remains unchanged. This can be shown in form of matrix notation

$$\begin{vmatrix} -1 & 0 \\ 0 & 1 \end{vmatrix}$$

$$[X'\ Y'] = [X\ Y] * \begin{vmatrix} -1 & 0 \\ 0 & 1 \end{vmatrix}$$

3. Reflection about origin

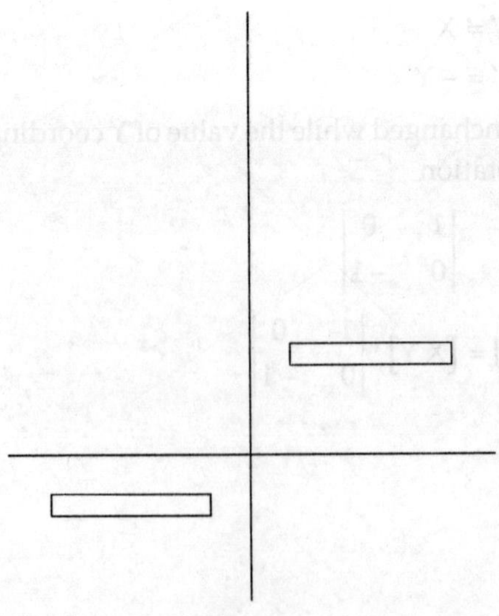

Fig. 3.6

From the figure, we know that

$$X' = -X$$

$$Y' = -Y$$

i.e. the value of X becomes negative while the value of Y also becomes negative. This can be **shown in form** of matrix notation

$$\begin{vmatrix} -1 & 0 \\ 0 & -1 \end{vmatrix}$$

$$[X'Y'] = [X\ Y] * \begin{vmatrix} -1 & 0 \\ 0 & 1 \end{vmatrix}$$

4. Reflection about the line Y = mX + C

For such reflection, we have to follow the following sequence of steps:

1. Translate the line by $T_x = 0$ and $T_y = -C$ as C is the Y intercept at point (0, C) so that line passes through the origin
2. Rotate by an angle "A" where tan A = m about origin
3. Take the reflection against X or Y axis depending upon the direction of rotation
4. Again rotate in reverse direction
5. Retranslate by $T_x = 0$ and $T_y = C$

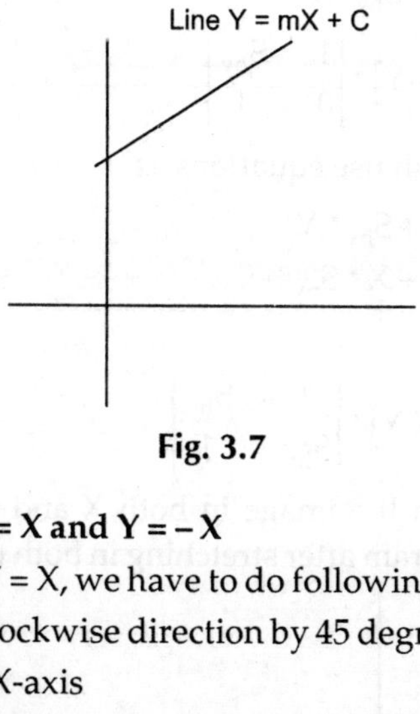

Fig. 3.7

5. Reflection about the line Y = X and Y = – X

Let's consider the first case Y = X, we have to do following sequence of steps

1. Rotate about origin in clockwise direction by 45 degree
2. Take reflection against X-axis
3. Again rotate it in anticlockwise direction by the same angle

Matrix for such reflection would be

$$\begin{vmatrix} 0 & 1 \\ 1 & 0 \end{vmatrix}$$

Let's consider the first case Y = – X, we have to do following sequence of steps

1. Rotate about origin in clockwise direction by 45 degree
2. Take reflection against Y-axis

3. Again rotate it in anticlockwise direction by the same angle of 45

Matrix for such reflection would be

$$\begin{vmatrix} 0 & -1 \\ -1 & 0 \end{vmatrix}$$

SHEARING TRANSFORMATION

The shearing transformation makes the object to distort the shape in either X or Y or both the directions. It can be imagined as the object which is made of very thin layers and they are moved (slide) over each other fixing the base in case of single dimensional shearing. One can assume it to be like stretching a chewing gum in either one direction or both directions.

To shear in X direction only use equations and shearing matrix as

$$X' = X + S_{hx} * Y$$

$$Y' = Y$$

$$[X'\ Y'] = [X\ Y] * \begin{vmatrix} 1 & 0 \\ S_{hx} & 1 \end{vmatrix}$$

To shear in Y direction only use equations and shearing matrix as

$$X' = X$$

$$Y' = X * S_{hy} + Y$$

$$[X'\ Y'] = [X\ Y] * \begin{vmatrix} 1 & S_{hy} \\ 0 & 1 \end{vmatrix}$$

To shear in X and Y direction both use equations as

$$X' = X + S_{hx} * Y$$

$$Y' = Y + X * S_{hy}$$

or putting in matrix form as

$$[X'\ Y'] = [X\ Y] * \begin{vmatrix} 1 & S_{hy} \\ S_{hx} & 1 \end{vmatrix}$$

The above equation will stretch the image in both X and Y direction simultaneously and a rectangle will look like a parallelogram after stretching in both directions.

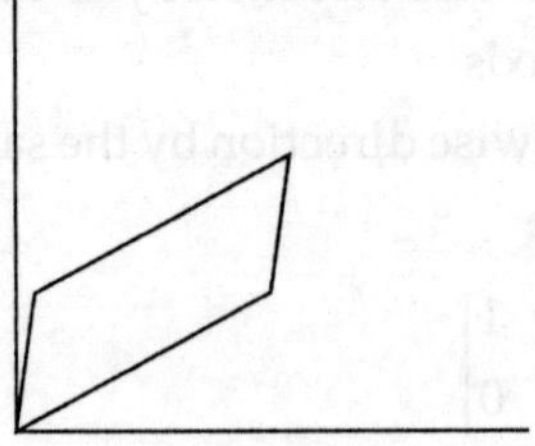

Fig. 3.8

Zooming and panning are some camera related transformations. Zoom in and out shows the image in reduced and enlarged size respectively. It is an important transformation in which object or a part of object can be selected and shown bigger than its size. For example, an architect wants to see a particular block of the building then he can use the zoom option of camera. AutoCAD and other graphics packages support Zooming of images. Panning is a transformation that translates the camera parallel to the plane of the background. Zooming and panning are used in tandem.

Taking the example from AutoCAD (which has been covered in the last chapter), some options associated with Zoom and Pan are listed below. Zooming is a tool that helps us to move around the drawing area.

Most of the operations involved in moving around the drawing area are embodied in one command called ZOOM. This command has a number of options as set out in its data prompt:

```
All/Centre/Dynamic/Extents/Left/Previous/Vmax/Window/<Scale(X/XP)>:
```

Each of these options is described in the following paragraphs.

Zoom Scale

This is the default option and simply requires the entry of a number which represents a magnification factor. Note that the factor is applied to the entire drawing (as defined by the LIMITS command). Numbers less than 1 will reduce the displayed size of the drawing, while numbers greater than 1 will enlarge it.

Zoom Extents

This option causes AutoCAD to display all the graphics that is contained in the drawing (referred to as the drawing extent) with the largest image possible. It does not necessarily extend to the defined drawing limits.

Zoom All

This option causes AutoCAD to display the whole drawing as far as its drawing limits or drawing extents (whichever is greater).

Zoom Window

This option prompts the user to point to the lower left and upper right corners of a box on the existing view in order to define that part which is to be enlarged to fill the display.

Zoom Centre

This option requires a point which is taken to be the centre of the new display, followed by a value to be its new height in drawing units. The existing height is offered as the default for the new height to allow for panning across the drawing.

Zoom Left Corner

This option operates in the same way as "ZOOM Centre" except that the point specified is taken as the lower left corner of the new display.

Zoom Previous

This option reverts to the displayed view prior to the current one. For the purpose of this option, up to 5 views are "stacked" so that the last five views can be recalled.

Zoom Dynamic

This is the most powerful ZOOM option once it is understood. It permits very quick movement around the drawing.

Another very useful command that can be used to alter the currently displayed view is the PAN command.

Pan

This command permits panning across the drawing without changing the display scale. A displacement must be specified either by pointing or typing.

Three other commands are available for creating 3D views of the drawing. These are really only of interest if you have taken the trouble to enter a three-dimensional description of an object. However, even if your drawing is only 2D, you can still look at it from any 3D point in space and view it as either a parallel projection or as a full perspective.

PERFORM SOME PRACTICE

1. Represent the matrix that performs rotation by 30 degrees about the origin. Later write a program to represent such matrix.
2. What are the new coordinates of the point P (2, – 4) after the rotation by 30 degrees?
3. Perform a 45 degree rotation of A(0, 0) B(1, 1) C(5, 2)
   (*a*) About the origin
   (*b*) About point P(– 1, – 1)
4. Magnify the with vertices A(0, 0) B(1, 1) & C(5, 2) to twice its size keeping C(5,2) fixed.

Solutions:

1.

$$R_{30} = \begin{vmatrix} \text{Cos } 30 & \text{Sin } 30 \\ -\text{ Sin } 30 & \text{Cos } 30 \end{vmatrix}$$

$$= \begin{vmatrix} \sqrt{3}/2 & 1/2 \\ -1/2 & \sqrt{3}/2 \end{vmatrix}$$

2. The given point is (2,–4) and it has to be rotated by 30 degrees so

$$[2, -4] * \begin{vmatrix} \sqrt{3}/2 & 1/2 \\ -1/2 & \sqrt{3}/2 \end{vmatrix}$$

$$= \left[\sqrt{3} + 2, 1 - 2\sqrt{3}\right]$$

The new coordinates of the point are $\left(\sqrt{3} + 2 \text{ and } 1 - 2\sqrt{3}\right)$

3. (*a*) The triangle has to be rotated by 45 degrees about the origin. We represent the triangle with the following matrix

$$\begin{vmatrix} A & B & C \\ 0 & 0 & 1 \\ 1 & 1 & 1 \\ 5 & 2 & 1 \end{vmatrix}$$

$$\text{Rotation Matrix R 45} = \begin{vmatrix} \text{Cos } 45 & \text{Sin } 45 & 0 \\ -\text{Sin } 45 & \text{Cos } 45 & 1 \\ 0 & 0 & 1 \end{vmatrix}$$

$$= \begin{vmatrix} \sqrt{2}/2 & \sqrt{2}/2 & 0 \\ -\sqrt{2}/2 & \sqrt{2}/2 & 1 \\ 0 & 0 & 1 \end{vmatrix}$$

So the co-ordinates A′ B′ C′ of the new transformed triangle can be calculated as (ABC) × R45

$$A'B'C' = \begin{vmatrix} 0 & 0 & 1 \\ 1 & 1 & 1 \\ 5 & 2 & 1 \end{vmatrix} \begin{vmatrix} \sqrt{2}/2 & \sqrt{2}/2 & 0 \\ -\sqrt{2}/2 & \sqrt{2}/2 & 1 \\ 0 & 0 & 1 \end{vmatrix}$$

$$= \begin{vmatrix} 0 & 0 & 1 \\ 0 & \sqrt{2} & 1 \\ 3/\sqrt{2} & 7/\sqrt{2} & 1 \end{vmatrix}$$

So new coordinates $A_, = (0, 0)$ $B_, = \left(0, \sqrt{2}\right)$ & $C_, = \left(3/\sqrt{2}, 7/\sqrt{2}\right)$ and with their help we can display rotated triangle.

(*b*) In the previous example, rotation was performed with respect to the origin but in this example it has to be performed with respect to (– 1, – 1)

(Refer back to the topic rotation about arbitrary axis and look at the concate-nation of matrices)

$$R = \begin{vmatrix} 1 & 0 & 0 \\ 0 & 1 & 0 \\ -1 & -1 & 1 \end{vmatrix} \begin{vmatrix} \sqrt{2}/2 & \sqrt{2}/2 & 0 \\ -\sqrt{2}/2 & \sqrt{2}/2 & 1 \\ 0 & 0 & 1 \end{vmatrix} \begin{vmatrix} 1 & 0 & 0 \\ 0 & 1 & 0 \\ 1 & 1 & 1 \end{vmatrix}$$

Left multiplying them, we get

$$= \begin{vmatrix} \sqrt{2}/2 & \sqrt{2}/2 & 0 \\ -\sqrt{2}/2 & \sqrt{2}/2 & 0 \\ -1 & \sqrt{2}-1 & 1 \end{vmatrix}$$

Now multiply the triangle matrix with the result obtained above to get new coordinates

$$= \begin{vmatrix} 0 & 0 & 1 \\ 1 & 1 & 1 \\ 5 & 2 & 1 \end{vmatrix} \begin{vmatrix} \sqrt{2}/2 & \sqrt{2}/2 & 0 \\ -\sqrt{2}/2 & \sqrt{2}/2 & 0 \\ -1 & \sqrt{2}-1 & 1 \end{vmatrix}$$

So the new coordinates of triangle have been evaluated as

$$A' = \left(-1, \sqrt{2}-1\right) B' = \left(-1, 2\sqrt{2}-1\right) C' = \left(3\sqrt{2}-1, 9/2\sqrt{2}-1\right)$$

4. To magnify triangle with vertices A(0, 0) B(1, 1) & C(5, 2) to twice its size while keeping vertex C(5, 2) fixed, we can do the following:

   First perform the operations (as in previous example) of translating the point to the origin, scaling and then translating back to the required position

$$S = \begin{vmatrix} 1 & 0 & 0 \\ 0 & 1 & 0 \\ -5 & -2 & 1 \end{vmatrix} \begin{vmatrix} 2 & 0 & 0 \\ 0 & 2 & 0 \\ 0 & 0 & 1 \end{vmatrix} \begin{vmatrix} 1 & 0 & 0 \\ 0 & 1 & 0 \\ 5 & 2 & 1 \end{vmatrix}$$

$$S = \begin{vmatrix} 2 & 0 & 0 \\ 0 & 2 & 0 \\ -5 & -2 & 1 \end{vmatrix}$$

$$\text{Now Triangle ABC} = \begin{vmatrix} 0 & 0 & 1 \\ 1 & 1 & 1 \\ 5 & 2 & 1 \end{vmatrix}$$

So ABC multiplied S gives

$$A'B'C = \begin{vmatrix} -5 & -2 & 1 \\ -3 & 0 & 1 \\ 5 & 2 & 1 \end{vmatrix}$$

So new coordinates are **A′ = (– 5, – 2) B′ = (– 3, 0) C′ = (5, 2), so C′ is fixed at (5, 2).**
A′ = (– 5, – 2) B′ = (– 3, 0) C′ = (5, 2)

INTERACTION (INPUT TECHNIQUES)

Interaction is the way user communicates with the system and that's what we call interactive systems. Interactivity is a must for Graphics as actions have to change rapidly. Computer graphics adds depth to communication between the user and computer machine. As we know **communication is always a two way process,** it is desirable to allow the user to respond to the output or displayed material.

There can be different sorts of **responses a user might wish** to make to such a display like selecting a particular part of the display, entering a new object on the display, specifying the position on the display, wishing to alter an object's orientation, size or location or there can be so many other options.

Some effective methods are there for the input of graphic information. **A user might move a STYLUS** a penlike device and see the lines appear on the display as if real pen and ink were being used for drawing. Scale and direction might be changed or the position of the display may be selected by pointing or indicating to it.

HARDWARE DEVICES USED IN INTERACTION

Various hardware devices enable the user to interact in the above stated manner with ease. These devices can be separated into two classes : **Locators and Selectors.**

Locators are devices giving us position information on the screen. The Computer machine receives from a locator the co-ordinates for a point. Using locators, we can indicate a position on the screen which is helpful in manipulating the screen coordinates.

Selector devices are used to select a particular graphical object from an image. A selector may pick a particular item and it does not provide information about where that item is located on the screen.

Some location devices are :

A pair of THUMBWHEELS containing two potentiometers mounted on the keyboard, which the user can adjust. One potentiometer is used for x direction and the other for y direction. Analog to digital converters change the potentiometer setting into a digital value which the computer can use to find the coordinates of a point.

Another location device is a JOYSTICK. A joystick has two potentiometers, just as a pair of thumb wheels. They have been attached to a single lever. Moving the lever forward or back changes the setting of the potentiometer.

Some other location devices are mouse and track balls. Digitizer or a tablet can also be used for location.

Some selector devices are :

Light Pen : A light pen is composed of a photocell. This pen may be poised at the screen on a refresh display.

The pen sends a pulse whenever the phosphor below it is illuminated. **When the light pen senses the phosphor beneath it being illuminated, it can interrupt the display processor's interpreting of the display file.**

DEVICES USED FOR EVENT HANDLING

A light pen is so popular and is an example of an event driven devices. There are other devices like keyboard which is also an example of driven devices. The machine must wait for a key to be pressed before it can judge which character the user wishes to send to the system.

Buttons & Switches may also be available as input devices as we have seen in Visual Basic and other programming languages. Whatever button is clicked, only the code behind that is executed. These are also event drivers.

Now the question arises how event handling is possible. It is possible through **INTERRUPT** approach. In this approach, interrupt is enabled and sent by the device when an event occurs. **An interrupt is an electrical signal that causes the processor to be interrupted from regular sequence and transfer control to a designated or special interrupt handling routine already fed into the system.**

By using the interrupt method, **central processing unit is free to carry out some other operation while it is waiting for an event to occur.** When the event occurs, processing is interrupted and the devices which caused the interrupt is serviced. After servicing the devices, CPU can proceed with its own incomplete task.

An interrupt method of event handling allows handling of events which may occurs at time other than when the CPU is expecting them.

INPUT DEVICE HANDLING ALGORITHM

Let us consider the routine to handle input devices. Basically graphics developers classify the devices into classes. We shall consider five classes of devices. They are

(1) button (2) pick (3) Keyboard (4) Locator (5) Valuation.

Now the method followed is as follows :

We will consider flags each classes. The value of flags will determine whether or not a particula class is enabled.

Algorithm for INPUT DEVICE handling

Variables class containing value/code for Buttons, KeyBoard, Locator, etc// Value of class wil change in the algorithm.

```
{
    If  class = 1 then
    {
    Perform all operation needed to permit input from the button devices
    Button = true ;
    End
    }
    If class = 2 then
    {
    Perform all operation needed to permit input from any other input device
    ......
    ......
    End;
    }
    And so on
    .
    .
    }
```

EVENT HANDLING

In principle, we call an event driven device as the one which generates an interrupt. The CPU detects the interrupt and stops the current activity or job and services the interrupting device. When the device has been serviced, normal processing resumes.

A brief outline is given below to show as above process. Assume that there is a single event queue.

```
Algorithm EVENT for processing an input device's interrupt.
{
Disable Physical Interrupt So That No Other Device Can Interrupt;
Save Processor Status Onto The Stack;
Determine Which Device Caused The Interrupt ;
{
Process The Interrupting Process
}
Restore Processor Status;
Reenable Physical Interrupts So That Other Device Can Interrupt;
Return ;
}
```

SAMPLED DEVICE

The locator is a sampled devices and therefore, may be read at any time; there is no need to wait for an event to be placed on the event queue. We only need a routine which read the locator and returns its X,Y values.

DETECTIBILITY ATTRIBUTE

There are times when we see multiple choices before us. The ability to pick up an item from a subset of items actually appearing on the display is delectability.

ECHOING

An important part of an interactive system is echoing. Echoing provides the user with information about his actions. This allows the user to compare what he has done against what he wanted to do. For keyboard input, echoing takes the form of displaying the type characters. Locators may be echoed by a screen cursor displayed at the current locator position.

A pick may be echoed by identifying the selected objects on the display. The selected objects may be flashed, made brighter or determine whether or not he has selected the intended objects.

INTERATIVE TECHNIQUES

We should include some techniques for interactively creating and modifying pictures. Let us first consider how to add new picture elements to the image.

Point plotting techniques gives the user the capability of selecting a particular point on the display screen. One use for point plotting routine is to enter line segments. The concept here is to connect the successive points selected by the user with line segments.

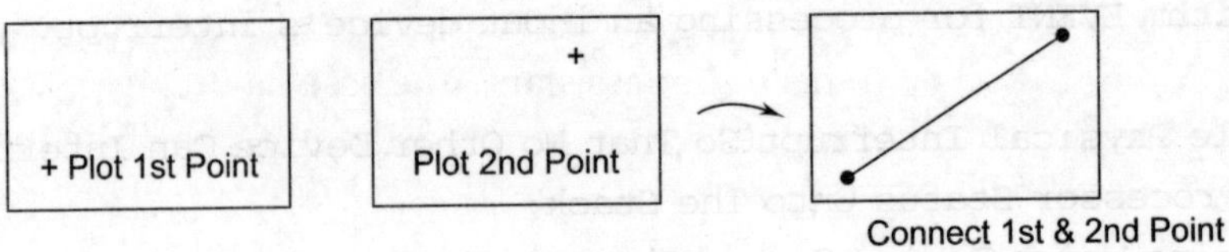

Fig. 3.9

A variation of this technique is called INKING. Inking makes the locator automatically leave a trial of line segments the way a pen leaves a trial of ink Sometimes you must have experienced it in Pain brush or in Corel Draw Software. It doesn't require the user to push a button for every line segment. Instead a segment is drawn whenever the locator moves a sufficient distance.

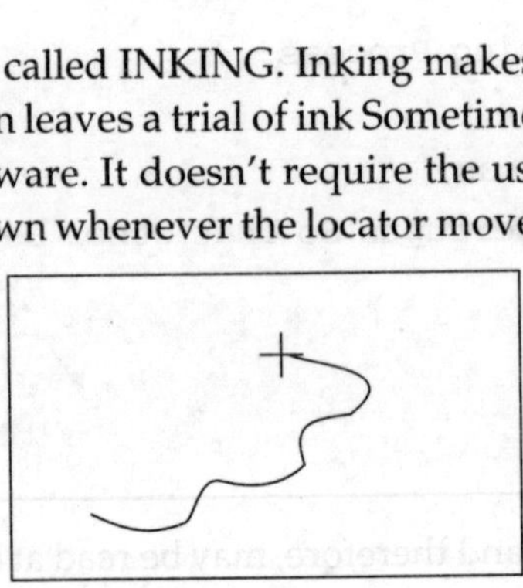

Fig. 3.10 *Figure for Inking*

Raster displays can extend inking to painting with a brush. A brush is a pattern of fixed patterns. When painting, we repeatedly sample the location position. Each time the position changes we copy the brush pattern into the frame buffer. The effect is to draw this pattern repeatedly on the display along the path of a locator. You must have experienced it in Paint Brush.

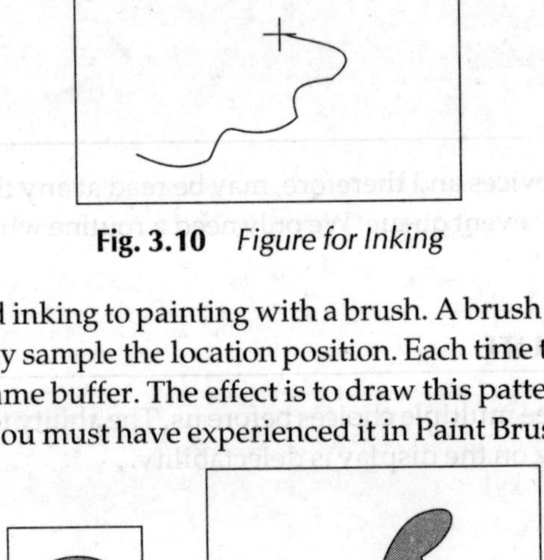

Fig. 3.11 *Figure for painting*

These methods are also referred to as rubber band methods of interaction. Flexibility is the key to rubber band methods. Inking and painting are examples of rubber band methods.

Dragging is a technique in by which we can drag an object on the screen to any point on the screen. Drag and drop technique is important for Graphics systems.

Tweening technique

Tweening, short for in-betweening, is the process of generating intermediate frames between two images to give the appearance that the first image evolves smoothly into the second image. **Inbetweens** are the drawings between the keyframes which help to create the illusion of motion. Tweening is a key process in all types of animation, including computer animation.

Sophisticated animation software enables one to identify specific objects in an image and define how they should move and change during the tweening process. Software may be used to manually render or adjust transitional frames by hand or use to automatically render transitional frames using interpolation of graphic parameters.

In the inbetweening workflow of traditional hand-drawn animation, the senior or key artist would draw the keyframes which define the movement, then, after testing and approval of the rough animation, hands over the scene to his or her assistant. The assistant does the clean-up and the necessary inbetweens, or, in really big studios, only some breakdowns which define the movement in more detail, then handing down the scene to his assistant, the inbetweener who does the rest.

Contrary to popular belief, no animator really draws inbetweens for all 24 frames required for one second of film. Only very fast movements require animation "on ones", as it is called. Most movements can be done with 12 drawings per second, which is called animating "on twos". Too few inbetweens distort the illusion of movement, like in cheap TV animation series where there can be as few as 4 drawings for a second of film.

Computer generated animation is always animated on ones. The decision about the number of inbetweens is also an artistic one, as certain styles of animation require a not-so-smooth fashion of movement.

Traditional inbetweening involves the use of drawing tables with underneath lighting to draw a set of pencil-on-paper pictures, but in more recent times computers may be used to speed up the inbetweening process. The use of computers for inbetweening was pioneered by Nestor Burtnyk and Marceli Wein at the National Research Council of Canada. They received a Technical Achievement Academy Award in 1997, for "pioneering work in the development of software techniques for computer assisted key framing for character animation".

In the context of Adobe Flash, the process is simply called "tweening," and the resultant animation is called a "tween."

We will now focus on graphics operations covering Windowing, Clipping and filling. These operations are important part of any graphics system.

WINDOWING AND CLIPPING

The method for selecting and enlarging portions of a drawing is called Windowing and the technique for not showing that part of the drawing which one is not interested in is called Clipping.

VIEWING TRANSFORMATION

It is often useful to think of two models of the item we are displaying. There is the object model and there is the image of the object, which appears on the display.

The object model is said to reside in object space and this model represents the object using physical units of length.

The image model is measured in screen co-ordinates (we have normalized the screen co-ordinates so that they have range between 0 & 1)

We must have some way of converting from the object space units of measure to those of the image space (Screen space). This can be done by the scaling transformations. The physical dimensions of the object are scaled until they are suitable for display.

It may be, however, that the object is too complex to show in its entirety or that we are particularly interested in just a portion of it. We would like to imagine a box and would only display what is enclosed in the box and such a box is called Window.

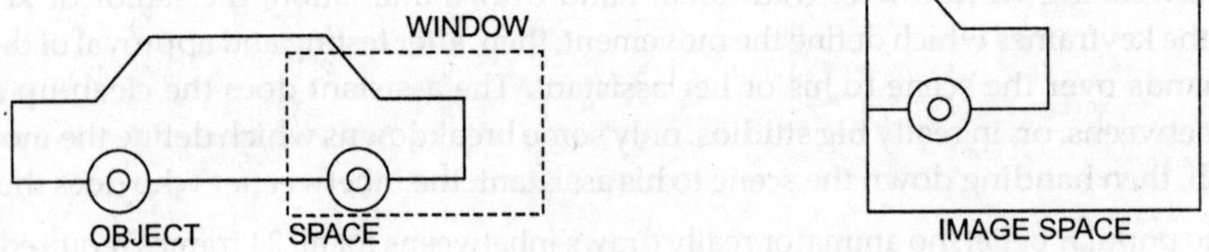

Fig. 3.12

It might also happen that we don't wish to use the entire screen for display. We would like to imagine a box on the screen and have the image confined to that box. Such box in the screen space is called a view port.

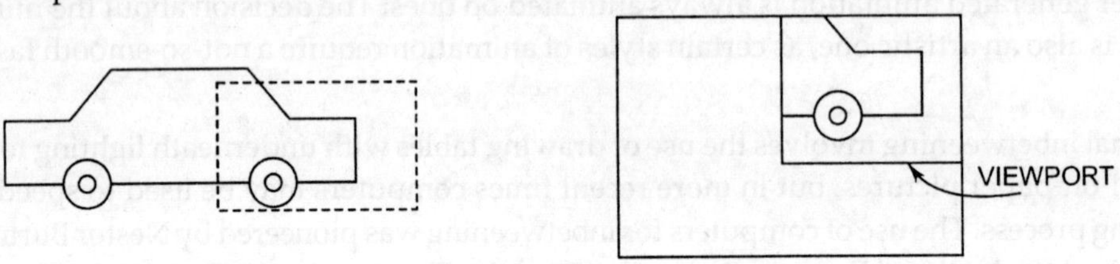

Fig. 3.13

When the window is changed we see a different part of the object shown at the same portion on the display. If we change the View port, we see the same part of the object drawn at a different place on the display.

Fig. 3.14

In specifying both window and view port, we have enough information to determine the translation and scaling transformations necessary to map from the object space to the image space. This can be done with the following steps:

1. First the object together with its window is translated until the lower left corner of the window is at the origin.
2. Second the object and window are scaled until the window has the dimension of a view port. This converts object and window into image and view port.
3. The final transformation step is another translation to move the view port to its correct position on the screen.

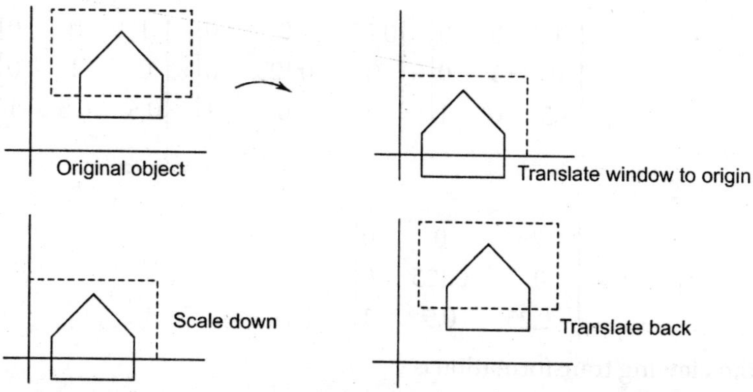

Fig. 3.15

We are trying to do two things: We are changing the window size to become the size of the view ort (scaling) and we are positioning it at the desired location (translating). The overall transformaion, which performs these steps, is called the viewing transformation.

Let us consider an example of viewing transformation. If our window has left and right boundaies of 3 & 5 and lower and upper boundaries of 0 & 4 then the first translation matrix would be

$$\begin{vmatrix} 1 & 0 & 0 \\ 0 & 1 & 0 \\ -3 & 0 & 1 \end{vmatrix}$$

Matrix

uppose the view port is the upper right quadrant of the screen with boundaries at 0.5 and 1.0 for oth x & y directions

$$S_x = (1.0 - 0.5)/(5.0 - 3.0)$$
$$= (0.5)/2.0)$$
$$= 0.25$$

Similarly $S_y = 0.125$

So scaling transformation matrix will be

$$\begin{vmatrix} 0.25 & 0 & 0 \\ 0 & 0.125 & 0 \\ 0 & 0 & 1 \end{vmatrix}$$

Matrix

inally to position the view port requires the translations of

$$\begin{vmatrix} 1 & 0 & 0 \\ 0 & 1 & 0 \\ 0.5 & 0.5 & 1 \end{vmatrix}$$

Matrix

The viewing transformation is then

$$\begin{vmatrix} 1 & 0 & 0 \\ 0 & 1 & 0 \\ -3 & 0 & 1 \end{vmatrix} \times \begin{vmatrix} 0.25 & 0 & 0 \\ 0 & 0.125 & 0 \\ 0 & 0 & 1 \end{vmatrix} \times \begin{vmatrix} 1 & 0 & 0 \\ 0 & 1 & 0 \\ 0.5 & 0.5 & 1 \end{vmatrix}$$

Matrices

$$= \begin{vmatrix} 0.25 & 0 & 0 \\ 0 & 0.125 & 0 \\ -0.25 & 0.5 & 1 \end{vmatrix}$$

In general form the viewing transformation is

$$\begin{vmatrix} 1 & 0 & 0 \\ 0 & 1 & 0 \\ -W_{XL} & -W_{YL} & 1 \end{vmatrix} \times \begin{vmatrix} \left(\frac{V_{XH} - V_{XL}}{W_{XH} - W_{XL}}\right) & 0 & 0 \\ 0 & \left(\frac{V_{YH} - V_{YL}}{W_{YH} - W_{YL}}\right) & 0 \\ 0 & 0 & 1 \end{vmatrix}$$

$$\times \begin{vmatrix} 1 & 0 & 0 \\ 0 & 1 & 0 \\ V_{XL} & V_{YL} & 1 \end{vmatrix}$$

Matrix

where W is used for Window, V for a view port, X for position of vertical boundary, Y for horizontal boundary, H for horizontal and L for lower boundary.

C language supports in built functions like window (int left, int top, int right, int bottom) and the same hods good for view port also.

CLIPPING

We shall now consider how to cut off the lines, which are outside the window so that only the lines within the window are displayed. This process is called clipping.

In clipping we examine each line of the display to determine whether or not it is completely inside the window, lies completely outside the window or crosses the window boundary.

If it is inside, the line is displayed. If it is outside nothing is drawn. If it crosses the boundary., we must determine the point of intersection and draw only the portion which lies inside.

Cohen-Sutherland Line Clipping

This algorithm makes clever use of bit operations (out-codes) to perform the test efficiently. Line segments endpoints are each given 4 bit binary codes.

The Cohen-Sutherland line clipping algorithm quickly detects and dispenses with two common and trivial cases. To clip a line, we need to consider only its endpoints. If both endpoints of a line lie inside the window, the entire line lies inside the window. It is **trivially accepted** and needs no clipping. On the other hand, if both endpoints of a line lie entirely to one side of the window, the line must lie entirely outside of the window. It is **trivially rejected** and needs to be neither clipped nor displayed.

Inside-Outside Window Codes

To determine whether endpoints are inside or outside a window, the algorithm sets up a **half-space code** for each endpoint. Each edge of the window defines an infinite line that divides the whole space into two half-spaces, the **inside half-space** and the **outside half-space,** as shown below.

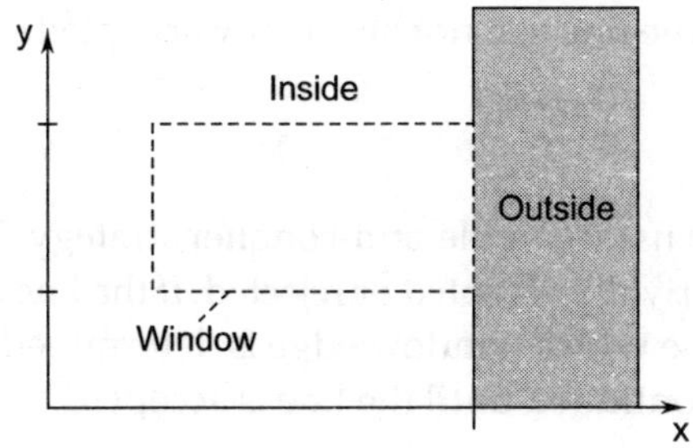

Fig. 3.16

As you proceed around the window, extending each edge and defining an inside half-space and an outside half-space, nine regions are created - the eight "outside" regions and the one "inside"region. Each of the nine regions associated with the window is assigned a 4 bit code to identify the region. Each bit in the code is set to either a 1(true) or a 0(false). If the region is to the **left** of the window, the **first** bit of the code is set to 1. If the region is to the **top** of the window, the **second** bit of the code is set to 1. If to the **right,** the **third** bit is set and if to the **bottom**, the **fourth** bit is set. The 4 bits in the code then identify each of the nine regions as shown below.

1001	0001	0101
1000	0000 Window	0100
1010	0010	0110

Fig. 3.17

For any endpoint **(*x*, *y*)** of a line, the code can be determined that identifies which region the endpoint lies. The code's bits are set according to the following conditions:

- First bit set **1** : Point lies to **left** of window $x < x_{min}$
- Second bit set **1** : Point lies to **right** of window $x > x_{max}$
- Third bit set **1** : Point lies to below**(bottom)** of window $y < y_{min}$
- Fourth bit set **1** : Point lies to above**(top)** of window $y > y_{max}$

The sequence for reading the codes' bits is **LRBT** (Left, Right, Bottom, Top).

Once the codes for each endpoint of a line are determined, the logical **AND** operation of the codes determines if the line is completely outside of the window. If the logical AND of the endpoint codes is **not zero,** the line can be trivally rejected. For example, if an endpoint had a code of 1001 while the other endpoint had a code of 1010, the logical AND would be 1000 which indicates the line segment lies outside of the window. On the other hand, if the endpoints had codes of 1001 and 0110, the logical AND would be 0000 and the line could not be trivally rejected.

The logical **OR** of the endpoint codes determines if the line is completely inside the window. If the logical OR is **zero,** the line can be trivally accepted. For example, if the endpoint codes are 0000 and 0000, the logical OR is 0000 - the line can be trivally accepted. If the endpoint codes are 0000 and 0110, the logical OR is 0110 and the line can not be trivally accepted.

Algorithm

The Cohen-Sutherland algorithm uses a divide-and-conquer strategy. The line segment's endpoints are tested to see if the line can be trivally accepted or rejected. If the line cannot be trivally accepted or rejected, an intersection of the line with a window edge is determined and the trivial reject/accept test is repeated. This process is continued until the line is accepted.

To perform the trivial acceptance and rejection tests, we extend the edges of the window to divide the plane of the window into the nine regions. Each end point of the line segment is then assigned the code of the region in which it lies.

1. Given a line segment with endpoint $P_1 = (x_1, y_1)$ and $P_2 = (x_2, y_2)$
2. Compute the 4-bit codes for each endpoint.

   If both codes are **0000,** (bitwise OR of the codes yields 0000) line lies completely **inside** the window: pass the endpoints to the draw routine.

   If both codes have a 1 in the same bit position (bitwise AND of the codes is **not** 0000), the line lies **outside** the window. It can be trivially rejected.
3. If a line cannot be trivially accepted or rejected, at least one of the two endpoints must lie outside the window and the line segment crosses a window edge. This line must be **clipped** at the window edge before being passed to the drawing routine.
4. Examine one of the endpoints, say $P_1 = (x_1, y_1)$. Read P_1's 4-bit code in order: **Left-to-Right, Bottom-to-Top.**
5. When a set bit (1) is found, compute the **intersection I** of the corresponding window edge with the line from P_1 to P_2. Replace P_1 with **I** and repeat the algorithm.

Intersection of Line Segment

If the line cannot be trivially accepted or rejected, we must compute the intersection of the line with an appropriate window edge.

We need two equations for the line

- $y = mx + b$ where b, c are constant
- $x = 1/_m y + c$

Find the intersection with the top edge of the window:

$$y = \text{T (Top) or } y = y_{max}$$
$$x = 1/_m \text{T} + c$$

Then, find the intersection with the bottom edge:

$$y = \text{B (Bottom) or } y = y_{min}$$
$$x = 1/_m\text{B} + c$$

Now, find the intersection with the left edge:

$$x = \text{L (Left) or } x = x_{min}$$
$$y = m\text{L} + b$$

Finally, find the intersection with the right edge:

$$x = \text{R (Right) or } x = x_{max}$$
$$y = m\text{R} + b$$

There is no significance in the sequence of which edge to examine.

ILLUSTRATION OF LINE CLIPPING

Before Clipping

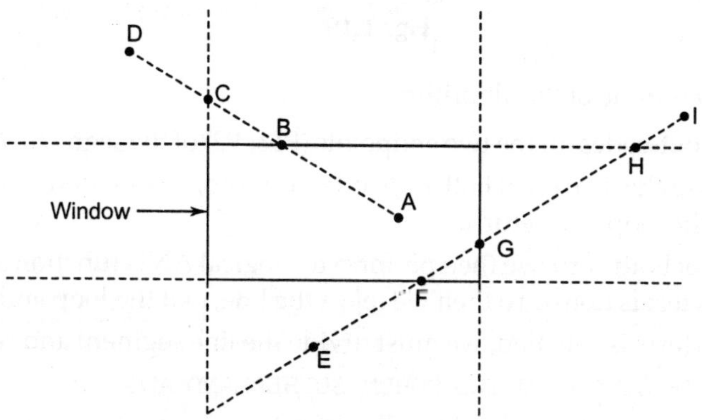

Fig. 3.18

1. Consider the line segment **AD:**

   Point **A** has an outcode of **0000** and point **D** has an outcode of **1001**. The logical AND of these outcodes is zero; therefore, the line cannot be trivally rejected. Also, the logical OR of the outcodes is not zero; therefore, the line cannot be trivally accepted. The algorithm then chooses **D** as the outside point (its outcode contains 1's). By our testing order, we first use the top edge to clip **AD** at **B**. The algorithm then recomputes **B's** outcode as **0000**. With the next iteration of the algorithm, **AB** is tested and is trivially accepted and displayed.
2. Consider the line segment **EI:**

   Point **E** has an outcode of **0100,** while point **I's** outcode is **1010**. The results of the trivial tests show that the line can neither be trivally rejected or accepted. Point **E** is determined to be an outside point, so the algorithm clips the line against the bottom edge of the window. Now line **EI** has been clipped to be line **FI**. Line **FI** is tested and cannot be trivially accepted or rejected. Point F has an outcode of **0000,** so the algorithm chooses point **I** as an outside point since its outcode is **1010.** The line **FI** is clipped against the window's top edge, yielding a new line **FH.** Line **FH** cannot be trivally accepted or rejected. Since **H's** outcode is **0010,** the next iteration of the algorthm clips against the window's right edge, yielding line **FG.** The next iteration of the algorithm tests FG and it is trivially accepted and display.

After Clipping

After clipping the segments **AD** and **EI**, the result is that only the line segment **AB** and **FG** can be seen in the window.

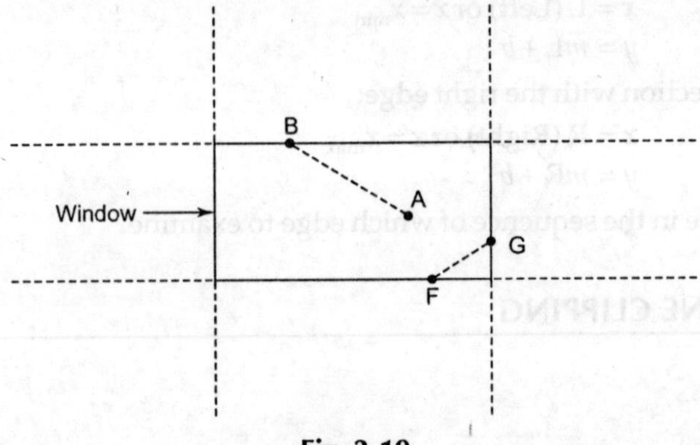

Fig. 3.19

Following is the brief outline of the algorithm :

1. First we compute out-codes for the two endpoints (PI & P2) of the segment. Next we enter a loop
2. Within the loop, we check to see if both out-codes are zero, if yes we enter the segment into the display file, exit the loop and return.
3. If out-codes are not both zero, we then perform the logical AND function and check for a non-zero result. If this test is non-zero then we reject the line, exit the loop and return.

   If neither of these tests is satisfied, we must divide the line segment and repeat the loop.

```
//TO DO CLIPPING OF LINE BY USING COHEN-SUTHERLAND ALGO..
# include<conio.h>
# include<stdio.h>
# include<dos.h>
# include<graphics.h>
typedef unsigned int outcode;
enum boolean {false, true};
enum{top=0x1,bottom=0x2, right=0x4,left=0x8} ;
outcode compoutcode (double, double, double, double, double, double);
void cohen (double x0, double y0, double x1, double y1, double xmin, double
xmax, double ymin, double ymax)
{
outcode outcode0, outcodel, outcodeout;
boolean aocept=false, done=false;
outcode0=compoutcode (x0, y0, xmin, xmax, ymin, ymax) ;
outcodel=compoutcode (x1, y1, xmin, xmax, ymin, ymax) ;
do {
If (! (outcode 0| outcode 1) )
{
accept=true;  //accept and exit (means line is totally in
```

```
(0000) )..
done=true;
}
else if (outcode 0 & outcode 1) //reject and exit (means line is totally
out).
done=true;
else   //failed both tests, so calculate the
line
{                        // segment to clip.
double x,y;
double m;                //atleast one endpoint is outside the clip
m=(yl-y0)/(xl-x0);          // rectangle;pick it...
outcodeout=outcode0? outcode0: outcodel;
if (outcodeout & top)
{
x=x0+(ymax-y0)/m;      //x=x0+(y-y0)/m;
y=ymax;
}
else if(outcodeout&bottom)
{
x=x0+ (ymin-y0) /m;
y=ymin;
}
else if(outcodeout & right)
y=y0+(xmax-x0)*m;          //y=y0+(x-x0)m;
x=xmax;
}
else
{
y = y0+ (xmin-x0) m;
x = xmin;
}
if(outcodeout==outcode0)
{
x0=x;y0==y; outcode0=compoutcode (x0, y0, xmin, xmax, ymin, ymax);
}
else
{
xl=x;yl=y,òoutcodel=compoutcode (xl, yl, xmin, xmax, ymin, ymax);
}
} //for else. . .
```

```
} while (done==faise);
if (accept)
line (x0,y0,xl,yl) ;
}
outcode compoutcode (double x, double y, double xmin, double xmax, double
ymin double ymax)
{
outcode code=0;
if (y>ymax)
code | =top;
else if(y<ymin)
code | =bottom;
if(x>xm+x)
code | =right;
else if (x<xmin)
code | =left;
return code;
}
void main ( )
{
clrscr ( );
int x0,y0,xl,y1, x2, y2,x3,y3, xmin, xmax, ymin, ymax, t;
int gd=DETECT,gm;
char str1 [50]="after clipping the view port is";
 initgraph(&gd,&gm,"c:\\tc\\bgi");
setbkcolor(4);
printf ("/n enter the coordinates for line: ");
scanf ("%d %d %d %d", %x0, &y0, &x1, &y1);
printf ("\n enter the coordinates for another line: ");
scanf ("%d %d %d %d", &x2, &y2, &x3, &y3);
print f ("\n enter the coordinates for window : ");
scanf ("d %d %d %d",&xmin,&ymin,&xmax,&ymax);
printf ("\n before clipping the line is:\n");
rectangle (xmin, ymin, xmax, ymax) ;
line(x0,y0,x1,y1);
line(x2,y2,x3,y3);
delay(3000);
clrscr ( );
setbkcolor(6);
setcolor(1);
cleardevice ( ) ;
```

```
setlinestyle(DOTTED_LINE, 1,1) ;
for(t=0; strl [t] != '\0'; t++)
{
gotoxy(16,2+t*1);
printf (" % c",strl[t]);
delay(100);
}
delay(200);
rectangle (xmin, ymin, xmax, ymax) ;
cohen (x0, y0, x1, y1, xmin, xmax, ymin, ymax) ;
cohen (x2, y2, x3, y3, xmin, xmax, ymin, ymax) ;
getch ( ) ;
```

SUTHERLAND HODGMAN ALGORITHM

The Cohen-Sutherland algorithm works well for lines and we would like a method, which may be used with polygons as well. The method un-bundles the clipping test to clip against each of the four boundaries individually. The idea behind the algorithm is that we can easily clip a line segment against any one of the window boundaries.

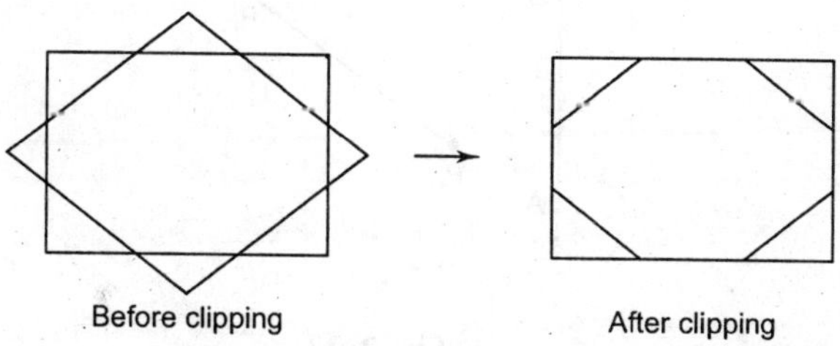

Fig. 3.20

A simple algorithm works as follows:

A polygon is called convex if the line joining any two interior points of a polygon lies completely inside the polygon. By convention, a polygon with vertices P_1 ....P_N and edges $P_{i-1}P_i$ and P_NP_i is said to be positively oriented if a tour of the vertices in the given order produces a counter clockwise circuit.

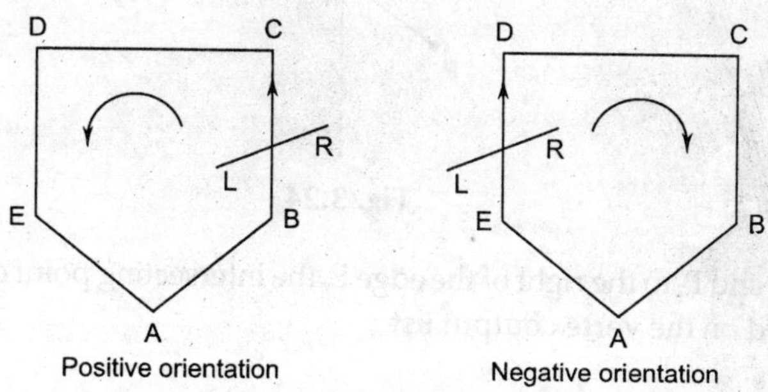

Fig. 3.21

Let P_1 .....P_N be the vertex list of the polygon to be clipped. Let edge E, determined by endpoint and B, be any edge of the positively oriented, convex clipping polygon. We clip each edge of the polygon in turn against edge E of the clipping polygon, forming a new polygon whose vertices are determined as follows:

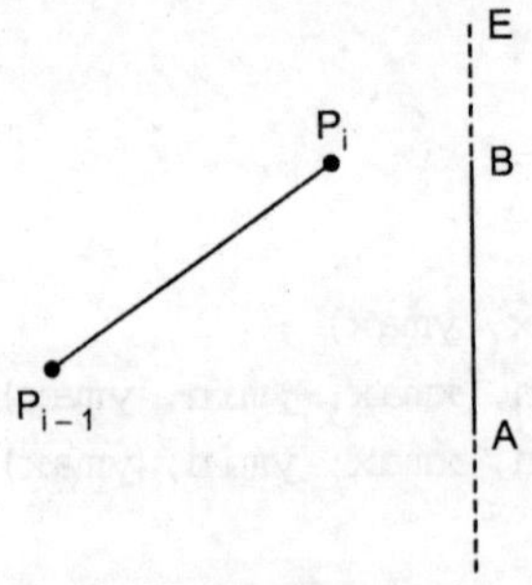

Fig. 3.22

If both P_{i-1} and P_i and to the left of the edge, vertex P_i is placed on the vertex output list of the clipped polygon (*i.e.*, vertex P_i will be considered).

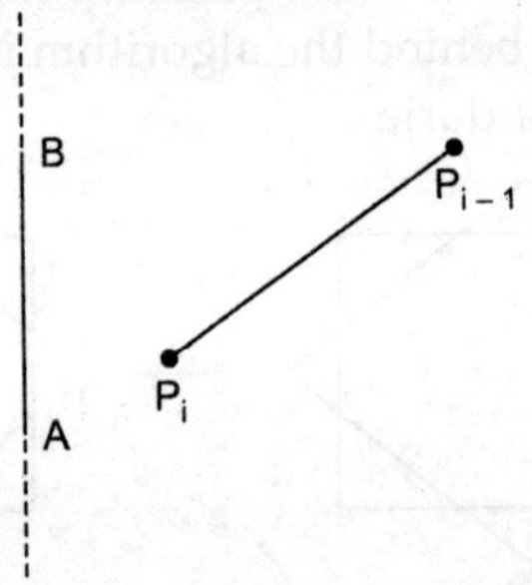

Fig. 3.23

If both P_{i-1} and P_i are to the right of the edge, nothing is placed on the vertex output list

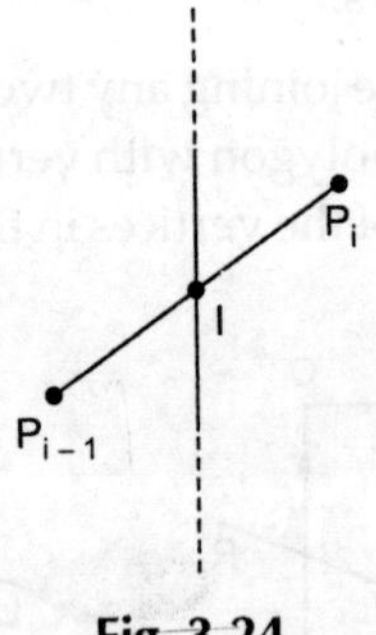

Fig. 3.24

If P_{i-1} is to the left and P_i to the right of the edge E, the intersecting point of line segment $P_{i-1}P_i$ with E is calculated placed on the vertex output list.

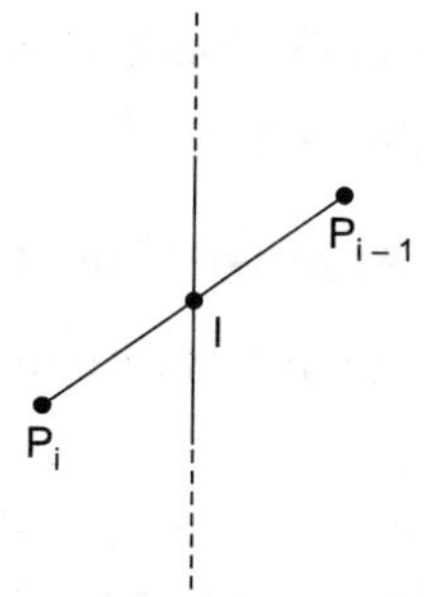

Fig. 3.25

If P_i is to the left, the intersection point I of line segment is calculated. Both I and P_i are placed on the vertex output list.

And this process continues till polygon is clipped against all window boundaries.

An algorithm that clips a polygon must deal with many different cases. The case is particularly noteworthy in that the concave polygon is clipped into two separate polygons. All in all, the task of clipping seems rather complex. Each edge of the polygon must be tested against each edge of the clip rectangle; new edges must be added and existing edges must be discarded, retained, or divided. Multiple polygons may result from clipping a single polygon. We need an organized way to deal with all these cases.

The following example illustrate a simple case of polygon clipping.

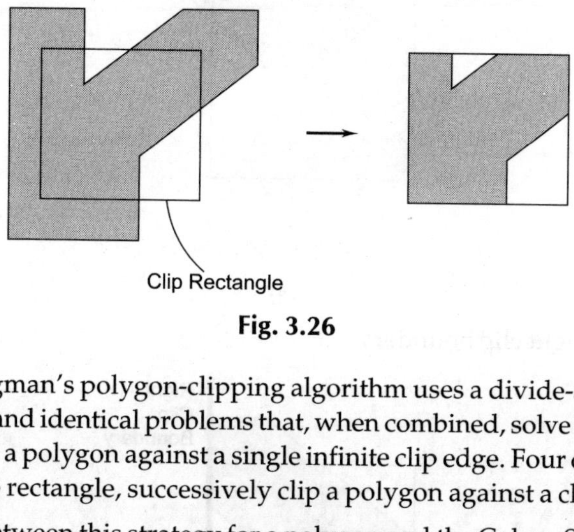

Fig. 3.26

Sutherland and Hodgman's polygon-clipping algorithm uses a divide-and-conquer strategy: It solves a series of simple and identical problems that, when combined, solve the overall problem. The simple problem is to clip a polygon against a single infinite clip edge. Four clip edges, each defining one boundary of the clip rectangle, successively clip a polygon against a clip rectangle.

Note the difference between this strategy for a polygon and the Cohen-Sutherland algorithm for clipping a line: The polygon clipper clips against four edges in succession, whereas the line clipper tests the outcode to see which edge is crossed, and clips only when necessary.

Steps of Sutherland-Hodgman's Polygon-Clipping Algorithm

- Polygons can be clipped against each edge of the window one at a time. Windows/edge intersections, if any, are easy to find since the X or Y coordinates are already known.
- Vertices which are kept after clipping against one window edge are saved for clipping against the remaining edges.

- Note that the number of vertices usually changes and will often increases.
- We are using the Divide and Conquer approach.

Four Cases of Polygon Clipping Against One Edge

The clip boundary determines a visible and invisible region. The edges from vertex i to vertex $i + 1$ can be one of four types:

- Case 1 : Wholly inside visible region - save endpoint
- Case 2 : Exit visible region - save the intersection
- Case 3 : Wholly outside visible region - save nothing
- Case 4 : Enter visible region - save intersection and endpoint

Because clipping against one edge is independent of all others, it is possible to arrange the clipping stages in a pipeline. The input polygon is clipped against one edge and any points that are kept are passed on as input to the next stage of the pipeline. This way four polygons can be at different stages of the clipping process simultaneously. This is often implemented in hardware.

Step by Step Example of Polygon Clipping

The original polygon and the clip rectangle.

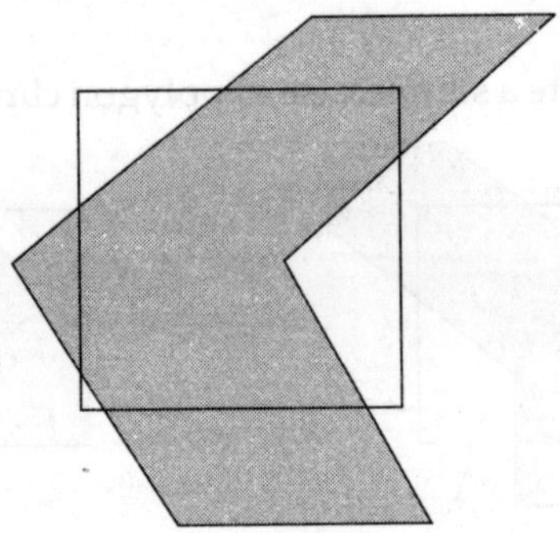

(a)

After clipped by the right clip boundary.

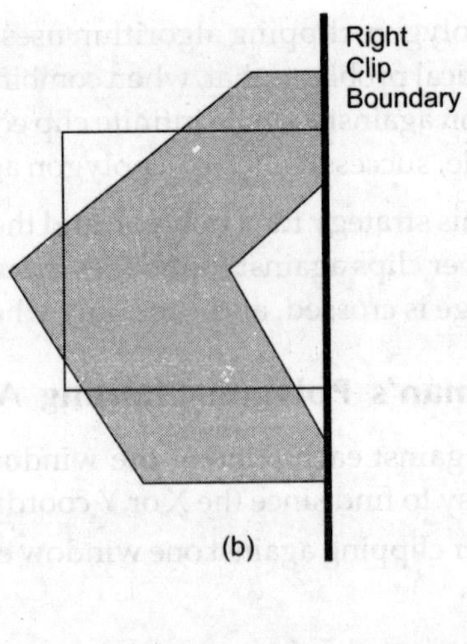

(b)

After clipped by the right and bottom clip boundaries.

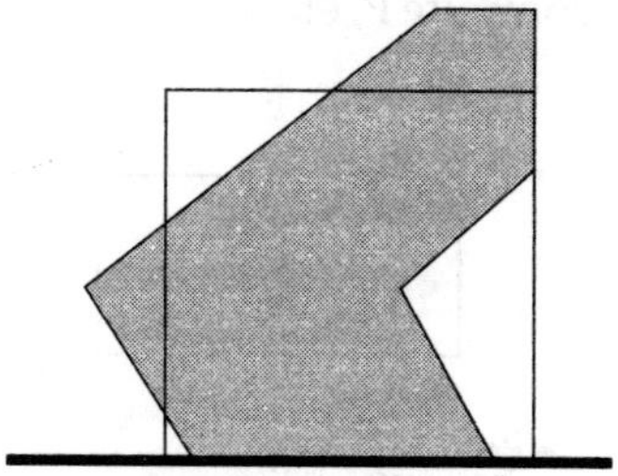

(c)

After clipped by the right, bottom and left clip boundaries.

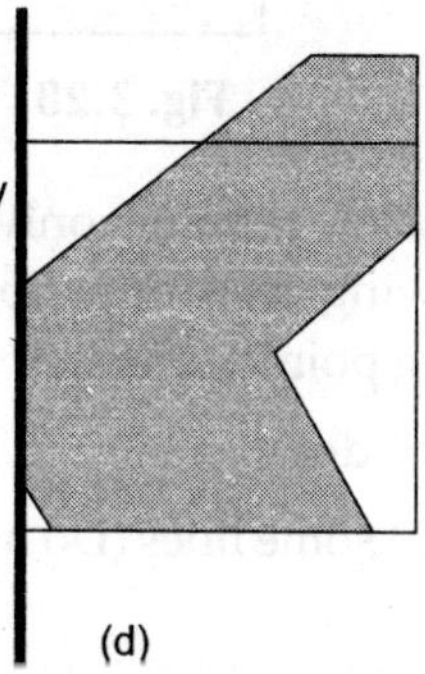

(d)

After clipped by all four boundaries.

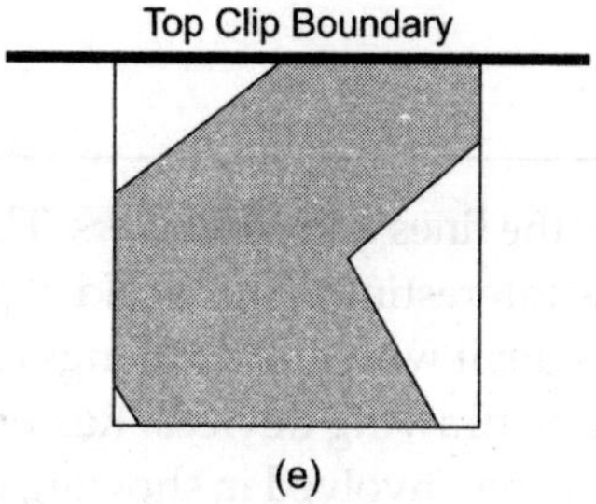

(e)

Fig. 3.27

Mid-Point Subdivision Clipping Algorithm (Binary Search)

The steps of the algorithm are:

Algorithm

1. Compute region codes for endpoints.
2. Check for trivial accept or reject.
3. If step 2 -> no then compute midpoint of line segment

$$xm = (x1 + x2)/2 \; ym = (y1 + y2)/2$$

4. Redo step 1 -> 3 for each 1/2 of line.

Example 1. 1) P1 -> 1000 2) no 3) Compute Pm P2 -> 0000 for Pm -> P2 1) Pm -> 0000 , P2 -> 0000 2) yes accept & display

Example 2. for P1 –> Pm 1) P1 –> 1000; Pm –> 0000 2) no 3) Compute new midpoint P Do step 1, 2 for P1 –> P and reject. for P –> Pm, compute P, etc.

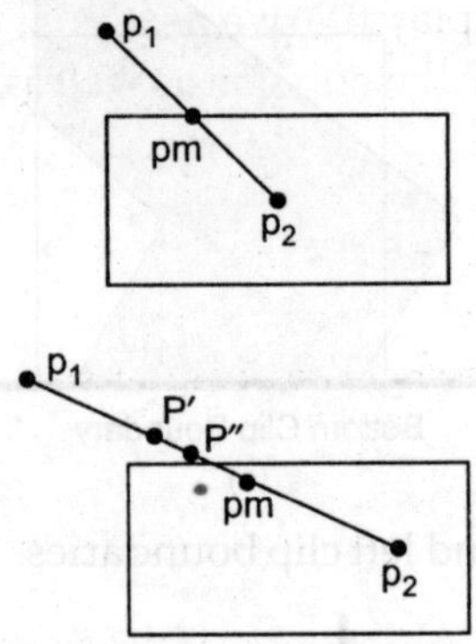

Fig. 3.28

With integers, Midpoint Subdivision requires only addition, right shift (/ 2). So it is a good method if perform clipping after viewing transformation to PDC (use integers). But it is not efficient for clipping against window (floating point numbers).

Advantages of clipping against window:

- May be able to completely reject some lines (Do not have to do viewing transformation [WC – > NDC] on them.)
- Device independence if clip to either viewport or window.

But a disadvantage is that we must do real number arithmetic and division and hence, it is slower.

POLYGON FILLING

So far discussion has dealt with only the lines and characters. The world might seem rather dull if it were made out of straight lines. How interesting is the world of patterns, colors and shading, Unfortunately, much of the early graphics dealt with line drawings only. This was because the available devices (DVST, Plotters etc.) were line drawing devices. Raster display can display solid patterns and objects with no greater effort than that involved in showing their outlines. Coloring and shading is possible with raster technology.

We introduced new graphic primitive, the Polygon in the first chapter. We have already discussed what polygons are and how to represent them? We shall now learn how to determine if a point is inside a polygon. Finally, a method for filling in all inside pixels will be developed.

We wish to be able to represent a surface. One basic surface primitive is a polygon, a many sided figure. A polygon may be represented as a number of line segments connected end to end to form a closed figure. The line segments that make up the polygon boundary are called sides or edges. The endpoint of the sides are called the polygon's vertices. The simplest polygon is the triangle, having three sides and three vertex points.

We have already discussed that polygon can be divided into two classes: Concave and Convex. A Convex polygon is a polygon such that for any two points inside the polygon, all points on the line segment connecting them are also inside the Polygon. A concave polygon is the one, which is not convex. A triangle is always convex.

INSIDE TEST (FOR DETERMINING POINTS INSIDE THE POLYGON)

Having entered commands in the display file, we next might wish to be able to show polygon as solid object by setting the pixels inside the polygon as well as those on boundary.

Let us consider how we can determine whether or not a point is inside the polygon?

EVEN-ODD Method : One way of doing so is to construct a line segment between the point in question and a point known to be outside the polygon Then we count how many intersections of the line segment with the polygon boundary occur.

If there are odd numbers of intersections then the point is INSIDE, an even number indicates that point is OUTSIDE. This is called the ODD-EVEN test for determining polygon interior points.

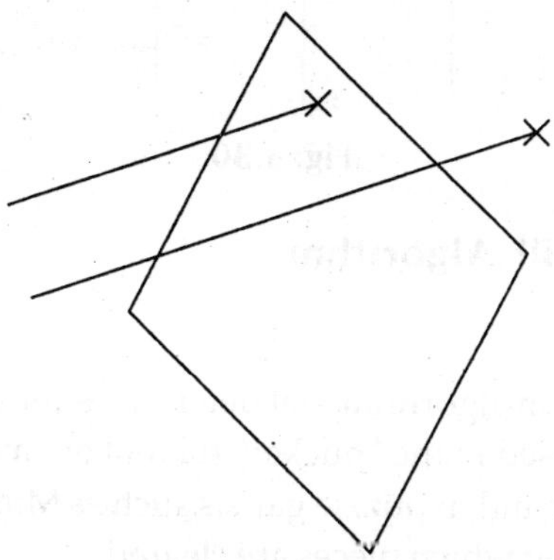

Fig. 3.29

If point of intersection is also the vertex then to handle such a case, we must look at the other endpoints of the two line segments which meet at this vertex. If these points lie on the same side of the constructed line then the point in question counts as even number of intersections. If they lie on the opposite side of the constructed line, the point is counted as single intersection.

There are many methods to fill a polygon, some of them are:

FLOOD FILL METHOD : One way of filling the polygons is to first draw the edges of the polygon in a blank frame buffer. Then starting with some "Seed" point known to be inside the polygon, we set the intensity to the interior style and examine the neighboring pixels. We continue to set the pixel values in an increasing area until we encounter the boundary pixels. This method is called Flood fill because color flows from the "seed" pixel until reaching the polygon boundary.

When flood filling is used, the user will generally provide an initial pixel called a seed, the algorithm will inspect each of the surrounding eight pixels to determine whether the extent has been reached.

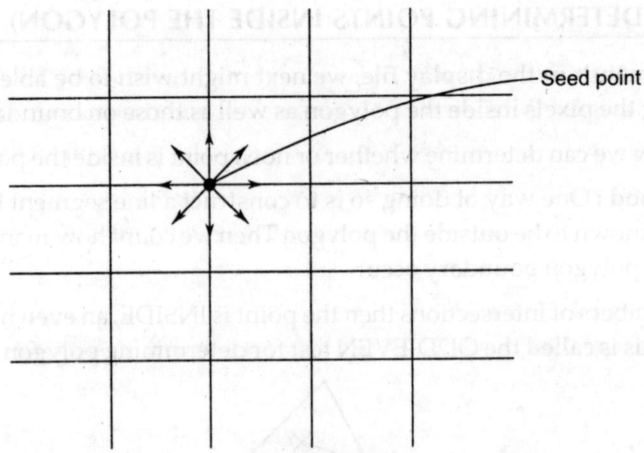

Fig. 3.30

Implementing the Flood Fill Algorithm

Flood Fill

Flood fill, also called **seed fill,** is an algorithm that determines the area connected to a given node in a multi-dimensional array. It is used in the "bucket" fill tool of paint programs to determine which parts of a bitmap to fill with color and in puzzle games such as Minesweeper, Puyo Puyo, Lumines, and Magical Drop for determining which pieces are cleared.

The flood fill algorithm takes three parameters: a start node, a target color and a replacement color. The algorithm looks for all nodes in the array which are connected to the start node by a path of the target color and changes them to the replacement color. There are many ways in which the flood-fill algorithm can be structured, but they all make use of a queue or stack data structure, explicitly or implicitly. One implicitly stack-based (recursive) flood-fill implementation (for a two-dimensional array) goes as follows:

Flood-fill (node, target-color, replacement-color):

1. If the color of *node* is not equal to *target-color*, return.
2. Set the color of *node* to *replacement-color*.
3. Perform **Flood-fill** (one step to the west of *node, target-color, replacement-color*).
   Perform **Flood-fill** (one step to the east of *node, target-color, replacement-color*).
   Perform **Flood-fill** (one step to the north of *node, target-color, replacement-color*).
   Perform **Flood-fill** (one step to the south of *node, target-color, replacement-color*).
4. Return.

Though easy to understand, this implementation is impractical in languages and environments where stack space is severely constrained (*e.g.*, Java applets).

An explicitly queue-based implementation might resemble the following:

Flood-fill (node, target-color, replacement-color):

1. Set Q to the empty queue.
2. If the color of *node* is not equal to *target-color*, return.

3. Add *node* to the end of *Q*.
4. For each element *n* of *Q*:
5. Set the color of *n* to *replacement-color.*
6. If the color of the node to the west of *n* is *target-color,* add that node to the end of *Q*.
   If the color of the node to the east of *n* is *target-color,* add that node to the end of *Q*.
   If the color of the node to the north of *n* is *target-color,* add that node to the end of *Q*.
   If the color of the node to the south of *n* is *target-color,* add that node to the end of *Q*.
7. Continue looping until *Q* is exhausted.
8. Return.

Most practical implementations use a loop for the west and east directions as an optimization to avoid the overhead of stack or queue management:

Flood-fill (node, target-color, replacement-color):

1. Set *Q* to the empty queue.
2. If the color of *node* is not equal to *target-color,* return.
3. Add *node* to *Q*.
4. For each element *n* of *Q*:
5. If the color of *n* is equal to *target-color:*
6. Set *w* and *e* equal to *n.*
7. Move *w* to the west until the color of the node to the west of *w* no longer matches *target-color.*
8. Move *e* to the east until the color of the node to the east of *e* no longer matches *target-color.*
9. Set the color of nodes between *w* and *e* to *replacement-color.*
10. For each node *n* between *w* and *e*:
11. If the color of the node to the north of *n* is *target-color,* add that node to *Q*.
    If the color of the node to the south of *n* is *target-color,* add that node to *Q*.
12. Continue looping until *Q* is exhausted.
13. Return.

Adapting the algorithm to use an additional array to store the shape of the region allows generalization to cover "fuzzy" flood filling, where an element can differ by up to a specified threshold from the source symbol. Using this additional array as an alpha channel allows the edges of the filled region to blend somewhat smoothly with the not-filled region.

Another method to fill is called **SCAN LINE** Method. One need to consider only the pixels which lie inside the polygon.

The algorithm can be sped up by filling lines. Instead of pushing each potential future pixel coordinate into the stack, it inspects the neighbour lines (previous and next) to find adjacent segments that may be filled in a future pass; the coordinates (either the start or the end) of the line segment are pushed on the stack. In most of cases this scanline algorithm is at least an order of magnitude faster than the per-pixel one.

Let us suppose that we start with the largest Y value and work our way down, scanning from left to right as we go in the raster manner. Our constructed test lines will be the horizontal lines at the current Y scanning value. Many problems in computer Graphics can be approached a scan line at a time. Algorithms, which take this approach, are called SCAN LINE algorithms.

We can draw to boundary of the polygon in a blank frame buffer and then examine the pixels in the box around the polygon, scan line by scan line. Moving around the scan line, when we encounter a pixel with the intensity of the boundary, we enter the polygon. Subsequent pixels are given the interior intensity until we encounter a second boundary pixel.

The problem with this scheme is that we must start with a frame buffer free of pixels with the polygon boundary intensity and we must be careful about cases where two polygon edges meet at a single point. We can avoid this problem by determining the polygon boundary values directly from the polygon instruction instead of from the frame buffer. Using the display file instructions, we can determine where the scan line crosses the polygon boundary.

"Consider only the sides which intersect the scan line. Our task becomes setting those pixels on the horizontal scan line which lie inside the polygon."

OUTLINE FOR SCAN LINE FILLING ALGORITHM

The algorithm for filling a polygon should begin by ordering the polygon on the largest Y value. It should begin with the largest Y value and scan down the polygon with decreasing Y. For each Y, it should determine which sides can be intersected and determine the X values for these intersection points. The X values are sorted, paired and passed to the line drawing algorithms.

The algorithm which performs the YX scan and fills in the polygon is called FILL-POLYGON.

It starts by retrieving the polygon information from the display file and sorting it by the largest Y value. This is achieved by means of picking the value through algorithm specially designed for this purpose. The filling, in of the polygon is done by repeating these five steps:

1. First check if any additional polygon sides should be considered for this scan line algorithm.
2. The second step is to sort the X coordinates of the points where the polygon sides crosses the scan line.
3. The third step is to actually turn on or light the pixels between the polygon edges
4. Next the current scan line is decremented.
5. And the process repeats.

These steps are repeated until the scanning process has passed all polygon edges.

SUMMARY

2D transformations are very important in Graphic systems. We need to enlarge or shrink the object so the concept of scaling has been discussed. Numerical problem on scaling are presented in the chapter Rotation is another process in which we rotate an image by certain degree according to our requirements. Students are advised to develop programs on rotation also. In translation, our object or image is displaced a given distance (x or y direction) on the screen.

Two more transformations have been described. They are reflection and shearing which are being used in computer graphics quite extensively.

Windowing is the method for selecting and enlarging portions of a drawing. The techniques for not showing that part of drawing in which one is not interested is clipping.

Instead of wasting entire screen for display, we can make use of viewport (a shall portion of window or screen) for display. As we have seen in the chapter, changing the window show us a different part of the object shown at same position on the display. If we change the viewport, we see the same part of the object drawn at a different place on the display.

In clipping, two algorithms are discussed. They are Cohen Sutherland and Sutherland Hodgman algorithms.

A program for Cohen Sutherland algorithm is presented in the chapter for ease of student.

Polygon is a many sides figure. The line segments that make up polygon boundary are called sides or edges. The end points of the sides are called Polygon's vertices.

We are mainly concerned with drawing polygons, checking points inside the polygon and then filling up the polygon. ODD EVEN test is given to check whether point is inside the polygon or outside.

Two methods of polygon filling are mentioned in the chapter. They are flood fill and scan line methods.

EXERCISE

1. What do you understand by 2D Transformations? Give matrices for scaling, translation and rotation.
2. What do you understand by Interaction? Explain some Input techniques that are interactive.
3. Why do matrices change under homogeneous Co-ordinate system? Give examples.
4. Enlarge a triangle with vertices A (1, 1) B(5, 1) and C (3, 5) to twice its size keeping point A(1,1) as fixed.
5. Develop programs in C for translation, rotation and scaling of a triangle
6. What do you understand by window and view port? Develop viewing transformation taking window and view port of your choice.
7. Explain line clipping and then develop a program for clipping a line using Cohen Sutherland algorithm.
8. Explain polygon clipping and then develop a program for clipping a polygon using Sutherland Hodgman algorithm.
9. What do you understand by polygon filling? Explain stack base fill algorithm.
10. Explain the advantage of scan line fill algorithm over stack base fill algorithm.

4

3-D TRANSFORMATIONS & HIDDEN SURFACES

3-D TRANSFORMATIONS

The process of finding which points on the flat screen correspond to the line and surface of the object involves a VIEWING TRANSFORMATION. We have already seen how useful it is to translate, scale and rotate images. We shall begin by considering these transformations in 3-D also and ultimately we shall extend our transformations to include parallel and perspective projections.

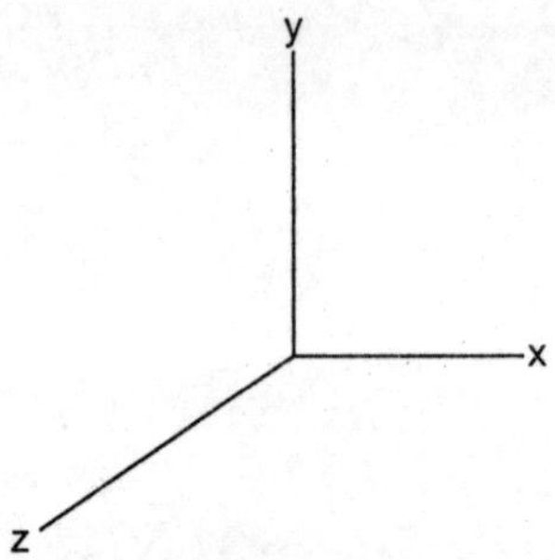

Fig. 4.1

SCALING TRANSFORMATION

The process of scaling changes the dimension of an object. The scale factors determines whether the scaling is a magnification where scaling factor S > 1 or a reduction where scaling factor S < 1.

$$S = \begin{vmatrix} Sx & 0 & 0 \\ 0 & Sy & 0 \\ 0 & 0 & Sz \end{vmatrix}_{3\times 3}$$

Matrix:

The above matrix is a 3 × 3 scaling matrix where Sx is the scale factor in x direction, Sy in y direction and Sz in Z direction.

There are times where we require homogeneous coordinates. Homogeneous coordinates are required when we have to concatenate two matrices of different order as we will see after translation matrix which is a 4×4 matrix. If using homogeneous coordinates, a 4×4 matrix is required (including a dummy row and column).

$$S = \begin{vmatrix} Sx & 0 & 0 & 0 \\ 0 & Sy & 0 & 0 \\ 0 & 0 & Sz & 0 \\ 0 & 0 & 0 & 1 \end{vmatrix}_{4\times 4}$$

Matrix:

This Scaling matrix behaves the same way as in 2-D.

Practice: Try out some mathematics on the same and check its correctness.

TRANSLATION TRANSFORMATION

Using translation an object is displaced a given distance and direction from its original position on the screen. The effect is required when we want our image to be shifted from one point to the other.

$$T = \begin{vmatrix} 1 & 0 & 0 & 0 \\ 0 & 1 & 0 & 0 \\ 0 & 0 & 1 & 0 \\ tx & ty & tz & 1 \end{vmatrix}_{4\times 4}$$

Matrix:

Practice: Try out some operations on translation matrix as we have done in 2-D transformations.

ROTATION TRANSFORMATION

Rotating an image by some angle is different in 3-D transformations. Here we have to rotate individually about each axis. If we rotate about Z axis, the matrix is

$$\begin{matrix}Rz = \\ (\text{Matrix})\end{matrix} \begin{vmatrix} \cos\theta & \sin\theta & 0 & 0 \\ -\sin\theta & \cos\theta & 0 & 0 \\ 0 & 0 & 1 & 0 \\ 0 & 0 & 0 & 1 \end{vmatrix}$$

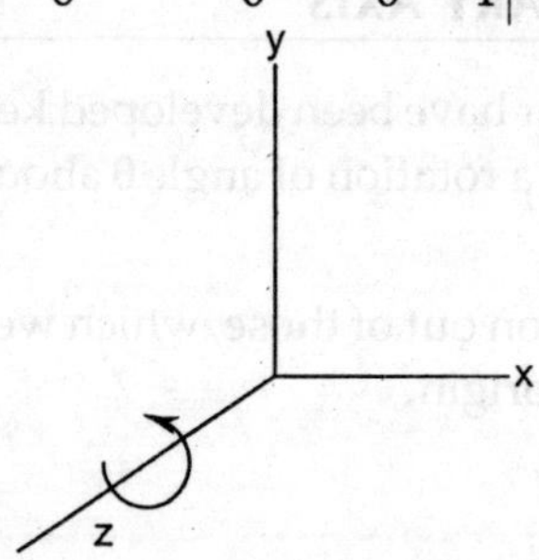

Fig. 4.2 *For z axis rotation*

If we rotate about x axis, the matrix is

$$Rx = \begin{vmatrix} 1 & 0 & 0 & 0 \\ 0 & \cos\theta & \sin\theta & 0 \\ 0 & -\sin\theta & \cos\theta & 0 \\ 0 & 0 & 0 & 1 \end{vmatrix}$$
(Matrix)

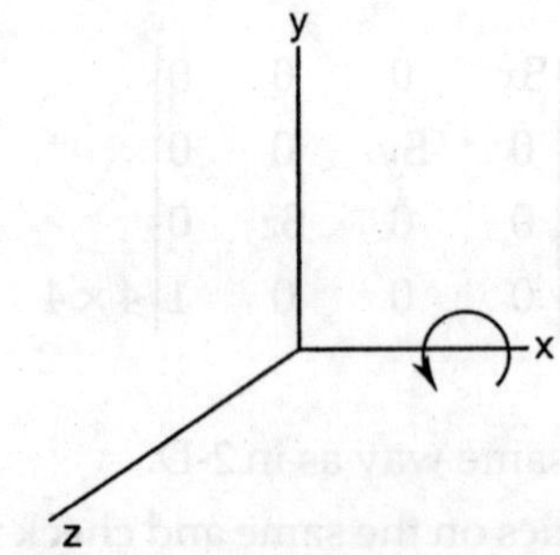

Fig. 4.3 *For x axis rotation*

If we rotate about y axis, the matrix is

$$Ry = \begin{vmatrix} \cos\theta & 0 & -\sin\theta & 0 \\ 0 & 1 & 0 & 0 \\ \sin\theta & 0 & \cos\theta & 0 \\ 0 & 0 & 0 & 1 \end{vmatrix}$$
(Matrix)

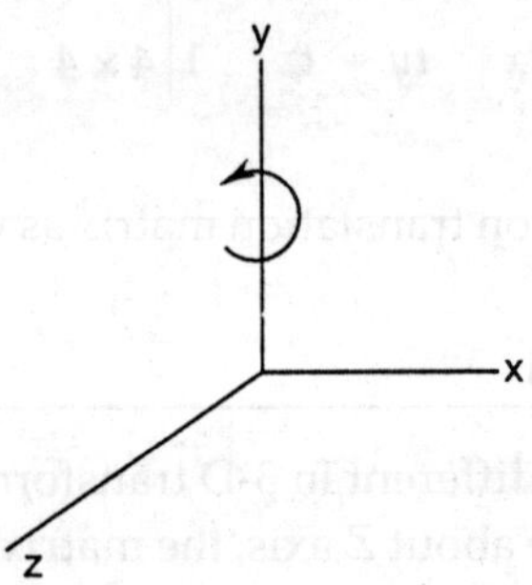

Fig. 4.4 *For y axis rotation*

Exercise: Try and develop programs on 3-D translation as have been developed for 2-D.

ROTATION ABOUT AN ARBITRARY AXIS

The rotation matrices developed so far have been developed keeping origin in mind. Problem here is to derive a transformation matrix for a rotation of angle θ about an arbitrary line (a line which is not at the origin).

We will develop this transformation out of those, which we have already encountered. We shall perform a translation to move to the origin.

(first translate the axis to rotation)

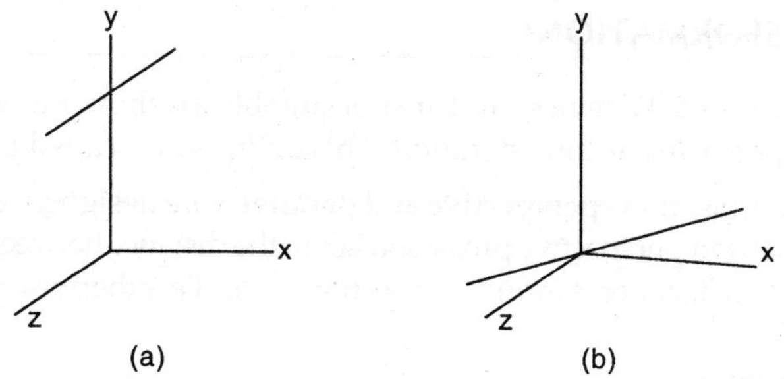

Fig. 4.5

We shall then have to make rotations about x and y axes to align the z axis with the line. The rotation about the line then becomes a rotation about z axis

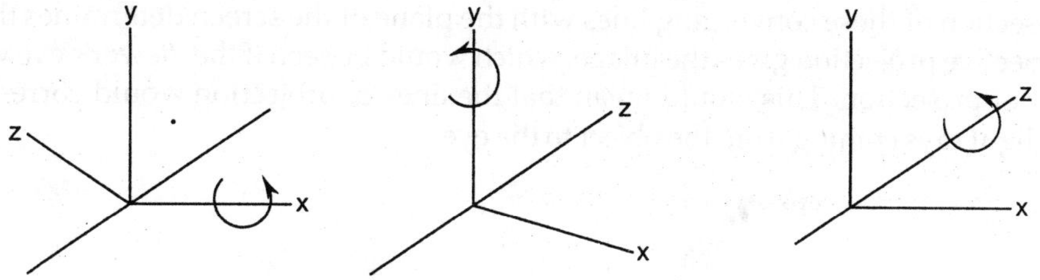

Fig. 4.6

Finally we apply inverse transformation for the rotation about y and x axes.

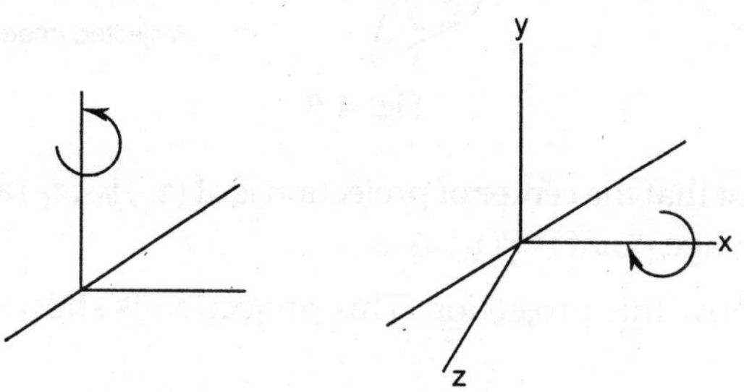

Fig. 4.7

Now translate to restore the line and co-ordinate to their original orientation.

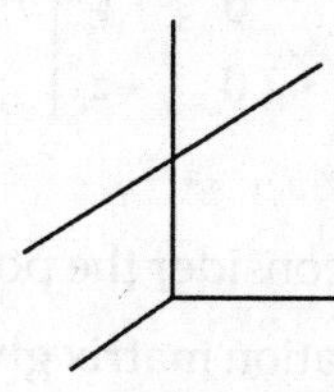

Fig. 4.8

The actual transformation for a rotation about an arbitrary axis is given by the product

$$R = TR_x R_y R_z R_y^{-1} R_x^{-1} T^{-1}$$

PROJECTION (TRANSFORMATION)

The output devices we use are 2-D devices and are not suitable for showing 3-D objects and this is the reason why we have to perform certain operation. This operation is called projection of the object.

Two basic methods of projection - **perspective and parallel** were designed to solve the problem. The difference between parallel and perspective projection lies in the distance between the center of projection to the projection plane. If this distance is infinite, projection is parallel otherwise projection is perspective.

PERSPECTIVE PROJECTION

In a perspective projection, the farther away an object is from the viewer, the smaller it appears. For example the railway tracks seem to meet at a point on the horizon. The result for the viewer is a depth cue, lines of projection coverage at a single point called **CENTER OF PROJECTION.**

The intersection of these converging lines with the plane of the screen determines the projected image. Perspective projection gives the image, which would be seen if the viewer's eye were located at the center of projection. This would mean that the lines of projection would correspond to the paths of the light rays coming from the object to the eye.

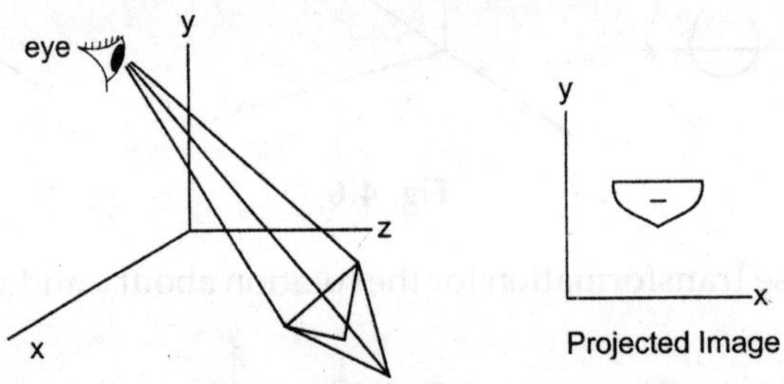

Fig. 4.9

We'll assume throughout that the center of projection is at (x_C, y_C, z_C) and the point on the object is (x_1, y_1, z_1) then projected image point is $P(x_2, y_2, z_2)$.

We'll use matrices to show this projection. This projection is shown in form of transformation matrix as

$$P_{at} = \begin{vmatrix} -z_c & 0 & 0 & 0 \\ 0 & -z_c & 0 & 0 \\ x_c & y_c & 0 & 1 \\ 0 & 0 & 0 & -z_c \end{vmatrix}$$

Matrix:

To show that this transformation works, consider the point (x_1, y_1, z_1)

Multiply the point (x_1, y_1, z_1) by transformation matrix given above and we would realize that the matrix is in the correct form as we get $z_2 = 0$ which shows that the third coordinate of the triplet disappears and resulting point (x_2, y_2) is then indeed the correctly projected point.

PERSPECTIVE ANOMALIES

The process of constructing a perspective view introduces certain anomalies which enhance realism in terms of depth cues but also distort actual sizes and shapes.

1. Perspective foreshortening: The farther an object is from the center of projection, the smaller it appears (*i.e.*, its projected size becomes smaller)

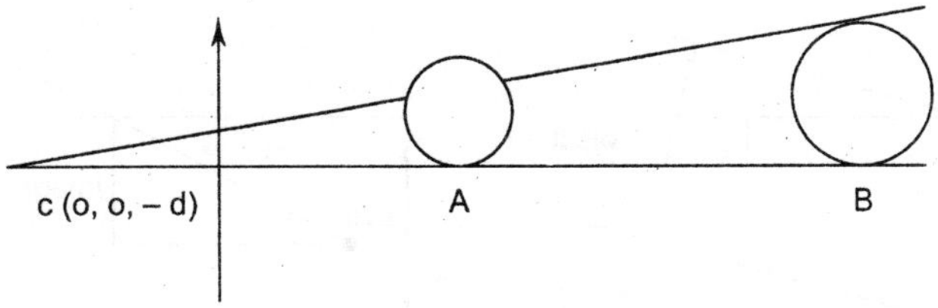

Fig. 4.10

We look at equations

$$x' = \frac{x}{1+\frac{z}{v_z}} \quad y' = \frac{y}{1+\frac{z}{v_z}}$$

where x' and y' are newly projected points, v_z is the view point along the z axis.

If objects is translated away from viewpoint (Z co-ordinate value increases), the image dimension (x' y') decreases. This is perspective foreshortening.

2. Vanishing Points: Perspective shortening situation gives rise to framing where parallel lines appear meet at a virtual point, commonly known as vanishing point.

For 3-D of a realistic display, there could be maximum of 3 vanishing points along the three orthogonal axes.

Projection of lines that are not parallel to the view plane appear to meet at same point on the view plane. A common manifestation of this anomaly is the illusion that rail road tracks meet at a point on the horizon.

This situation gives rise to framing where parallel lines appear to meet at a virtual point, commonly known as vanishing point.

For 3-D of a realistic display, there could be maximum of 3 vanishing points along the three orthogonal axes.

PARALLEL PROJECTION

We extend parallel lines from each vertex on the object until they intersect the plane of the screen to form a parallel projection. The point of intersection is the projection of the vertex.

We connect the projected vertex points by line segments, which correspond to connections on the original object.

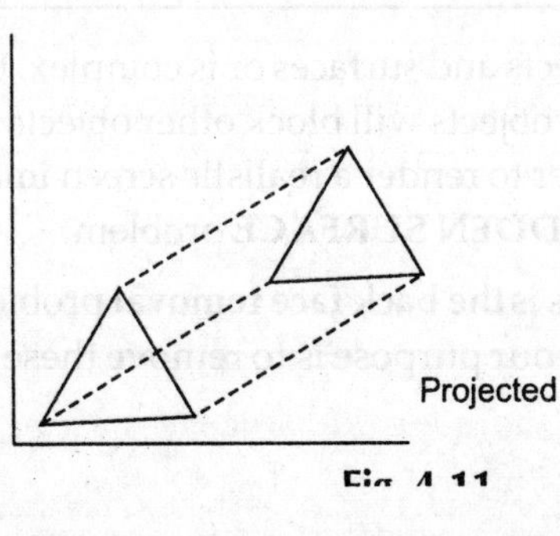

Fig. 4.11

Difference between parallel and perspective projection lies in the centre of projection as shown in the Fig. 4.12 (if centre of projection is at infinity then it is parallel otherwise perspective).

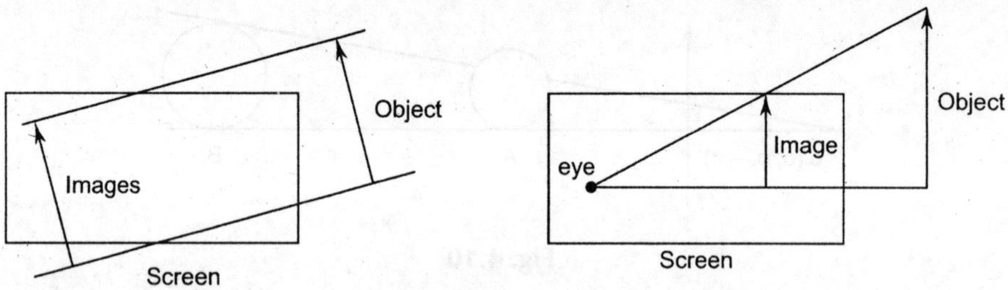

Fig. 4.12

Three types of parallel projections are popular. They are front view, side view and top view. Readers are requested to study them too.

SPECIAL PROJECTION

The problem of rendering a 2-D view of 3-D object existed long before the computer was used.

One class of projection used often in drafting is called an axonometric projection. This is parallel projection for which the direction of projection is perpendicular to the view plane.

If we change one direction of projection slightly to the side, then one of the side faces will become visible while some of the edges will shorten.

Changes the point of view shortens some edges and lengthen others.

ISOMETRIC PROJECTION

There is a particular direction of projection for which all edges will appear shortened from their 3-D length by the same factor. This is called **isometric projection**.

Isometric projection shortens all axes equally.

If a viewing transformation is chosen such that edges parallel to only two of the axes are equally shortened then the projection is called **dimetric**.

Dimetric projection shortens two axes equally.

A **tri-metric** projection is one in which none of the three edges directions is equally shortened. Tri-metric projection shortens all axes differently.

HIDDEN SURFACES

Whenever a picture contains opaque objects and surfaces or is complex, those objects that are closer to the eye and in the line of sight of other objects will block other objects from view. The blocked or hidden surfaces must be removed in order to render a realistic screen image. The identification and removal of these surfaces is called the **HIDDEN SURFACE** problem.

The problem central to hidden surfaces is **the back face removal** problem. There can be light faces and dark faces both in our problems and our purpose is to remove these dark faces.

Hidden surface removal can be a costly and time-consuming process and so we must apply easy tests to find out whether the face is dark or light. There is a simple test that we can perform which will eliminate most of the faces that cannot be seen.

This test identifies surfaces that face away from the viewer. They are the surfaces that make up the back of the object.

Only polygons will be considered as they make up the core of our images so now a polygon has two surfaces, a front and a back just as a mouse pad does.

There is a convention that is being followed by graphics developers for determining which face is dark or light. The convention says that when we are looking at the light surface, the polygon will appear to be drawn with anti-clock or counter-clockwise motions and if we look at the dark face, the pen drawing the polygon will appear to move clockwise.

There are two methods to find out whether the face is light or dark. They make use of vectors and arithmetic applied on them. One uses the vector cross product and the other uses the vector dot product. Both of these methods give us the **normal** in which we are interested.

Method-I

This method uses an operation called VECTOR CROSS PRODUCT. The cross product of two vectors is a third vector with the length equal to the product of the length of the two vector's times the Sine of the angle between them.

It gives us a normal perpendicular to the plane containing the two vectors so if we apply all this to two adjacent vertices of a polygon then we get a resultant that gives the product of those two adjacent vertices.

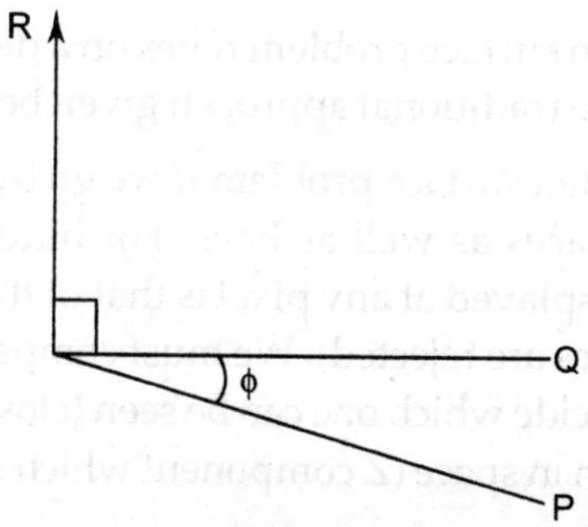

Fig. 4.13

Now two sides of a polygon describe two vectors of the polygon so the cross product of two polygon sides forms a vector pointing out from the polygon face.

Now hundred marks question is ***Will this vector point out from the dark face or the light face ?*** The answer to that depends on whether the two sides form a ***convex*** or **concave angle.**

The convex vertices are the ones that make obtuse angle(>= 90 degrees) so if the two vertices **make obtuse or convex angle** then resultant vector will point out of **light face** and the resultant will point out of the **dark face** if the vertices in question makes **a concave angle.**

Method-II

This method makes use of vector dot product.

$$C = A.B$$
$$= |A| \, |B| \cos\theta$$

In the above equation Cosine factor here is important because if vectors are in the same direction ($0 \le \theta < \pi/2$) the Cosine is positive and overall dot product is positive, but if directions are opposing ($\pi/2 \le \theta < \pi$) the Cosine is negative and so is the dot product.

This method says if a polygon is visible, the light surface should face towards us and the dark surface should face away from us.

So if the **normal vector** coming out of two polygon vertices or sides (discussed previously) points **towards the** viewer, the face is **visible** (a front face) otherwise the face is **hidden** (a back face) and should be removed.

So now how does all this apply to our back face removal process? How can we tell whether or not a normal or resulting vector points toward the viewer?

Next we examine the *z* component of the normal vector. If the component is positive then polygon faces towards the viewer and if negative, it faces away.

The back face algorithm computes the *z* components of the vector normal to the polygon. It then checks the sign and enters the polygon only if the *z* component is positive and in this way only front faces are entered.

Z BUFFERS

One simple approach to the hidden surface problem relies on a device called Z buffer which makes our work easier as compared to the traditional approach given below.

It is quite difficult to solve hidden surface problem if we go by the traditional approach. Raster displays are used to display surfaces as well as lines. For hidden surface removal, we want to arrange the FB so that the color displayed at any pixel is that of the surface closest to the viewer for that point (the farther away surfaces are rejected). We must compare all overlapping surfaces which are projected onto the pixel and decide which one can be seen (closest to us). We then have to sort the polygon according to their position in space (Z component which signifies the depth) but this is very tedious and time consuming.

One simple approach to this problem relies on a device called Z buffer. It is a large array with Z entry for each pixel on the display. The Z buffer can be used to save the Z coordinate values and then helps us to sort out the polygons by keeping track of the Z position.

Z BUFFER ALGORITHM (DEPTH BUFFER ALGO)

The Z buffer algorithm sets up a 2D array (like frame buffer discussed previously) but the Z buffer stores the depth value at each pixel rather than the color, which is stored in the frame buffer so we mean to say that pixel depth value is stored in Z buffer and pixel color value is stored in the frame buffer.

By initilizing the value of the Z buffer to some large negative number (say of the background), the problem of determining which surfaces are closer is cut down to simply comparing the present depth value stored in Z buffer at pixel (x, y) with the newly calculated depth value at pixel (x, y). If this new value is greater or more positive than the present Z buffer value (*i.e.*, closer along the line of sight), this value replaces the present value and the pixel color is changed to the color of the new surface.

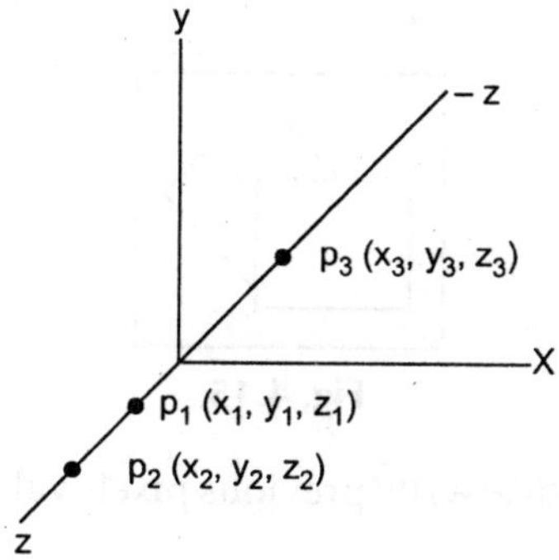

Fig. 4.14

SCAN LINE ALGORITHM

There are situations when we want to simultaneously process polygons and if we are willing to collect the polygons and process them together, then a full screen Z buffer is not needed. A scan line Z buffer is sufficient for us and requires much less memory. The **scan line hidden surface** is the solution to our problem.

The idea was suggested by Carpenter. The reason a large amount the memory is needed for a Z buffer is that we process each polygon independently.

We can reduce the memory requirements by processing all of the polygons together on a scan line by scan line basis. This gives the effect of repeatedly doing a Z buffer hidden surface removal for a screen that is only one pixel high (a single scan line). The Z buffer only needs to store one scan line worth of depth information.

When the scan line is over, we save the result, reinitialize the Z buffer, more to the next scan line and do the next scan line Z buffer sort until screen is solved. The key here is that all polygons are processed together.

THE PAINTER'S ALGORITHM

There is a property of frame buffers used by NEWELL, which has became to be known as the Painter's algorithms. The algorithm gets its name from the manner in which an oil painting is created.

The artist starts with the background. He can, if he wishes, fill the entire canvas with the background scenes. The artist then paints the fore ground objects, there is no need to remove portion of the background, the artist simply paints on top of them. The new paint covers the old so that only the newest layer of the paint is visible.

A frame buffer has this same property of painting. We store a filled polygons into the frame buffer by changing the proper pixels to value corresponding to polygons interior style. If we then enter a second polygons "on top of" the first, some of those pixels will be changed to correspond to the second polygon's interior style. The second polygon has "Covered up" the first.

The painter's algorithms tells us to enter first those polygons which are farthest from the viewer (the background) and enter the last the objects closest to the viewer (the foreground). Hidden surfaces are covered up by choosing the correct order to draw them and taking full advantage of the properties of frame buffers.

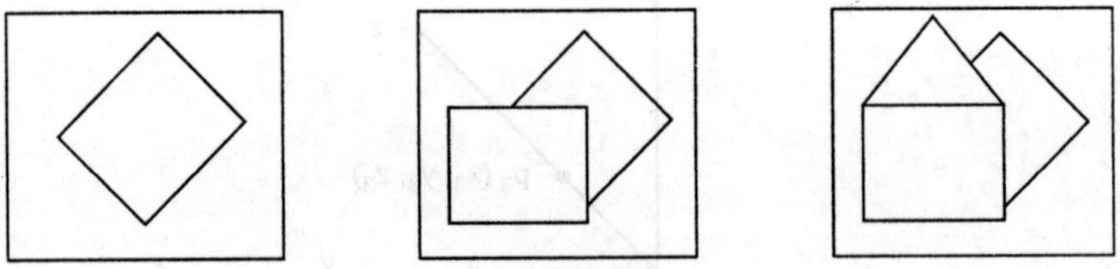

Fig. 4.15

The most recent filled polygons overwrite previous pixels values.

WARNOCK'S ALGORITHM

The basic idea behind the Warnock's algorithm is based on the hypothesis of how the human eye-brain combination process information in a scene. The hypothesis says "very little time is spent on areas that contain little information".

As example, consider an otherwise empty table top with a notebook on it. Our attention is focused on the notebook instead of the table and rest of the table is just ignored.

The Warnock algorithm and its derivatives attempt to take advantage of area coherence in the above discussion. This characteristic of "area coherence" says that adjacent areas (pixels) in both x and y directions tend to be the same and needn't be processed time and again and approximations would do.

Since the Warnock's algorithm is concerned with that is displayed, it works in IMAGE SPACE. It considers a window in large space and seeks to determine if the window is empty or if the contents of the window are simple enough to display. If not, a sub window is sub-divided until either the contents of a sub-window are simple enough to display or the sub-window size is at the limit of desired resolution.

In Warnock's original algorithm, each window is sub-divided into four equal sub-windows. It makes clever use of Quad tree data structure. The window is divided until either the contents of a sub-window are simple enough to display or the sub-window size is at the limit of desired resolution.

SUMMARY

In 2-D transformations, we were interested in x and y coordinates but in 3-D transformations x, y and z axis are all used. Z co-ordinate is used for depth of an object. Scaling, translation and rotation are the same operations but with additional z-coordinates entry in matrices.

Since display devices are 2-D so objects or images in 3-D have to be projected onto the screen. Projection is the process by which 3-D objects are presented onto the 2-D display device. Whenever z coordinate is zero, image has been properly projected. Two methods of projection are used: Perspective and parallel projections. Perspective projections are much closer to reality of life and have certain anomalies as discussed in the chapter. Railway tracks appearing to meet at some point in horizon is example of perspective projection. The difference between the two lies in the centre of projection as discussed in the chapter with the help of a diagram.

Hidden surfaces are another important area of graphics. The blocked or hidden surfaces must be removed in order to render a realistic screen image. We are interested in back face removal. We apply different techniques to find out whether a face is back/dark or front/light. After finding the dark faces, we remove them.

Different algorithms for hidden surfaces are given in the chapter. Most important of them is z-buffer algorithm.

EXERCISE

1. What do you understand by 3D transformation? Give matrices for scaling, translate and rotation.
2. What do you understand by Quadtree and Octtree ?
3. How are back faces detected and why do we need to remove them?
4. Implement z-buffer algorithm using 'C'.
5. Use Perspective matrix and apply it to a point $(x_1 y_1 z_1)$, then show that $z_1 = 0$ after multiplication.

5

INTERACTION, RENDERING & ILLUMINATION

INTERACTION

Interaction is the way user communicates with the system and that's what we call interactive systems. Interactivity is a must for Graphics as actions have to change rapidly. Computer graphics adds depth to communication between the user and computer machine. As we know **communication is always a two way process**, it is desirable to allow the user to respond to the output or displayed material.

There can be different sorts of **responses a user might wish** to make to such a display like selecting a particular part of the display, entering a new object on the display, specifying the position on the display, wishing to alter an object's orientation, size or location or there can be so many other options.

Some effective methods are there for the input of graphic information. **A user might move a STYLUS** a penlike device and see the lines appear on the display as if real pen and ink were being used for drawing. Scale and direction might be changed or the position of the display may be selected by pointing or indicating to it.

HARDWARE DEVICES USED IN INTERACTION

Various hardware devices enable the user to interact in the above stated manner with ease. These devices can be separated into two classes : **Locators and Selectors.**

Locators devices are giving us position information on the screen. The Computer machine receives from a locator the co-ordinates for a point. Using locators, we can indicate a position on the screen which is helpful in manipulating the screen coordinates.

Selector devices are used to select a particular graphical object from an image. A selector may pick a particular item and it does not provide information about where that item is located on the screen.

Some location devices are :

A pair of THUMBWHEELS containing two potentiometers mounted on the keyboard, which the user can adjust. One potentiometer is used for x direction and the other for y direction. Analog to digital converters change the potentiometer setting into a digital value which the computer can use to find the coordinates of a point.

Another location device is a JOYSTICK. A joystick has two potentiometers, just as a pair of thumb wheels. They have been attached to a single lever. Moving the lever forward or back changes the setting of the potentiometer.

Some other location devices are mouse and track balls. Digitizer or a tablet can also be used for location.

Some selector devices are :

Light Pen : A light pen is composed of a photocell. This pen may be poised at the screen on a refresh display.

The pen sends a pulse whenever the phosphor below it is illuminated. *When the light pen senses the phosphor beneath it being illuminated, it can interrupt the display processor's interpreting of the display file.*

DEVICES USED FOR EVENT HANDLING

A light pen is so popular and is an example of an event driven devices. There are other devices like keyboard which is also an example of driven devices. The machine must wait for a key to be pressed before it can judge which character the user wishes to send to the system.

Buttons and Switches may also be available as input devices as we have seen in Visual Basic and other programming languages. Whatever button is clicked, only the code behind that is executed. These are also event drivers.

Now the question arises how event handling is possible. It is possible through **INTERRUPT** approach. In this approach, interrupts is enabled and sent by the device when an event occurs. *An interrupt is an electrical signal that causes the processor to be interrupted from regular sequence and transfer control to a designated or special interrupt handling routine already fed into the system.*

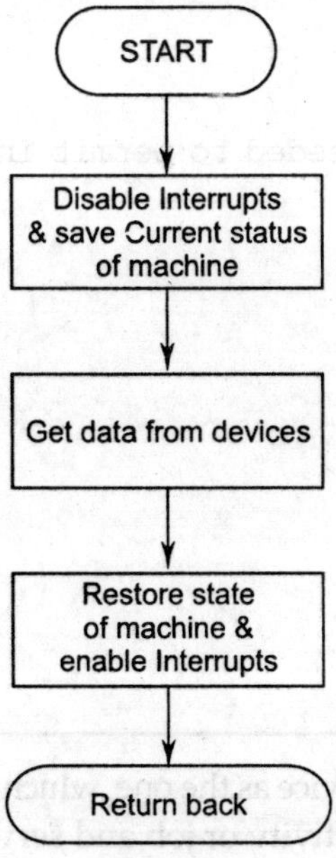

Fig. 5.1

By using the interrupt method, *central processing unit is free to carry out some other operation while it is waiting for an event to occur.* When the event occurs, processing is interrupted and the devices which caused the interrupt is serviced. After servicing the devices, CPU can proceed with its own incomplete task.

An interrupt method of event handling allows handling of events which may occurs at times other then when the CPU is expecting them.

INPUT DEVICE HANDLING ALGO

Let us consider the routine to handle input devices. Basically graphics developers classify the devices into classes. We shall consider five classes of devices. They are:

(1) button (2) pick (3) Keyboard (4) Locator (5) Valuation.

Now the method followed is as follows :

We will consider flags each classes. The value of flags will determine whether or not a particular class is enabled.

Algorithm for INPUT DEVICE handling

Variables class containing value/code for Buttons, Keyboard, Locator, etc// Value of class will change in the algorithm.

```
{
        If  class = 1 then
        {
        Perform all operation needed to permit input from the button devices
        Button = true ;
        End
        }
        If class = 2 then
        {
        Perform all operation needed to permit input from any other input
device
        ......
        ......
        End;
        }
        And so on
        .
        .
        }
```

EVENT HANDLING

In principle, we call an event driven device as the one, which generates an interrupt. The CPU detects the interrupt and stops the current activity or job and services the interrupting device. When the devices has been serviced normal processing resumes.

A brief outline is given below to show as above process. Assume that there is a single event quene. Algorithm EVENT for processing an input device's interrupt.

```
{
Disable Physical Interrupt So That No Other Device Can Interrupt;
Save Processor Status Onto The Stack;
Determine Which Device Caused The Interrupt ;
{
Process The Interrupting Process
}
Restore Processor Status;
Reenable Physical Interrupts So That Other Device Can Interrupt;
Return ;
}
```

ECHOING

An important part of an interactive system is echoing. Echoing provides the user with information about his actions. This allows the user to compare what he has done against what he wanted to do. For keyboard input, echoing takes the form of displaying the type characters. Locators may be echoed by a screen cursor displayed at the current locator position.

A pick may be echoed by identifying the selected objects on the display. The selected objects may be flashed, made brighter or determine whether or not he has selected the intended objects

INTERACTIVE TECHNIQUES

We should include some techniques for interactively creating and modifying pictures Let us first consider how to add new picture elements to the image.

Point plotting techniques gives the user the capability of selecting a particular point on the display screen. One use for point plotting routine is to enter line segments. The concept here is to connect the successive points selected by the user with line segments.

A variation of this technique is called INKING. Inking makes the locator automatically leave a trial of line segments the way a pen leaves a trial of ink Sometimes you must have experienced it in Pain brush or in Corel Draw Software. It doesn't require the user to push a button for every line segment. Instead a segment is drawn whenever the locator moves a sufficient distance.

Raster displays can extend inking to painting with a brush. A brush is a pattern of fixed patterns. When painting, we repeatedly sample the location position. Each time the position changes we copy the brush pattern into the frame buffer. The effect is to draw this pattern repeatedly on the display along the path of a locator. You must have experienced it in Paint Brush.

RENDERING

To put it in simple words, rendering is the process of producing images or pictures. Producing realistic images involves both physical theory and psychology. Light *i.e.*, electromagnetic energy, reaches the eye after interacting with the physical environment to give us a realistic view.

When light energy falls on a surface, there are three possibilities. It can be absorbed, reflected or transmitted. Some of the light energy incident on a surface is absorbed and converted to heat. The rest is either reflected or transmitted. **It is the reflected or transmitted light that makes an object visible.**

If all the incident light energy is absorbed, the object is invisible. The object is then called a BLACK BODY. Reflected or transmitted light energy makes an object visible. According to physics, the amount of energy absorbed, reflected or transmitted depends on the wavelength of the light.

If some wavelengths are selectively absorbed, the light leaving the object has a different energy distribution. The object appears COLOURED. The colour of the object is determined by the wavelengths selectively absorbed.

The character of the light reflected from the surface of an object depends on the composition, direction and geometry of the light source.

The light reflected from an object is also characterized by being either **diffusely or specularly** reflected. Diffusely reflected light can be considered as the light that has penetrated below the surface of an object, been absorbed and then re-emitted. Diffusely reflected light is scattered equally in all directions.

Specularly reflected light is reflected from the outer surface of an object.

SHADING OF OBJECTS (LIGHT, COLOR AND SHADING)

Diffuse Illumination

Let us begin our discussion of illumination by considering an indirect lighting source. We will assume that our object is illuminated by light that does not come from any particular source, but that comes from all directions. This is background light, light that is reflected from walls, floor and ceiling. This light is uniform, that there is the same amount of light everywhere. There will be no bright spots and no particular direction will be favored. A surface will therefore receive the same amount of diffuse light energy no matter what its direction may be.

Now some of this energy will be absorbed by the surface while the rest will be reflected or re-emitted. The ratio of the light reflected from the surface to the total incoming light is called the **coefficient of reflection or reflectivity**. A white surface reflects nearly all of the incoming radiation; hence its coefficient of reflection is close to 1, a black surface on the other hand, absorbs most of the incoming light hence its reflectivity is near zero. A gray surface would have a the coefficient lying somewhere in between.

Brightness of an object illuminated by diffuse light is given by the expression

$$\mathbf{I = I_b * R_c}$$

Here I_b : intensity of the background light

R_c : object's reflectivity

I : intensity of the light coming from any visible surface

If user is allowed to set the values of I_b and R_c, he can create light or dark scenes and paint his objects in different shades or colors.

Every plane on a particular object will be shaded equally. This, however, is not the way real objects look and for a more realistic shading model, we must also include point sources of illumination.

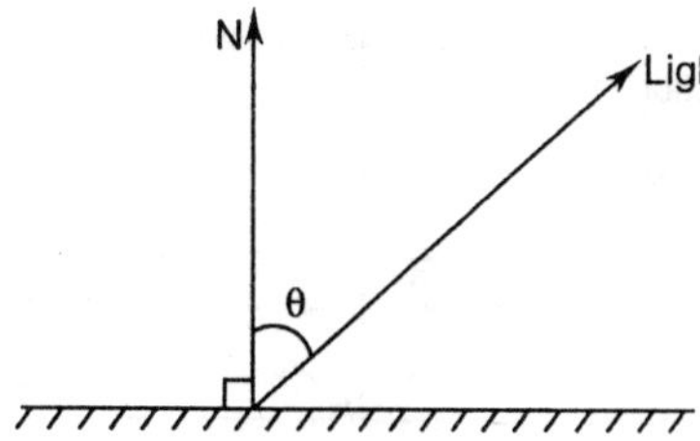

Fig. 5.2

Point Source Illumination

Point source illumination is an abstraction of real world. This type of illumination is obtained from sources such as light bulbs, candles or the sun. The light originates at a particular place, it comes from a particular direction over a particular distance. Surfaces facing us and positioned nearer to the light source will receive more light than those facing away from or far removed from the illumination.

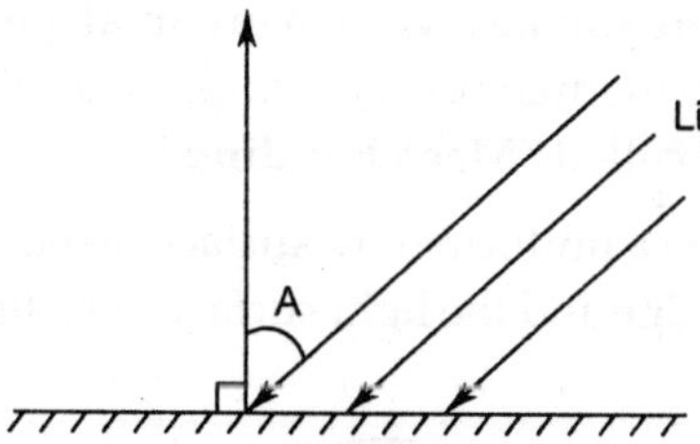

Fig. 5.3

$$\cos A = L.N$$

Suppose that P amount of light comes from the point source. I_b and R have already been defined in diffuse light then the shade of a surface of an object will be given by

$$\mathbf{I = I_b.R_c + P.R_c (L.N)}$$

The point source term in the above equation has the light from the point source times the cosine of an angle of incidence (giving us how much light illuminates each point on the surface), multiplied by the coefficient of reflection (giving us how much of this light is re-emitted to reach the viewer).

Specular Reflection

Light can be reflected from an object in two ways: there is a diffuse reflection and there is a Specular reflection. The diffuse reflection depends upon the angle of incidence and the reflected light can be colored since the coefficient of reflection is involved.

Specular reflection acts quite differently. It is the type of reflection which occurs at the surface of mirror.

Light is reflected in nearly a single direction(not spread out over all directions). Plastics and many metals have a specular reflection which is independent of color; all colors are equally reflected.

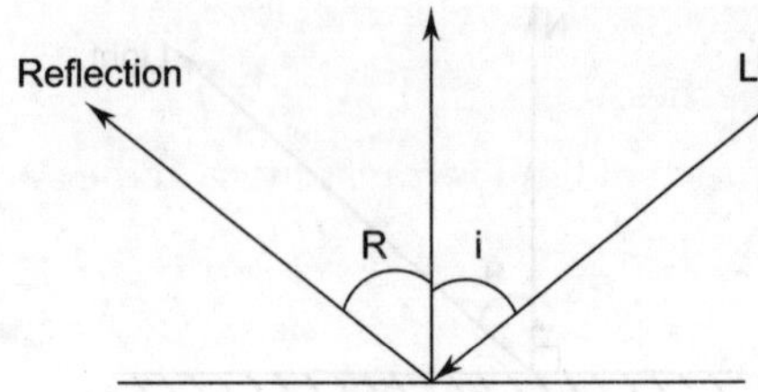

Fig. 5.4

For specular reflection, light comes in, strikes the surface and bounces right back off. The angle that reflected beam makes with surface normal is called angle of reflection R and is equal in magnitude to the angle of incidence (I).

SMOOTH SHADING OF SURFACE APPROXIMATIONS

So far we have dealt with only flat polygons. If we wanted to draw a carved shape (a doughnut, ball, can , cup or airplane) , we could approximate it with many small polygons. If we shade the approximate surface, we can often see the individual polygon edges. The edges are enhanced by the properties of our eyes to produce an effect called **"Mach Banding"**.

Mach banding is the process when a uniform dark surface meets a uniform light surface, the dark surface appears even darker along edge and the light surface even lighter. This makes the edge stand out.

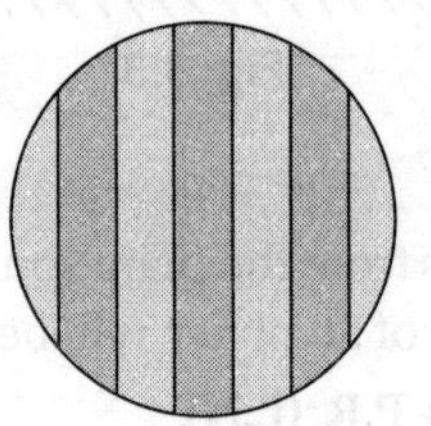

Fig. 5.5

A method was suggested by Henri Gouraud for varying the shade across polygon surfaces so that the shade at polygon's edge matches that of its neighbors. To do this, we need more information than just a single shade value per polygon. Instead, need a shade value at each vertex. We could for *e.g.*, extend our polygon routines to enter an intensity value at each vertex, along with the position. This information would have to be included in the display file. The rest of the work would be done by the polygon filling routines.

TRANSPARENCY

Our shading model has not considered transparent objects so far. Surface of a transparent object may receive light from behind as well as from in front. Such objects have a transparency coefficient T as well as values for reflectivity and specular reflection.

The transparency coefficient may depend upon the thickness of the object. If one layer of tinted lets through only half of the light, then two layers will let through only one quarter. The transmission of light depends exponentially on the distance which the light ray must travel within the objects.

$$\mathbf{T} = t \cdot e^{-ad}$$

Where d: the distance the light must travel in the object

t and a : coefficient of properties of material

t: determines how much of light is transmitted at the surface (instead of reflected)

a : it tells how quickly the material absorbs or attenuates the light

A proper treatment of transparent objects should also consider the fact that light changes direction when it crosses the boundary between two media, this effect is called **Refraction.** The change in direction is related to a property of materials called the Index of Refraction (n). The law is called Snell's Law.

$$\sin \theta_1 / \sin \theta_2 = \frac{n_1}{n_2}$$

the light ray is bent both when it enters a transparent object and when it leaves. To correctly show transparent objects, then, we have to retain back faces so that we can calculate the light path in and out of objects and also determine the length of the path within the object.

If we assume that :

1. for a given surface, the transparency coefficient for the object is a coefficient
2. refraction effects can be ignored and
3. no light source can be seen directly through the object

then the light coming through is just the transparent coefficient times the light coming from objects behind it.

The shade actually displayed will correspond to the light from the new object's plus the light behind, which is transmitted through the object.

$$V = v_r + t.vt$$

Where v is the total amount of light

V_r : amount refracted from the surface

$V(t)$: the light coming from behind the object

Transparent objects have a low reflectivity and the refracted light (v_r) comes from specular reflection.

SHADOWS

The problem of shadows is very much similar to the hidden surface problem. A shadowed object is one, which is hidden from the light source. Shadow and hidden surface calculations are performed together for efficient computation.

One approach to the shadow problem is to repeat the hidden surface calculation using light source as the viewpoint. This hidden surface calculation divides the polygons into shadowed and unshadowed groups. Surfaces which are visible and which are also **visible** from the light source are shown with both the background illumination and the light source illumination. Surfaces which are **visible** but are hidden from the light source are displayed with only the background illumination.

Another approach to the shadow problem is the use of Shadoe Volumes. Consider a polygon and a light source. There is a volume of space hidden from the light by the polygon. This is the polygon's shadow volume. We can construct this volume from the polygon itself and from the rays from the light which touch the polygon edges.

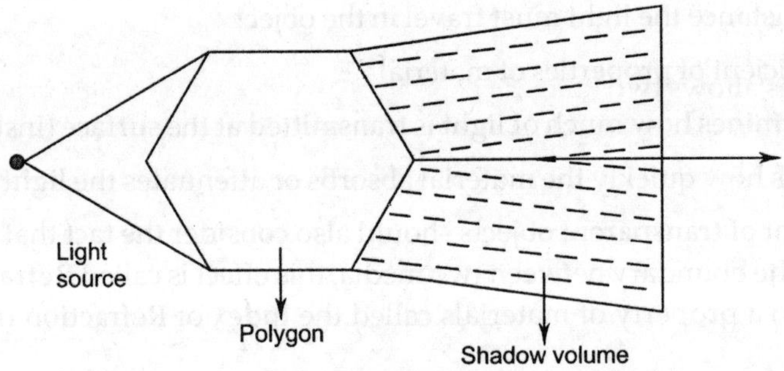

Fig. 5.6

We can compare all other visible polygons to this volume. Positions which lie inside the volume are shadowed. The intensity calculation should not include a term from this light source. Polygons which lie outside the shadowed volume are not shaded by this polygon but might be shaded by some other polygon so they must still be checked against the other shadow volumes.

IMPORTANCE OF SHADOWS

1. Shadows contribute greatly to the realism of the scene by increasing depth perception.
2. Shadows are also important in simulation, for *e.g.*, a specific area of interest may be invisible because it is in a shadow

Much of the current work on shadows is in modeling finite light sources to give more realistic results.

RAY TRACING

There is a simple brute, force techniques that can yield startlingly realistic computer generating images. Its basic form is easy to implement and requires little of the graphic system we have been constructing. It can handle curved surfaces as well as flat polygons. It includes perspective projection, hidden surface removal, reflections, shadows and transparency. The technique is called **Ray Tracing.**

The idea is to determine the intensity for each pixel one at a time by following a ray back from a viewpoint through the pixel and into the object space. We can compute the intersection of that ray with all surfaces. If none is encountered then the pixel has the background shade. If the ray impacts one or more surfaces, we find the one closest to the viewpoint. It is the one which will be seen (the rest are hidden by it). This in effect solves the hidden surface problem for every pixel.

Most of the time spent in ray tracing is in finding the intersection of a ray with the nearest surface. As the complexity of the image goes up, the number of surfaces that must be checked against the ray also increases. There is much interest and research into ray tracing techniques both in modeling the properties of objects and light surface to make them more realistic and in finding data structures and algorithms which make it more efficient.

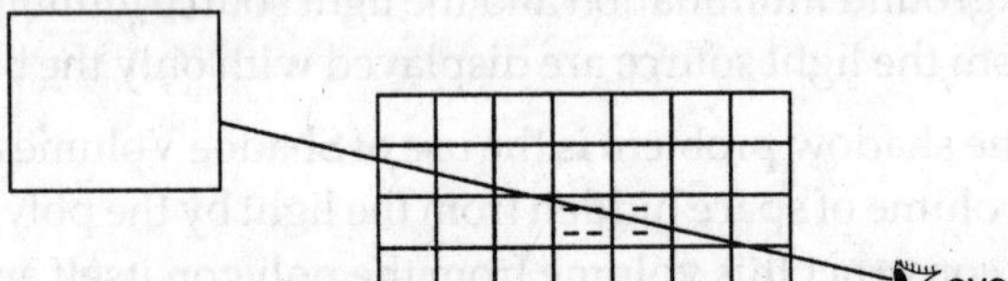

Fig. 5.7

HALF TONES

Many display devices allows two imaging states per pixel (on or off, black or white). This is fine for line drawings but when displaying surfaces, we would often like more variety than just black or white. Photographs are routinely reproduced in books and newspapers using only two states (ink or no ink). This technique is called **Half Toning**.

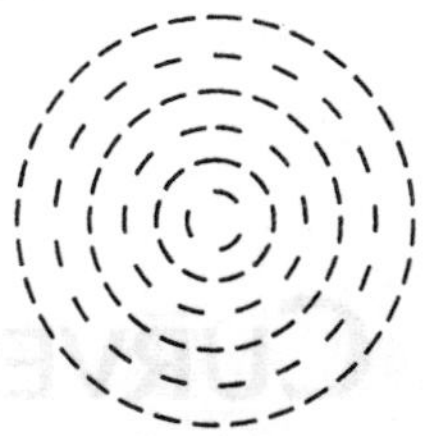

Fig. 5.8

A continuous tone image is shown through a screen. This produces a regularly spaced pattern of small dots. The dots vary in size according to the original image intensity; so where the image is light, the dots are small and the background color of the paper predominates. Where the image is dark, the dots are large and merge together to cover the paper with ink.

SUMMARY

This chapter focuses on making one graphics system interactive. Interaction is a two way process. The user must be able to respond to the system. Certain interactive techniques are given in this chapter. Interrupts are also handled here. They provide for event handling. Event handling algorithm is given in the chapter.

Rendering is the process of producing images or pictures. Producing realistic images involves both physical theory and psychology.

Illumination is the process of lighting an object. It can be diffuse illumination and point source illumination.

Some other topics have also been discussed like ray tracing, half tones, mach banding etc.

EXERCISE

1. What is interaction? Discuss various hardware devices used in interaction.
2. What is event handling? How is it accomplished?
3. Write a program for input device handling.
4. What do you understand by Rendering and illumination? Explain & discuss various types of illumination.
5. Write short notes on :
   (*a*) MACH banding
   (*b*) Specular reflection.
   (*c*) Shadow & shadow volumes
   (*d*) Ray tracing
   (*e*) Half tones.

6

CURVES & ANIMATION

CURVES AND FRACTALS

The real world is not made up of stick figures or straight lines otherwise the world would have been a boring place to live in. Many of the things which we might like to model or display involve curves or curve like structures. We might like to plot a mathematical function or the path of a aero-plane or we might wish to design a car or the wing of an airplane or we might desire to draw a woman's face. Natural objects are neither perfectly flat nor smoothly curved but often have rough, jagged contours.

In this chapter, we shall introduce methods for generating curved lines. We shall develop spline interpolation algorithm for drawing curved lines and fractal curve generators for rough and natural looking objects.

CURVE GENERATION

There are two approaches which can be taken to draw curved lines.

1. One approach is to develop a curve generation algorithm such as DDA, with this approach a true curve is created.
2. A second method is to approximate a curve by a number of small straight line segments. The numerical interpolation techniques are used for this approach.

Suppose we have a curve such as the arc of a circle that we wish to draw. If we know a differential equation for this curve, we can write digital differential analyzer algorithm which will calculate the co-ordinates of points on the curve. We can change the intensity values of the pixel which contains these points and an image of the curve will appear on the screen.

The differential equation for simple curves such as circles and ellipses are fairly easy to solve and generation algorithm for them can be implemented in hardware also. A display device may be capable of drawing arcs as well as line segments.

Let us step through the development of DDA algorithm for generating circular arcs. The equations for the arc co-ordinates can be written in terms of an angle parameter B as follows:

$$x = R \cos A + x_o$$
$$y = R \sin A + y_o \quad \text{...(1)}$$

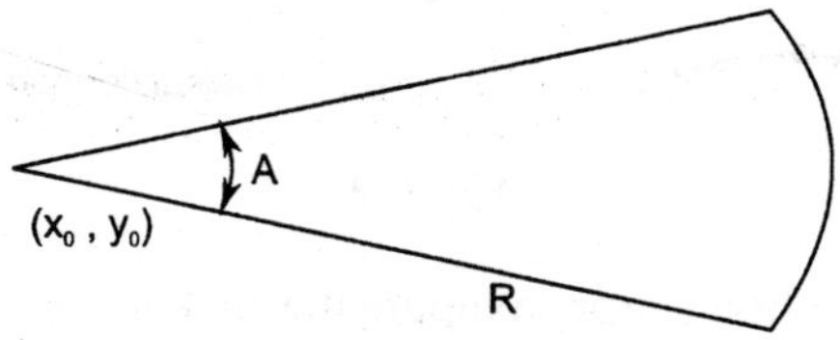

Fig. 6.1

Where (x_o, y_o) is the center of curvature & R is the arc radius.

Differentiating tell us to change x by d_x and y by d_y.

If we change A by dA

$$d_x = -R \sin A \, d_A$$
$$d_y = R \cos A \, d_A \quad \text{...(2)}$$

equation (1) gives

$$R \cos A = x - x_o$$
$$R \sin A = y - y_o \quad \text{...(3)}$$

So

$$d_x = -(y - y_o) \, d_A$$
$$d_y = (x - x_o) \, d_A \quad \text{...(4)}$$

Now the changes dx and dy tell us the amount to add to an old point on the arc to get a new point.

$$x_2 = x_1 + dx = x_1 - (y_1 - y_o) \, d_A$$
$$y_2 = y_1 + dy = y_1 + (x_2 - x_o) \, d_A$$

Now these equations are is implemented through the algorithm.

Problem with this method is that we need more information that just its end points. This may mean that a different display file structure should be used.

INTERPOLATION

Above problem was solved because we had known equations for the curve. How can we express a curve, which has no simple mathematical definition?

We can draw an approximation to such a curve if we have an array of sample points. We can then guess what the curve should look like between the sample points. If the curve is smooth and one samples are close enough together, we can make pretty good guess as to what missing portion should like. One guess will probably not be exactly right but it will be close enough for appearances.

We can fill in a gap between the sample points by finding the co-ordinates along the known approximating curve and connecting these points with line segments.

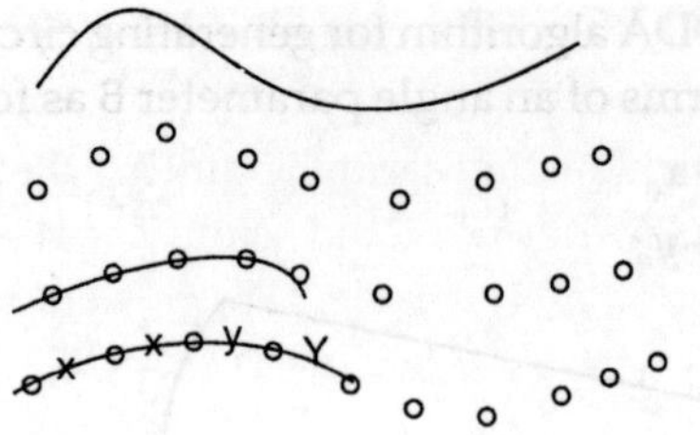

Fig. 6.2

We shall use polynomial function to approximate the curve.

Functions are often expressed in the form $y = f(x)$ but we shall prefer a parametric form.

$$x = fx(u)$$
$$y = fy(u)$$
$$z = fz(u)$$

The parametric form treats all these directions equally and it allows multiple values (several y or z values for a given x) so that curves can double back or even cross themselves.

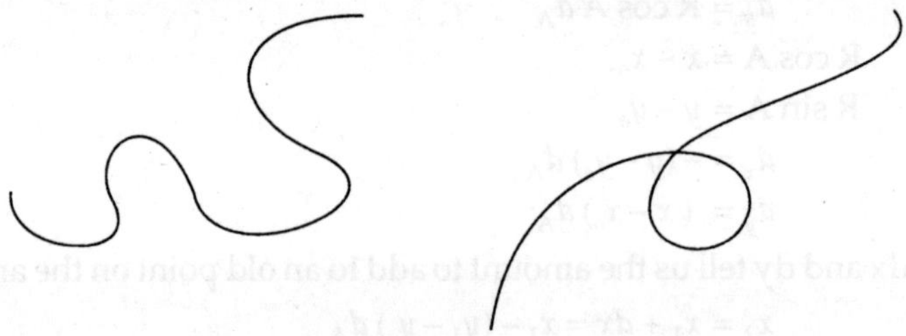

Fig. 6.3

Now let's use a function which can be used for interpolation.

Suppose we want a polynomial curve that will cross through n sample points.

$(x_1\ y_1\ z_1), (x_2\ y_2\ z_2), \ldots\ldots\ldots\ldots\ldots\ldots\ldots, (x_n\ y_n\ z_n)$

We shall build the function as the sum of terms, one term for each sample points.

$$fx(u) = \sum_{i=1}^{n} x_i\, B_i(u)$$

$$fy(u) = \sum_{i=1}^{n} y_i\, B_i(u)$$

$$fz(u) = \sum_{i=1}^{n} z_i\, B_i(u)$$

The function $B_i(u)$ are called **Blending Functions** for each value of u, they calculate & give us how much the ith sample points affects the position of the curve. We can think of each sample point as trying to pull the curve in its direction. The $B_i(u)$ function tells us how hard the ith sample point is pulling.

Note: If for some value of u, $B_i(u) = 1$ for each $j \neq 1$, $B_j(u) = 0$ then the ith sample point has complete control of the curve.

We shall create blending function for which the first sample point $(x_1\ y_1\ z_1)$ has complete control when $u = -1$, the second when $u = 0$, the third when $u = 1$ and so on. The reason for this selection of u values is to make the actual implementation a bit simpler. For this choice, we need for $B_i(u)$ a function which is 1 at $u = -1$ and 0 for $u = 0, 1, 2, \ldots\ldots\ldots\ldots, n-2$.

B – SPLINES

There are a set of blending functions and they always sum to 1. They generate curve sections which have continuous slopes so that they fit together smoothly.

Cubic B - Spline functions are adequate for most applications. The cubic B - Spline blending functions interpolate over four sample points and are cubic polynomials in u.

The cubic B - Spline functions for the middle of the curve are as follows:

$$B_1(u) = \frac{(1-u)^3}{6}$$

$$B_2(u) = \frac{u^3}{2} - u^2 + \frac{2}{3}$$

$$B_3(u) = \frac{-u^3}{2} + \frac{u^2}{2} + \frac{u}{2} + \frac{1}{6}$$

$$B_4(u) = \frac{u^3}{6}$$

The following functions should be used for the very first section of the curve

$$B'_1(u) = (1-u)^3$$

$$B'_2(u) = 21 . \frac{u^3}{12} - 9 . \frac{u^2}{2} + 3u$$

$$B'_3(u) = -11 . \frac{u^3}{12} - 3 . \frac{u^2}{2}$$

$$B'_4(u) = \frac{u^3}{6}$$

We can use Lagrange's Interpolation method.

Let's consider the case where there are four sample points. Then we will need four blending functions.

$$B_1(u) = \frac{u(u-1)(u-2)}{(-1)(-2)(-3)}$$

$$B_2(u) = \frac{(u+1)(u-1)(u-2)}{(1)(-1)(-2)}$$

$$B_3(u) = \frac{(u+1)(u)(u-1)}{(2)(1)(-1)}$$

$$B_4(u) = \frac{(u+1)(u)(u-1)}{(3)(2)(1)}$$

Using these functions and four sample points, we can construct a curve which passes through the four sample points.

$$x = x_1B_1(u) + x_2B_2(u) + x_3B_3(u) + x_4B_4(u)$$
$$y = y_1B_1(u) + y_2B_2(u) + y_3B_3(u) + y_4B_4(u)$$
$$z = z_1B_1(u) + z_2B_2(u) + z_3B_3(u) + z_4B_4(u)$$

Cubic B splines helps to Smoothen the curve.

BEIZER CURVES

Cubic Beizer curves are commonly used in graphics system. A Beizer curve is described in terms of control polygon whose vertices are commonly called control points.

A Beizer curve begins at exactly the first control point P_o and terminates at exactly the last control point P_3.

The formula for converting form control points into a pair of parametric equations will be of the form.

$$x(t) = axt^3 + bxt^2 + c_xt + dx$$
$$y(t) = ayt^3 + byt^2 + c_yt + d_y$$

where
$$a_x = -x_o + 3 * x_1 + (-3 * x_2) + x_3;$$
$$a_y = -y_o + 3 * y_1 + (-3 * y_2) + y_3;$$

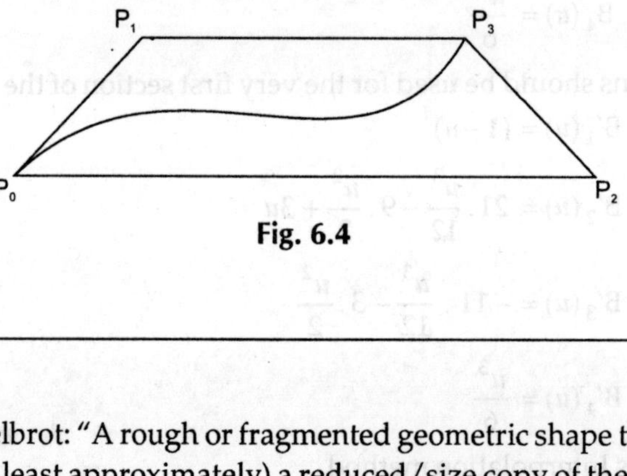

Fig. 6.4

THE FRACTAL MAGIC

What is a Fractal?

According to B. Mandelbrot: "A rough or fragmented geometric shape that can be subdivided in parts, each of which is (at least approximately) a reduced/size copy of the whole."

Fractals are geometric figures, just like rectangles, circles and squares, but fractals have special properties that those figures do not have.

Fractal Properties

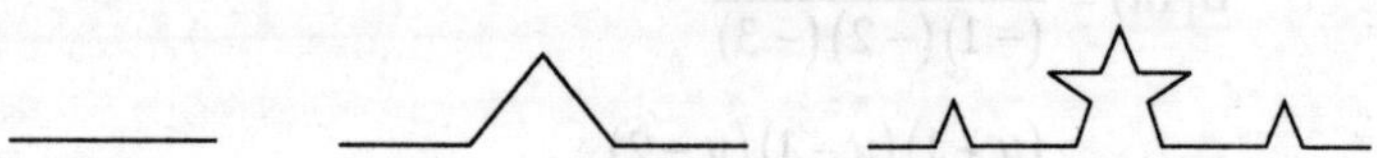

Fig. 6.5

A **point** has no dimensions - no length, no width, no height. That dot is obviously way too big to really represent a point. But we'll live with it, if we all just agree what a point really is.

A line has one dimension - length. It has no width and no height, but infinite length.

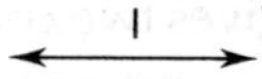

Fig. 6.6

Again, this model of a line is really not very good, but until we learn how to draw a line with 0 width and infinite length, it'll have to do.

A **plane** has two dimensions - length and width, no depth.

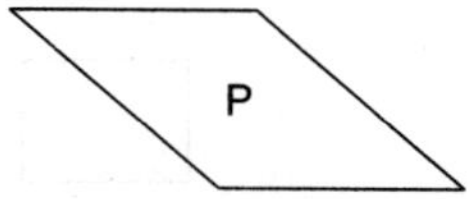

Fig. 6.7

It's an absolutely flat tabletop extending out both ways to infinity.

Space, a huge empty box, has three dimensions, length, width, and depth, extending to infinity in all three directions.

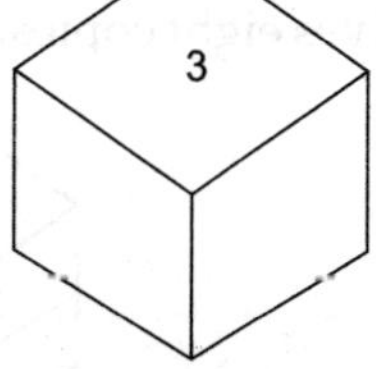

Fig. 6.8

Obviously this isn't a good representation of 3-D. Besides its size, it's just a hexagon drawn to fool you into thinking it's a box.

Fractals can have ***fractional (or fractal) dimension***. A fractal might have dimension of 1.6 or 2.4. How could that be? Let's investigate below.

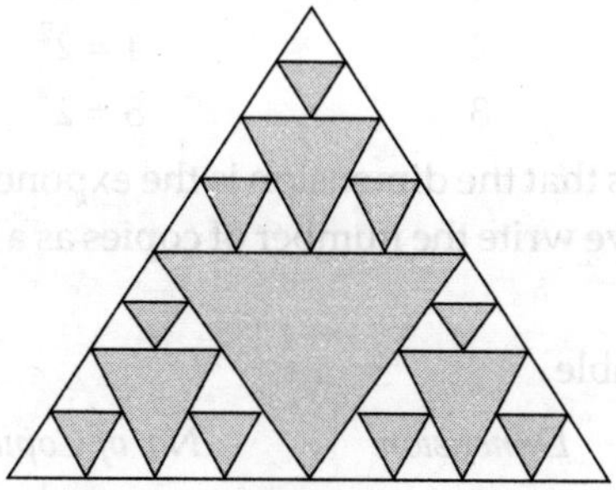

Fig. 6.9

Just as the images above weren't very good pictures of a point, line, plane, or space, the drawing meant to be the Sierpinski Triangle has limitations. Remember as we continue that fractals are really formed by infinitely many steps. So there are infinitely many smaller and smaller triangles inside the figure, and infinitely many holes (the black triangles).

Let's look further at what we mean by dimension. Take a self-similar figure like a line segment, and double its length. Doubling the length gives two copies of the original segment.

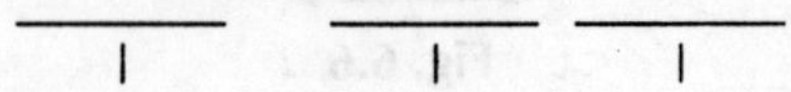

Fig. 6.10

Take another self-similar figure, this time a square 1 unit by 1 unit. Now multiply the length and width by 2. How many copies of the original size square do you get? Doubling the sides gives four copies.

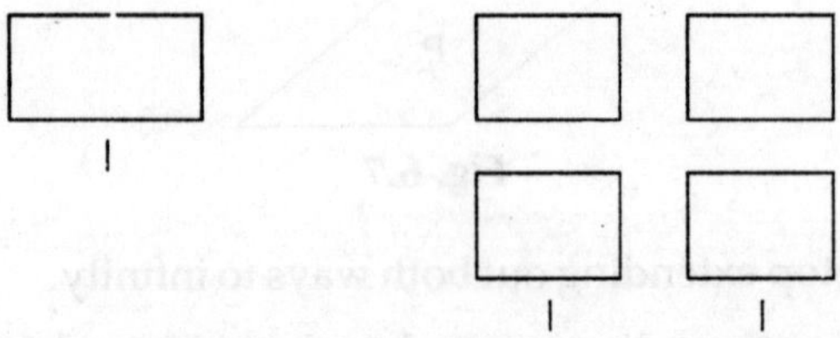

Fig. 6.11

Take a 1 by 1 by 1 cube and double its length, width, and height. How many copies of the original size cube do you get? Doubling the side gives eight copies.

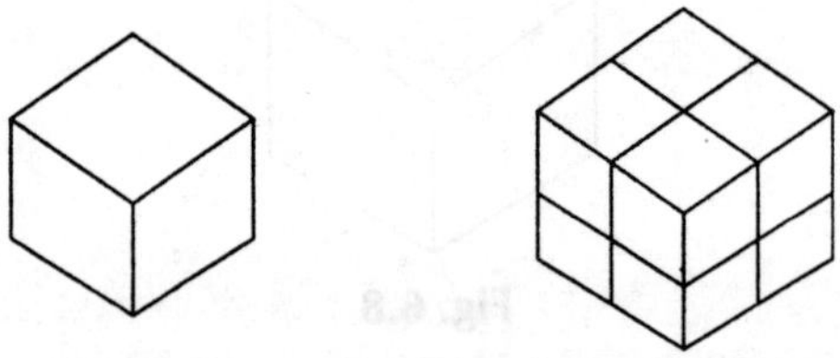

Fig. 6.12

Let's organize our information into a table.

Figure	*Dimension*	*No. of Copies*
Line	1	$2 = 2^1$
Square	2	$4 = 2^2$
Cube	3	$8 = 2^3$

Do you see a pattern? It appears that the dimension is the exponent - and it is! So when we double the sides and get a similar figure, we write the number of copies as a power of 2 and the exponent will be the dimension.

Let's add that as a row to the table.

Figure	*Dimension*	*No. of Copies*
Line	1	$2 = 2^1$
Square	2	$4 = 2^2$
Cube	3	$8 = 2^3$
Doubling Similarity	d	$n = 2^d$

We can use this to figure out the dimension of the Sierpinski Triangle because when you double the length of the sides, you get another Sierpinski Triangle similar to the first.

Start with a Sierpinski triangle of 1-inch sides. Double the length of the sides. Now how many copies of the original triangle do you have? Remember that the black triangles are holes, so we can't count them.

Doubling the sides gives us three copies, so $3 = 2^d$, where d = the dimension.

But wait, $2 = 2^1$, and $4 = 2^2$, so what number could this be? It has to be somewhere between 1 and 2, right? Let's add this to our table

Figure	*Dimension*	*No. of Copies*
Line	1	$2 = 2^1$
Sierpinski's Triangle	?	$3 = 2^?$
Square	2	$4 = 2^2$
Cube	3	$8 = 2^3$
Doubling Similarity	d	$n = 2^d$

So the dimension of Sierpinski's Triangle is between 1 and 2. Do you think you could find a better answer? Use a calculator with an exponent key (the key usually looks like this ^). Use 2 as a base and experiment with different exponents between 1 and 2 to see how close you can come. For example, try 1.1. Type 2^1.1 and you get 2.143547. I'll bet you can get closer to 3 than that. Try 2^1.2 and you get 2.2974. That's closer to 3, but you can do better.

That's how fractals can have fractional dimension.

FRACTAL GEOMETRY

Almost all geometric forms used for building man made objects belong to Euclidean geometry, they are comprised of lines, planes, rectangular volumes, arcs, cylinders, spheres, etc. These elements can be classified as belonging to an integer dimension, either 1, 2, or 3. This concept of dimension can be described both intuitively and mathematically. Intuitively we say that a line is one dimensional because it only takes 1 number to uniquely define any point on it. That one number could be the distance from the start of the line. This applies equally well to the circumference of a circle, a curve, or the boundary of any object.

A plane is two dimensional since in order to uniquely define any point on its surface we require two numbers. There are many ways to arrange the definition of these two numbers but we normally create an orthogonal coordinate system. Other examples of two dimensional objects are the surface of a sphere or an arbitrary twisted plane.

The volume of some solid object is 3 dimensional on the same basis as above, it takes three numbers to uniquely define any point within the object.

A more mathematical description of dimension is based on how the "size" of an object behaves as the linear dimension increases. In one dimension consider a line segment. If the linear dimension of the line segment is doubled then obviously the length (characteristic size) of the line has doubled. In two dimensions, if the linear dimensions of a rectangle for example is doubled then the characteristic size, the area, increases by a factor of 4. In three dimensions if the linear dimension of a box are doubled then the volume increases by a factor of 8. This relationship between dimension D, linear scaling L and the resulting increase in size S can be generalised and written as

$$S = L^D$$

This is just telling us mathematically what we know from everyday experience. If we scale a two dimensional object for example then the area increases by the square of the scaling. If we scale a three dimensional object the volume increases by the cube of the scale factor. Rearranging the above gives an expression for dimension depending on how the size changes as a function of linear scaling, namely

$$D = \log(S)/\log(L)$$

In the examples above the value of D is an integer, either 1, 2, or 3, depending on the dimension of the geometry. This relationship holds for all Euclidean shapes. There are however many shapes which do not conform to the integer based idea of dimension given above in both the intuitive and mathematical descriptions. That is, there are objects which appear to be curves for example but which a point on the curve cannot be uniquely described with just one number. If the earlier scaling formulation for dimension is applied the formula does not yield an integer. There are shapes that lie in a plane but if they are linearly scaled by a factor L, the area does not increase by L squared but by some non integer amount. These geometries are called fractals! One of the simpler fractal shapes is the von Koch snowflake. The method of creating this shape is to repeatedly replace each line segment with the following 4 line segments.

The process starts with a single line segment and continues for ever. The first few iterations of this procedure are shown below.

Fig. 6.13

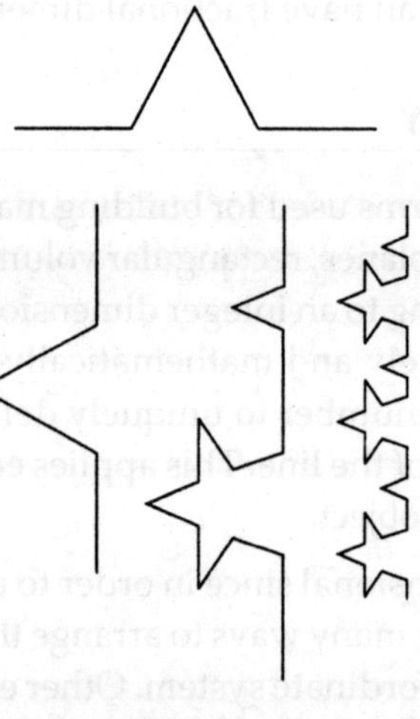

Fig. 6.14

This demonstrates how a very simple generation rule for this shape can generate some unusual (fractal) properties. Unlike Euclidean shapes this object has detail at all levels. If one magnifies an Euclidean shape such as the circumference of a circle it becomes a different shape, namely a straight line. If we magnify this fractal more and more detail is uncovered, the detail is self similar or rather it is exactly self similar. Put another way, any magnified portion is identical to any other magnified portion.

ITERATIVE FORMATION

Fractals are often formed by what is called an iterative process

To make a fractal: Take a familiar geometric figure (a triangle or line segment, for example) and operate on it so that the new figure is more "complicated" in a special way.

Then in the same way, operate on that resulting figure, and get an even more complicated figure.

Now operate on that resulting figure in the same way and get an even more complicated figure.

Do it again and again...and again. In fact, you have to think of doing it infinitely many times.

You can observe this iterative process in all the fractals that we make

- Sierpinski's Triangle
- Koch Snowflake

INTRODUCTION TO COMPUTER ANIMATION

Animation is the creation of the illusion of movement by assembling a sequence of still images.

To 'animate' is literally 'to give life to'. 'Animating' is moving something which can't move itself. These pictures do not really move -- they are composed of a series of static images that affect the eyes at the rate of 12 to 24 images per second. The illusion of movement is caused by a physiological affect known as 'persistence of vision'.

Animation adds to graphics the dimension of time which vastly increases the amount of information which can be transmitted. In order to animate something, the animator has to be able to specify, either directly or indirectly, how the 'thing' is to move through time and space. The basic problem is to select or design animation tools which are expressive enough for the animator to specify what he wants to specify while at the same time are powerful or automatic enough that the animator doesn't have to specify the details that he is not interested in. Obviously, there is no one tool that is going to be right for every animator, for every animation, or even for every scene in a single animation. The appropriateness of a particular animation tool depends on the effect desired by the animator. An artistic piece of animation will probably require different tools that an animation intended to simulate reality.

There are two main categories of computer animation: ***computer-assisted animation and computer generated animation***. This book is mainly concerned with computer-generated animation. For discussion purposes, motion specification for computer-generated animation is divided into two categories: low level techniques (techniques that aid the animator in precisely specifying motion), and high level techniques (techniques used to describe general motion behavior) .

Low level techniques consist of techniques, such as shape interpolation algorithms, which help the animator fill in the details of the motion once enough information about the motion has been specified by the animator. When using low level techniques, the animator usually has a fairly specific idea of the exact motion that he or she wants.

High level techniques are typically algorithms or models used to generate a motion using a set of rules or constraints. The animator sets up the rules of the model, or chooses an appropriate algorithm, and selects initial values or boundary values. The system is then set into motion, so to speak, and the motion of the objects is controlled by the algorithm or model. The model-based/algorithmic approaches often rely on fairly sophisticated computation, such as physically based motion control.

Any technique requires a certain amount of effort from the animator and a certain amount of effort from the computer. One of the things which distinguishes animation techniques is whether its the animator or the computer which bears most of the burden. Motion specification aids are those techniques which seem to require more input from the user and fairly straightforward computation. Model-based approaches, on the other hand, require less from the animator and more computation. But the categories are really artificial.

Another way to characterize the difference between techniques is to look at the level of abstraction at which the animator is working. In one extreme, at a very low level of abstraction, the animator could color in every pixel individually in every frame. At the other extreme, at a very high level of abstraction, the animator could tell a computer to 'make a movie about a dog'. Presumably, the computer would whirl away while it computes such a thing. A high level of abstraction frees the animator from dealing with all of the details. A low level of abstraction allows the animator to be very precise in specifying exactly what is displayed when. In reality, animators want to be able to switch back and forth and work at various levels of abstraction. The challenge to developing animation tools is designing the tools so that animators are allowed to work at high levels of abstraction when desired, while providing them the ability to work at low levels when needed.

PERCEPTION

Images convey a lot of information because the human visual system is a sophisticated information processor. It follows, then, that moving images have the potential to convey much more information.

When animation is recorded for later viewing, it is typcially presented in film or video formats by recording a series of still images. This is possible because the eye-brain assembles a sequence of images and interprets them as a continuous movement. Persistence of motion is created by presenting a sequence of still images at a fast enough rate to induce the sensation of continuous motion.

The receptors in the eye continually sample light in the environment. The only limitation on motion detection is the reaction time of those sensors and on certain mechanical limitations such as blinking and tracking. If an object moves fast enough, then the receptors in the eye will not be able to respond fast enough for the brain to distinguish a sharply defined, individual detail; motion blur results.

In either film or video, a sequence of images is recorded which can be played back at rates fast enough to fool the eye into interpreting them as continuous motion. Of course, in order to save resources, this rate is kept as low as possible while still maintaining the persistence of motion. Under some viewing conditions such as room lighting and viewing distance, the rate at which single images must be played back in order to maintain the perception of motion varies. The image is said to flicker when the perception of continuous motion fails to be created. The object appears as a rapid sequence of still images to the eye-brain.

There are actually two rates that are of concern. One is the number of images per second that are displayed in the viewing process. The other, is the number of different images that occur per second. The former is the *playback rate;* the latter is the *sampling rate or update rate*. For example, images are always played back at 30 images per second on a TV, but in some Saturday morning cartoons there may be only six different images per second with each image repeated five times.

THE EARLY DAYS OF ANIMATION

Persistence of vision was discovered in the 1800s. This led to such devices as the zoetrope, or "wheel of life." The zoetrope has a short, fat cylinder which rotated on its axis of symmetry. Around the inside of the cylinder were a sequence of drawings, each one slightly different from the one next to it. The cylinder had iong slits cut into its side in between each of the images so that when the cylinder was spun a slit would allow the eye to see the image on the oppose wall of the cylinder. As the cylinder was spun on its axis, the sequence of slits passing in front of the eye would present a sequence of images to the eye, creating the illusion of motion.

Another low-tech animation piece of equipment was the flipbook. The flipbook was a tablet of paper with an individual drawing on each page so the viewer could flip through them. This was also popular in the 1800s..

The earliest hint of using a camera to make lifeless things appear to move was by Meleis in 1890 using simple tricks. The earliest pioneers in film animation were Emile Cohl, a Frenchman who produced several vignettes, J. Stuart Blackton, an American, who actually animated 'smoke' in a scene in 1900 and who is credited with the first animated cartoon in 1906, and the first celebrated animator, Winsor McCay, an American best known for his works Little Nemo and Gertie the Dinosaur.

The first major technical developments in the animation process can be traced to the work (and patents) of John Bray starting in 1910. His work laid the groundwork for the use of translucent cels (short for celluloid) in compositing multiple layers of drawings into a final image as well as the use of grey scale (as opposed to black and white) drawings. Later developments by Bray and others enhanced the overlay idea to include multiple translucent pieces of celluloid (cels), added a peg system for registration, and the drawing of the background on long sheets of paper so that panning (translating the camera parallel to the plane of the background) could be performed more easily. Fleischer patented rotoscoping in 1915. Rotoscoping is drawing images on cells by tracing over previously recorded live action. Bray experimented with color in one 1920 short.

During this time, animation as an art form was still struggling. The first animated character with an identifiable personality is Felix the Cat by Otto Messmer which appeared in the early 1920s in Pat Sullivan productions. In the late 1920s however, new forces had to be reckoned with: sound and Walt Disney.

DISNEY

Walt Disney was, of course, the overpowering force in the history of animation. Not only did his studio contribute several technical innovations, but the Disney studio, more than anyone else, advanced animation as an art form.

Some of Disney's innovations in animation technology were the use of a storyboard to review the story, the use of pencil sketches to review motion, and the multi-plane camera stand In addition, Disney pioneered the use of sound and color in animation (although not the first to use color). Disney also studied live action sequences to create more realistic motion in his films. When he used sound for the first time in Steamboat Willie (1928), he gained an advantage over his competitors.

Camera stand animation is more powerful than you might think. A camera stand allows the parallax effect - moving of backgrounds at different rates as the observer pans across an environment to create the illusion of depth—and zooming. Each of the planes can move six directions (right, left, up, down, in, out) as well as the camera moving in and out. By keeping the camera lens open during movement, figures can be made to appear extruded into shapes of higher dimension, simulate motion blur, exhibit depth attenuation.

With regard to the art form of animation, Disney perfected the ability to impart unique, endearing personalities in his characters including Mickey Mouse, Pluto, Goofy, the three little Pigs, and the seven Dwarfs. He also developed mood pieces of animation including Skeleton Dance and Fantasia. He also promoted the idea that the mind of the character was the driving force of the action and that a key to believable animated motion was the analysis of real life motion.

OTHER MEDIA FOR ANIMATION

Computer animation is considered by many to be actually closer to other animation techniques rather than traditional hand-drawn animation. Often it is compared to stop motion animation, such as puppet animation, that builds and manipulates identifiable objects. Other stop motion techniques are claymation, pinhead animation and sand animation.

In this type of animation, a physical object is manipulated, the camera takes an image of it, the object is manipulated again, another image is taken of it, and the process repeats to produce the animated sequence.

ANIMATION PRODUCTION

Computer animation production has borrowed most of the ideas from conventional animation production including the use of a story board, test shots, and pencil testing. The use of key frames and in-betweening have also been adopted in certain computer animation systems.

Story boards have pretty much translated directly over to computer animation production although they may be kept on a computer. They still hold the same functional place in the animation process.

In computer animation there is usually a strict distinction between the creation of the models, the specification of their motion, and the rendering process which is applied to those models. In conventional animation, the model building, motion specification, and rendering are really all the same thing. In computer animation, speed-quality tradeoffs can be made in each of the three stages during the trial and error process that characterizes much of animation.

A test shot in computer animation is usually a high quality rendering of a highly detailed model to see a single frame of the final product. Pencil testing can be performed either by simplifying the sophistication of the models used, or by using low quality and/or low resolution renderings, or by using simple motion control algorithms. Place-holder cubes can be rendered in wire frame to present the gross motion of rigid bodies in space and to see spacial and temporal relationships among objects. This may also provide real-time calculation and playback of the animation. Similarly, high-quality rendering of low complexity models or low-quality renderings of highly detailed models, or some intermediate levels of both the model and the renderer can be used to give the animator clues to the finished product's quality without committing to the final computation. For example, a hardware z-buffer display can provide good turn-around time with decent quality images before going to a ray traced image. Solids of revolution objects lend themselves quite well to allowing for three, four or five levels of detail for a given model. Also, smooth shading, texture mapping, specular reflection and solid texturing can all be options presented to the animator for a given run. To simplify motion control, for example, simple interpolation between poses may be used instead of inverse dynamics.

TIME

When choreographing action in an animation or other production, the precise specification of time and temporal relationships is important. In everyday life, time is usually considered to be a continuous axis. In animation, however, because of the ultimate breakdown into frames, the time axis is discrete. It is important to keep this in mind when discussing temporal relationships of events in the animation production.

Because of the discrete nature of frames, there may be some ambiguity when saying, for example, a span ends exactly when another span begins. In the discrete world, we will take that to mean that a span ends on the frame before the frame that the other span begins on.

COMPUTER ANIMATION: FILMS AND VIDEOS

Early computer animation companies included Mathematical Applications Group, Inc. (MAGI), Information International Inc. (III, or Triple-I), Digital Productions, Digital Effects, Image West, Robert Abel and Associates, and Cranston-Csuri.

Current computer animation companies (who also contribute significantly to research in the area are: Pixar, Industrial Light and Magic (ILM), Pacific Data Images (PDI), Disney, Xaos, Rhythm & Hues, Digital Domain, Lamb & Company, Metrolight Studios, Boss Film Studios, deGraf/Wahrman, R/Greenberg Associates, Blue Sky Productions, Sony Pictures, Cinesite, Imageworks, and Apple. (One might also include Silicon Graphics. in that list since their equipment is used so extensively for computer animation.)

Early on, Computer Graphics (CG) appeared in a variety of movies in which it was used as computer graphics (that is, the CG was not intended to fool the audience into thinking it was anything other than CG). For example, ***Future World*** (1976) and ***Star Wars*** (1977, Image West) fall into this category. More recently, Lawnmower Man (1992, Xaos, Angel Studios) which has a segment of Hollywood's view of Virtual Reality in it, used CG in the same role, although a more sophisticated example.

Tron (1982, MAGI) was a little different. The CG was still supposed to be computer-like because the action takes place inside a computer. But in this case, it was an integral part of the environment that the actions (and actors) were taking place in. The CG was used throughout the movie. It integrated computer animation with live action, but, since the action took place in a computer, the CG didn't have to look realistic (and didn't). This was the first time CG was used as an integral part of a movie.

Along the same lines of *Tron* in using CG to create an 'inside the computer' environment is *Reboot* (1995, Limelight Ltd./BLT Productions). *Reboot* deserves special mention as the first Saturday morning cartoon that is full three-dimensional computer-generated animation. The action takes place inside a computer so they don't have to go for 'realism'. Still, there are several human-like main characters and, overall, The *Reboot* series is very impressive.

One main use of CG has been to replace physical models. In this case, CG is used to create realistic elements which are intermixed with the live action. *The Last Star Fighter* (1984, Gray Demos' Digital

Productions, even the Cray X-MP was in the credits) used computer animation instead of building models for special effects. The action takes place in space as well as on planets; CG was used for the scenes in space and physical models were used for the scenes on a planet. It's not hard to tell when the movie switched between CG models and physical models. There were probably 20 minutes of CG used in the movie. This was the first time CG was used as part of the live action in which it wasn't supposed to look computer generated. More recently, *Apollo 13* (1995, Digital Domain) used CG models of the return vehicle from the mission. In TV-land, special note should go to *Babylon 5* (1995, Newtek). *Babylon 5* is the first TV show to routinely use CG models as regular features of it's sci-fi show - and it's Amiga-based.

CG is also used to create 'alien' creatures. Creatures which are supposed to be realistic, but don't have to match anything that the audience is familiar with. *The Abyss* (1989, ILM) is one such movie in which CG is used to effect an alien creature which is integrated with the rest of the live action. Some of the CG in *Terminator II* served a similar purpose as well as *Casper* (1995, ILM), *Species* (1995, Boss Film Studios), *Mighty Morphin' Power Rangers* (VIFX), *Sexy Robot* (TV Commercial, Abel).

More challenging is the use of CG to create realistic models of creatures that are familiar to the audience. *Jurassic Park* (1993, ILM) was the first to completely integrate use of CG character animation in which the graphics were designed so as to blend in with the live action so that it was difficult to tell what was computer generated and what wasn't. *Jumanji* (1995, ILM) does the same thing with it's incredible modeling of animals. To a lesser extent, *Batman Returns* (1995), Digital Domain) also does the same thing by providing 'stunt doubles' of Batman in a few scenes. CG was used to create the face of *RoboCop 2* (1990, deGraf/Wahrman) and animated skeletons in *Total Recall* (Metrolight) as well.

Another popular CG technique for special effects is the use of particle systems. One of the best examples is in *Star Trek II: The Wrath of Khan* (Lucas Film computer division, later ILM) in which a wall of fire sweeps over the surface of a planet. Another example is *Lawnmower Man* in which a character disintegrates into a swirl of small balls. A more recent example from television is in the opening sequence of *Star Trek: Deep Space Nine* (1995) to model a comet's tail. *Twister* also uses particle systems to simulate a tornado.

Of course, one use of computer animation is simply to 'do animation.' By that I mean computer animation is used to produce animated pieces which would otherwise be done by more traditional means - essentially 3D cartoons (although the term cheapens the idea somewhat). Although I'd like to restrict my topic to 3D computer animation, I suppose that morphing should be mentioned. This is essentially a 2D procedure which warps control points (or feature lines) of one image into the control points (feature lines) of another image while the images themselves are blended. In Star Trek IV, one of the first commercial morphs was provided by ILM in the back in time dream sequence In *Willow* (1988, ILM), ILM provided the morph of several animals. This technique was also used by ILM *in Indiana Jones and the Last Crusade* (1989) and *Terminator 2*. PDI is known for its use of morphing in various commercials including a Plymouth Voyager commercial and an Exxon commercial in which a car changes into a tiger. Of course, morphing has gone on to become another Energizer Bunny of TV commercials - it keeps going and going and going... Full 3D morphing has yet to make it out of the research labs and into any production environment.

There is another class of movies in which CG plays a role - that of 'hidden special effect' (for lack of a better term). CG can be used to cover up mechanical special effects or to enhance the scene to integrate a mechanical special effect more completely. For the most part, this resides in the 2D realm and, as such, will not be the focus of this document. However, with the onset of digital techniques for 2D compositing, sequences will be routinely digitally available making them susceptible to a variety of digital post-processing techniques. The first digital blue screen matte extraction was in Willow (ILM). The first wire removal was in Howard the Duck (ILM). In *True Lies* (1994, Digital Domain), CG was used to erase support wires from suspended actors. In Forest Gump (1994, Digital Domain), CG was used to insert a ping pong ball in a sequence showing an extremely fast action game. In *Babe* (1995, Rythm & Hues), CG was used to move the mouths of animals and fill in the background uncovered by the movement. In *Interview with a Vampire* (1994, Digital Domain), CG was used to curl the hair of a woman during the transformation into a vampire. In this case, some of the effect was created using 3D graphics and then integrated into the scene by 2D compositing.

COMPUTER ANIMATION SOFTWARE

Here is a short list of some animation software.

GIFF Animator
Macromedia Flash
Softimage (Microsoft)
Alias/Wavefront (SGI)
3D Studio MAX (Autodesk)
Lightwave 3D (Newtek)
Prisms 3D Animation Software (Side Effects Software)
HOUDINI (Side Effects Software)
Apple's toolkit for game developers
Digimation

Here we are going to discuss **Macromedia Flash** and **GIFF Animator**

MACROMEDIA FLASH

Macromedia Flash is quickly becoming the standard for multimedia development for the web and the desktop. Flash is an extremely powerful drawing or illustration program, featuring all the creation and manipulation features you could want. You can introduce objects, move objects, and even morph objects over time. Flash allows you to easily incorporate text, graphics, sound, and animation into a compressed package that can be sent over the web or played from the desktop.

The core elements of the interface can be described in terms that lend themselves to a movie analogy. The desktop is the "stage," and the unfolding of your creation takes place along a timeline that is divided into "frames." You can set an object to exist for a specific number of frames, and you can assign actions (start/stop) to a frame. Larger subdivisions of the file are called "scenes." Flash provides tools for sketching and layout in a process called "storyboarding."

Objects are controlled using a series of "panels" that group the functions you might want to perform on an object you've created. The **Transform** panel, for example, lets you rotate, skew, scale, and duplicate elements. The **Align** panel controls the alignment, distribution, sizing, and spacing of objects. With the **Mixer**, you can define colors. Using the **Character** panel, you can edit fonts characteristics such as font size, font color, and kerning, as well as set links to text. Similar panels are available to create and control color and sound.

Some key concepts behind the features:

- The range of options for object manipulations is due to the program's ability to treat objects as either bitmap or vector, depending on the operation you want to perform. Imported bitmap art can be converted to a collection of vector drawings for extraction and further manipulation to suit the purposes of the presentation.
- A "key frame" is a space in the timeline where you can define the properties of an object (shape, color, transparency, position, etc.) for a chosen time duration. Another function of key frames is to introduce a layer in a timeline relationship to active layers. Different key frames can exist in different layers, but you need to line up key frames to give the appearance of motion and movement.
- A major consideration in developing web-based communication vehicles is the time required for downloading. This becomes crucial when using motion. The library feature of Flash serves to reduce the file size of the final product, because objects can be reused many times in the movie, but are downloaded only once. You can edit one instance of a library item and apply the change to the library item or leave the library item alone. Objects must be placed in a library before you can apply animation.
- Download time can also be saved by manipulating objects in layers so that part of an object or group is covered by another. Flash stores only the content that's visible at the surface.
- "Tweening" allows you to select two frames and then morph an object from one shape to another between the frames.

GIFF ANIMATOR

Key Features

Fast and easy animation

1. **Intuitive Interface:** Get around fast using a tab-based interface
2. **Easy composition:** Create dynamic multiple object animation with drag and drop precision
3. **Dynamic effects:** Apply various text effects, video effects, transitions etc.
4. **Powerful optimization:** Ensure fast loading animation with the latest image compression techniques
5. **Flexible output:** Export to a wide variety of file formats, including Flash, AVI, MPEG etc.

System Requirements for GIFF Animator

- Intel Pentium compatible processors
- Microsoft Windows 98, NT 4.0 SP5 or higher
- 64 MB of RAM
- 20 MB of available hard disk space
- CD-ROM drive
- True color or Hicolor display adapter
- Windows compatible pointing device

SOUND ANIMATION

Special bonds connect sound with moving images. In animation, these bonds are very special. The visual elements and the audio track seem to share a more intimate and more creative partnership than exists in other motion picture form.

This may be created by :

- High degree of synchronization
  The technology of animation encourages a higher degree of synchronization that is practical within other forms of moviemaking. In both visual and audio realms, the animator has total control. An image or a sound can be placed with accuracy down to the tenths of a second. [read about the Synchresis phenoma]
- Strong relationship between animation and music
  Animation and music have a basic mathematical foundation and move forward at a determined speed. The rhythm of a musical composition is measured, and beats are fitted into bar units of defined time length and are interpreted in time units.
- Sound metaphors
  The combination of fast moving animated visuals and unrealistic sound effects create audiovisual metaphors that often have humorous aspects. For example slow moving footsteps synched to cymbal crashes ...or ... fast moving hands digging to the sound of a roaring engine..
- Kinetic energy
  In animation synchronized sound effects are used as a source of kinetic energy.
  In the Classic Hollywood Studio Cartoon the sound track are mostly constructed from boinks, petangs, pings, and kerthuds to energize a scene.
  When these sounds are determinants of the scene's pacing, they are recorded prior to shooting and logged like a voice track; the animation is shot to the effects track.

Animation sound can be...

- Pre-synchronous
- Post-synchronous
- Non-synchronous

Pre-synchronous

Music and sound effects for key actions is recorded before the images are produced and the animation is "shoot to the track" The sounds are created "presynch"

Most voices are recorded presynch. Presynched is the best way to achieve the precise synchronization between pictures and sound that, for audience, is one of the most entertaining aspects of animation. For the animator, presynching also helps solve one of the most difficult problems encountered during shooting: how to pace action, or more precisely, how to determine the extent of each incremental movement. Once a voice or music track has been recorded, analyzed, and logged, it becomes a concrete determinant of when key actions must occur relative to those points.

Dramatic important sound are logged as voice track prior to shooting.

Post-synchronous

The images are shoot before the sounds.

Sound effects are used to complete the outer orientation (the spatial and temporal settings) established by the visuals. These sound effects are often added in postproduction, since they are rarely the primary determinant of the scene's pacing. If the animator is shooting to the voice track, particular actions in the picture that require a sound effect — such as doors closing, gunshots, telephones ringing, and so forth — are simply cut into the effects track at the appropriate frame.

Non-synchronous

Non-synchronous music has not been carefully timed to fit the picture. Because music and film both are "time arts", it is inevitable that any selection will synchronize with the picture at random points, and even non-synchronous music severs as a "bed" for the action throughout.

In animation actions are condensed

Standard libraries of sound effects are more and then useless for animation because the action of animation is for compact - a real car takes ages to go into the distance compared with the animation of the same action.

First Principle of animation sound

First Principle of animation sound effects is that there is no connection between the object in the picture and the origin of the sound.

SUMMARY

World is full of curves and curves like structures so generation of curves is an important area of computer graphics. We can generate curves using DDA like algorithm or by interpolation techniques.

In curves, blending functions play an important role. B-splines are a set of blending functions and always sum to 1. They generate curve sections which were continuous slopes so that they fit together smoothly.

Beizer curves are commonly used in graphics system. A Beizer curve is described in terms of central polygon who vertices are commonly called control points. It begins exactly at the first control point P_0 adn terminates exactly at last control point P_3.

Fractals stands for fractional dimensional and is a term widely associated in graphics with randomly generated curves and surfaces. They are used to provide materialistic shapes for representing objects such as coast lines, rugged mountains, grass etc.

Animation is the creation of the illusion of movement by assembling a sequence of still images. To animate is 'to give life to'. The illusion of movement is caused by physiological affect known as "PERSISTENCE of version". We are concerned with computer generated animation.

There are softwares for animation like Gif Animation and Macromedia Flash. They have been discussed in the chapter.

EXERCISE

1. What are curves ? How are they generated ?
2. What is animation ? Explain different types of softwares used for it.
3. Write a program to generate Beizer curves.
4. Write a program for generation of fractals.
5. Write short notes on :

   (*a*) Persistence of version
   (*b*) Animation and Movies
   (*c*) Animation Hardware
   (*d*) Multimedia
   (*e*) Fractals.

7

MULTIMEDIA

INTRODUCTION

This is an introduction to multimedia. Multimedia is very hard to define, but it does involve a combination of existing technologies. For this reason we will first look at the components that make up a multimedia application, text, graphics etc., what formats are used, what you should consider when buying hardware, and then at some multimedia applications.

History of Multimedia Systems

Newspaper were perhaps the first mass communication medium to employ Multimedia -- they used mostly text, graphics, and images.

In 1895, Gugliemo Marconi sent his first wireless radio transmission at Pontecchio, Italy. A few years later (in 1901) he detected radio waves beamed across the Atlantic. Initially invented for telegraph, radio is now a major medium for audio broadcasting.

Television was the new media for the 20th century. It brings the video and has since changed the world of mass communications.

Some of the important events in relation to Multimedia in Computing include:

- 1945 - Bush wrote about Memex
- 1967 - Negroponte formed the Architecture Machine Group at MIT
- 1969 - Nelson & Van Dam hypertext editor at Brown
- Birth of The Internet
- 1971 - Email
- 1976 - Architecture Machine Group proposal to DARPA: Multiple Media
- 1980 - Lippman & Mohl: Aspen Movie Map
- 1983 - Backer: Electronic Book

- 1985 - Negroponte, Wiesner: opened MIT Media Lab
- 1989 - Tim Berners-Lee proposed the World Wide Web to CERN (European Council for Nuclear Research)
- 1990 - K. Hooper Woolsey, Apple Multimedia Lab, 100 people, educ.
- 1991 - Apple Multimedia Lab: Visual Almanac, Classroom MM Kiosk
- 1992 - the first M-bone audio multicast on the Net
- 1993 - U. Illinois National Center for Supercomputing Applications: NCSA Mosaic
- 1994 - Jim Clark and Marc Andreesen: Netscape
- 1995 - JAVA for platform-independent application development. Duke is the first applet.
- 1996 - Microsoft, Internet Explorer.

It can be defined as "the combined use of several media, such as movies, slides, music and lighting, especially for the purpose of education or entertainment."

For our purposes, multimedia includes:

- Text
- Audio (narration, dialogue, or sound effects)
- Music
- Film, video, and photographs
- Animation and graphics

In this context multimedia can be thought of as the combination of text, graphics, sound, animation and video delivered by some form of computer. When the user has some control of what is presented it becomes interactive multimedia. Multimedia does not have to be interactive, for example a tutorial may just involve the student pressing enter to go on to the next screen in a linear fashion. The tutorial would become interactive if the student affects the tutorial, for example if their answer to a question determined which screen came up next.

Multimedia can have a many definitions these include:

Multimedia means that computer information can be represented through audio, video, and animation in addition to traditional media (*i.e.*, text, graphics drawings, images).

A good general definition is:

Multimedia is the field concerned with the computer-controlled integration of text, graphics, drawings, still and moving images (Video), animation, audio, and any other media where every type of information can be represented, stored, transmitted and processed digitally.

A ***Multimedia Application*** is an Application which uses a collection of multiple media sources *e.g.*, text, graphics, images, sound/audio, animation and/or video.

Hypermedia can be considered as one of the multimedia applications.

HYPERTEXT AND HYPERMEDIA

The concept of hypertext has been around a long time, and was first described by Vannevar Bush in 1945. The actual term hypertext was coined by Ted Nelson in the 60's to describe his Xanadu project. Hypertext is text based, and in a hypertext document there are links which when activated, often by clicking on with the mouse, take the user to a different area in the same document or even a different document. These links allow the user to navigate through the document in a non-linear or non-sequential fashion. Hypermedia is a hypertext system that is not restricted to text documents, but includes other media, effectively multimedia hypertext.

Hypertext is a text which contains links to other texts. The term was invented by Ted Nelson around 1965.

Hypertext is therefore usually non-linear (as indicated below).

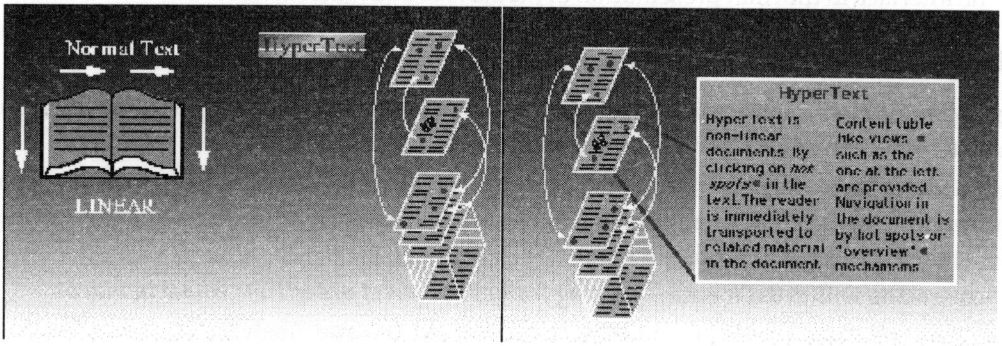

Fig. 7.1

Definition of Hypertext

HyperMedia is not constrained to be text-based. It can include other media, *e.g.*, graphics, images and especially the continuous media - sound and video. Apparently, Ted Nelson was also the first to use this term.

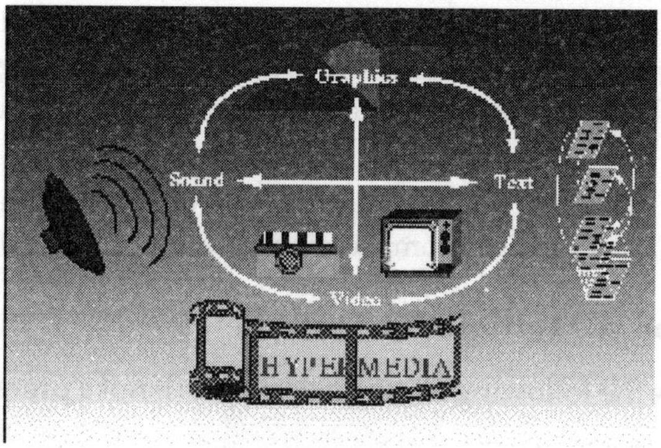

Fig. 7.2

Definition of HyperMedia

The World Wide Web (WWW) is the best example of hypermedia applications.

MULTIMEDIA SYSTEMS

A **Multimedia System** is a system capable of processing multimedia data and applications. It is characterized by the processing, storage, generation, manipulation and rendition of Multimedia information.

Characteristics of a Multimedia System

A Multimedia system has four basic characteristics:

- Multimedia systems must be ***computer controlled.***
- Multimedia systems are ***integrated.***
- The information they handle must be represented ***digitally.***
- The interface to the final presentation of media is usually ***interactive.***

Challenges for Multimedia Systems

Supporting multimedia applications over a computer network renders the application ***distributed.*** This will involve many special computing techniques -- discussed later.

Multimedia systems may have to render a variety of media at the same instant -- a distinction from normal applications. There is a temporal relationship between many forms of media (*e.g.*, Video and Audio). There 2 are forms of problems here.

- Sequencing within the media -- ***playing frames in correct order/time frame in video***
- ***Synchronisation*** -- inter-media scheduling (*e.g.*, Video and Audio). Lip synchronisation is clearly important for humans to watch playback of video and audio and even animation and audio. Ever tried watching an out of (lip) sync film for a long time?

The key issues multimedia systems need to deal with here are:

- How to represent and store temporal information.
- How to strictly maintain the temporal relationships on playback/retrieval
- What processes are involved in the above.

Data has to represented ***digitally*** so many initial source of data needs to be ***digitise*** -- translated from analog source to digital representation. The will involve scanning (graphics, still images), sampling (audio/video) although digital cameras now exist for direct scene to digital capture of images and video.

The data is ***large*** several Mb easily for audio and video -- therefore storage, transfer (bandwidth) and processing overheads are high. Data compression techniques very common.

Desirable Features for a Multimedia System

Given the above challenges the following feature a desirable (if not a prerequisite) for a Multimedia System:

Very High Processing Power

-- needed to deal with large data processing and real time delivery of media. Special hardware commonplace.

Multimedia Capable File System

-- needed to deliver real-time media -- *e.g.*, Video/Audio Streaming. Special Hardware/Software needed *e.g.*, RAID technology.

Data Representations/File Formats that Support Multimedia

-- Data representations/file formats should be easy to handle yet allow for compression/decompression in real-time.

Efficient and High I/O

-- input and output to the file subsystem needs to be efficient and fast. Needs to allow for real-time recording as well as playback of data. *e.g.*, Direct to Disk recording systems.

Special Operating System

-- to allow access to file system and process data efficiently and quickly. Needs to support direct transfers to disk, real-time scheduling, fast interrupt processing, I/O streaming etc.

Storage and Memory

-- large storage units (of the order of 50 – 100 Gb or more) and large memory (50 –100 Mb or more). Large Caches also required and frequently of Level 2 and 3 hierarchy for efficient management.

Network Support

-- Client-server systems common as distributed systems common.

Software Tools

-- user friendly tools needed to handle media, design and develop applications, deliver media.

Components of a Multimedia System

Now let us consider the Components (Hardware and Software) required for a multimedia system:

Capture Devices

-- Video Camera, Video Recorder, Audio Microphone, Keyboards, mice, graphics tablets, 3D input devices, tactile sensors, VR devices. Digitising/Sampling Hardware

Storage Devices

-- Hard disks, CD-ROMs, Jaz/Zip drives, DVD, etc.

Communication Networks

-- Ethernet, Token Ring, FDDI, ATM, Intranets, Internets.

Computer Systems

-- Multimedia Desktop machines, Workstations, MPEG/VIDEO/DSP Hardware.

Display Devices

-- CD-quality speakers, HDTV,SVGA, Hi-Res monitors, Colour printers.

APPLICATIONS OF MULTIMEDIA

Examples of Multimedia Applications include:

- World Wide Web
- Hypermedia courseware
- Video conferencing
- Video-on-demand
- Interactive TV
- Groupware
- Home shopping
- Games

- Virtual reality
- Digital video editing and production systems
- Multimedia Database systems

TRENDS IN MULTIMEDIA

Current big applications areas in Multimedia include:

World Wide Web

-- Hypermedia systems -- embrace nearly all multimedia technologies and application areas. Ever increasing popularity.

MBone

-- Multicast Backbone: Equivalent of conventional TV and Radio on the Internet.

Enabling Technologies

- developing at a rapid rate to support ever increasing need for Multimedia. Carrier, Switching, Protocol, Application, Coding/Compression, Database, Processing, and System Integration Technologies at the forefront of this.

WHERE CAN MULTIMEDIA BE USED?

Multimedia can be used in just about any situation where computers are being used to deliver information, and a number where they are not traditionally used. It may just be used to enhance areas that were previously text only, for example presentations or information kiosks. Multimedia email and video conferencing allows information to be communicated better. Collaborative working tools are becoming cheaper and more widely available, and many video conferencing applications now allow application sharing. Multimedia is widely used in education, from preschool to postgraduate. Interactive multimedia allows students to explore data, and simulations allow the students to work on experiments. This can be particularly useful in a distributed environment with distance learning. Multimedia can also be used to enhance data presentation and data analysis, for example, by converting the images from a satellite to sound, it becomes much easier to hear discrepancies in that data.

We are concerned with **interactive multimedia,** the use of varied media in combination with computer technology. This marriage creates an especially effective method of presenting information. By using interactivity to involve the user, more knowledge is retained, far more than the rate for most other instructional methods.

Forms of interactive multimedia include Web sites, CD-ROMs, programs, presentations, tutorials, help sections, and even games.

HARDWARE REQUIREMENT FOR INTERACTIVE MULTIMEDIA

When determining hardware or equipment requirements for interactive multimedia (IM) the main issues that should be taken care of are :

The User's computer

In are using an off-the-shelf IM program, the requirements for the **user's machine configuration** will be specified in the program's documentation.

In developing our own custom title, we have to determine our user's machine specifications **before designing the program.** We will have to test the program thoroughly on a similar machine and specify the requirements in our program documentation.

Platform

- Most programs have been developed for either the Mac or PC, and won't run on both.
- Hybrid programs (programs written for both Mac and PC programs) and World Wide Web pages can be run on both Macs and PC's.
- Developing a custom hybrid program is a bit tricky.

Display (Screen Requirements)

Most computers can show only 256 colors (referred to as 8-bit color.)

Multimedia projects that require more colors will look better but they need a monitor than can show the extra colors. They may not run at all on a 256 color monitor.

The most common screen sizes for Multimedia display are 640*480 pixels and 800*600 pixels, with resolution of about 72 pixels per inch.

Memory Requirements

Before the computer can run a program some memory (RAM) must be fixed for it.

Many multimedia programs require between 4 and 8 megabytes of RAM. Many computers have 8 MB or less. If the RAM requirement of our project starts climbing above about 4 MB on a machine with less than 8 MB RAM some users may have trouble

Speed

The cause of most response time delays is the process of getting data from the hard disk, the CD-ROM or the network.

Most multimedia programs are written for "MPC2" or higher standards, which covers most recent (1992 or later) computers. This means processors such as 486, Pentium, or for the Mac PowerPC, and a double spin CD-ROM drive is recommended.

Sound and Video Capability

The users computer should have sound and video capability.

Macintosh computers have integrated good quality sound and video capability built in for many years now. Microphones and external speakers can be plugged into the jacks provided.

With IBM compatible PCs the Sound and Video capability is not built in, so if we want these we'll probably have to purchase additional cards. Installing and configuring these cards can be troublesome for the layperson so these cards are often provided with the computer at purchase

Supporting Devices

Depending on what kind of multimedia program will be used, the computer will probably need one of the following:

- a CD-ROM drive
- access to data stored on a hard drive or server
- or access to the internet via modem or network

Delivery Method

How will the users access the project ? Will it be from a CD-ROM or floppy disk ? By downloading it from the internet or World Wide Web ? These are some of the **methods of delivery.** Some of these methods will **impose equipment choices on our users,** such as the need for a CD-ROM drive if the project is on CD-ROM. If we are unsure of how the delivery method will affect our requirements, then have a look at our delivery guidelines.

Development Computer

We'll have similar **hardware requirements** to a multimedia program user, but we may need more RAM, Hard drive space, or microprocessor speed.

For **web page authoring,** these requirements will be less, as compared to a **high end CD-ROM** including video and audio which may require specialized hardware.

Large projects may have several computers, each specified to do specific tasks such as audio/ video production, graphics and programming.

Development Platform

Choice of platform (Macintosh, PC, Unix, etc) is often determined by our audience and the types of computers they have access to. Multimedia projects can be designed to run on both Macs and PCs. This is known as cross-platform authoring.

For internet based projects the issue of platform is not as much a consideration because most of the necessary software (*e.g.*, web browsers) is available across all platforms.

Project Size

Projects under development can easily require many times more disk space than required by the end product.

To handle the amount of storage that may be needed, we could use: larger Hard drives, an external Hard drive shared by users, storage space on a server, or we can use portable media drives such as SyQuest cartridges or zip drives.

Peripheral Equipment

Common peripheral devices include: CD-ROM drives, modems, scanners, external Hard drives and portable media drives (WORM, MO, zip, DAT, SyQuest are all different forms of media used in portable drives).

External Hard Drives

Many projects will require extensive amounts of disk space, especially during development. External hard disks of very large capacity are relatively cheap and provide an easy way of moving a project's files from one computer to another.

CD-ROM drives, CD-ROM burners

Many computers don't come with CD-ROM drives and may need to have one attached externally to be able to play CD-ROMs. Most multimedia won't run from anything slower than a "double spin" drive, so don't forget to check the speed. Multimedia developers may use a CD-ROM burner to be able to "press" copies of programs, for testing or back-up. These devices require software to press the data and can't be used to playback multimedia programs because their usually too slow playback speeds.

What is Multimedia Authoring System?

An Authoring System is a program which has pre-programmed elements for the development of interactive multimedia software titles. Authoring systems vary widely in orientation, capabilities, and learning curve. There is no such thing (at this time) as a completely point-and-click automated authoring system; some knowledge of heuristic thinking and algorithm design is necessary. Whether you realize it or not, authoring is actually just a speeded-up form of programming; you don't need to know the intricacies of a programming language, or worse, an API, but you do need to understand how programs work.

Why should you use an authoring system?

It generally takes about 1/8th the time to develop an interactive multimedia project, such as a CBT (Computer Based Training) program, in an authoring system as opposed to programming it in compiled code. This means 1/8 the cost of programmer time and likely increased re-use of code (assuming that you pass this project's code to the next CBT project, and they use a similar or identical authoring system). However, the content creation (graphics, text, video, audio, animation, etc.) is not generally affected by the choice of an authoring system; any production time gains here result from accelerated prototyping, not from the choice of an authoring system over a compiled language.

Multimedia Authoring

Tools for making a complete multimedia presentation where users usually have a lot of interactive controls.

1. **Macromedia Director**
    - Movie metaphor (the cast includes bitmapped sprites, scripts, music, sounds, and palettes, etc.)
    - Can accept almost any bitmapped file formats
    - Lingo script language with own debugger allows more control including external devices, *e.g.*, VCRs and video disk players
    - Ready for building more interactivities (buttons, etc.)
    - Currently in version 7.0, this popular general market product follows the cast/score/scripting paradigm, which makes it the tool of choice for animation content. Its roots as a cel- and sprite-animation program are unmistakable; and its inclusion of Lingo, its object-based scripting language, has made it the animation-capable program to beat. The AfterBurner compression Xtra creates Shockwave files, allowing Web playback.
2. **Authorware**
    - Professional multimedia authoring tool
    - Supports interactive applications with hyperlinks, drag-and-drop controls, and integrated animation

- Compatibility between files produced from PC version and MAC version Other authoring tools include:
- Microcosm : Multicosm, Ltd. ; DOS, Windows Microcosm is a Hypermedia Linkage authoring system.
- Question Mark : Question Mark Computing Ltd ; DOS, Mac, Windows; WWW (via Perception) Question Mark is optimized for Electronic Assessment production.
- Emblaze Creator : Geo International ; JavaScript, Mac, Windows95, WWW.

  Emblaze Creator 2.5 is a cast/score/scripting tool which is designed for Web-based playback of interactive multimedia.
- Flash : Macromedia ; Mac, Windows95, NT, WWW (via Flash Player).
  Flash 3.0 is a cast/score/scripting tool, which primarily uses vector graphics (and can create vector graphics from imported bitmaps). It is optimized for Web delivery and is especially common for banner adds and small interactive web deliverables.
- HyperCard : Apple Computer ; Mac, WWW (via LiveCard!).
  HyperCard is a card/scripting authoring system currently in version 2.4.1. It runs natively on both 68 K and PowerMacintosh machines and is widely used because of its easy availability at a low price. Its largest drawback is the lack of integrated color; current color implementation is via the ColorTools XCMD set (included) or via third-party XCMDs.
- HyperGASP : Caliban Mindwear.

  HyperGASP is a card/scripting authoring system currently in version 3.0; the newest version no longer requires HyperCard. Supports export to HTML for Web authoring.
- HyperStudio ; Roger Wagner Publishing ; Mac, Windows, WWW (via HyperStudio plug-in).
  HyperStudio is a card/scripting paradigm authoring system, optimized for and focussed on the educational market.
- IconAuthor: Asymetrix ; Windows, NT, Solaris, UNIX, WWW (via Windows).
  IconAuthor follows the iconic/flow control paradigm. It is notable for its SmartObject editor, which tags content files (still graphics, RTF text, etc.) for interactivity. It has the option to either embed content files or leave them external in specified directories. The biggest strength of this program is its included data handling, which makes it unparalleled for CBT data tracking. The latest version should also provide WWW porting of existing content. Avoid its internal "Move Object" path animation feature due to jerky response — use a .FLC or .AVI instead.

SUMMARY

Newspaper were perhaps the first mass communication medium to employ Multimedia -- they used mostly text, graphics, and images.

Multimedia means that computer information can be represented through audio, video, and animation in addition to traditional media (i.e., text, graphics drawings, images).

Hypertext is a text which contains links to other texts. The term was invented by Ted Nelson around 1965.

A **Multimedia System** is a system capable of processing multimedia data and applications. It is characterized by the processing, storage, generation, manipulation and rendition of Multimedia information.

EXERCISE

1. Define multimedia and give brief history of its development.
2. Define Hypertex and Hypermedia.
3. What do you mean by multimedia system gives its characteristics and what are its challenges.
4. Give applications of multimedia and where it can be used?
5. What are the hardware requirement for interactive multimedia.
6. What is multimedia Authoring system why should you use an authorising system.

APPENDIX-1

AUTOCAD

AutoCAD is a general purpose computer aided drafting application program designed for use on single-user, desktop personal computers and graphic workstations. It was developed in the 1980's by Autodesk Inc., Sausalito, California.

Concepts and Definitions

AutoCAD is an interactive drawing system designed to permit a user to construct or edit a drawing on a graphics display screen. Principal functional component of AutoCAD is known as the *drawing editor*.

Up until Release 10, AutoCAD was essentially a two-dimensional drawing system. Following that release, it now supports a full three-dimensional database.

In order to understand AutoCAD, we must focus on a few specific concepts.

What's in an AutoCAD Drawing

An AutoCAD drawing is made up of *entities*. These can be either simple graphic primitives (such as lines, arcs, circles, text and so on) or blocks (which are groups of entities).

The graphic primitives are defined geometrically in terms of the normal cartesian coordinate system (right-handed system with positive X-axis to the right, positive Y-axis up the screen and positive Z-axis coming out of the screen towards the user). Hence, for example, lines are defined by their end- point coordinates (x, y and z), while circles are defined by their centre coordinates and radius. Each entity also has certain attributes associated with it, such as line style, text font or colour.

A *block* is a group of entities that can be manipulated as a **single unit**. Once created, a block may be moved, scaled, rotated, copied or deleted. A block can be created by collecting together a group of entities from the current drawing (the drawing being currently edited) and assigning a single name to that group. Alternatively, an existing drawing (from disk) can be inserted into the current drawing as a block. Equally, a block from the current drawing can be written out to a file as a new drawing.

As an alternative to inserting a drawing into another drawing as a block, AutoCAD now provides the facility to attach a drawing to the current drawing as an *external reference*. The external drawing is then treated like a block except that it is automatically updated each time the drawing to which it is attached is loaded. Naturally, if the external drawing is altered in the meantime, then the external reference will be updated to reflect those changes.

Another important feature of a block (including external reference blocks) is that it can be duplicated many times within a drawing, with each copy **pointing to the one graphic description,** but having its **own unique position, scale and rotation factor.** This is known as instancing. There are two advantages to this approach.

- **space saving** - the graphics description is only stored once; and
- **ease of re-definition** - the graphics description of a block can be altered and then re-defined in order to update each instance in the drawing.

It is also possible to associate named attributes with a block. For example, a block representing a door might have attributes such as type, manufacturer, finish, lock-type, etc. Each instance of the block would have a value associated with it for each defined attribute. AutoCAD provides facilities for scheduling the attribute data associated with inserted blocks in a drawing.

The final concept to be explained about blocks is the notion of exploding. Any instance of a block may be exploded in order to reduce it back to its separate graphic entities. Similarly, an external reference block can be unbound so that it becomes a local block and then, in turn, can be exploded.

UNITS, SCALES AND PAPER SIZES

A clear understanding of the way that AutoCAD handles units of measurement, scale and paper size is necessary before a drawing can be created or edited. AutoCAD provides complete control over these things by distinguishing between model space and paper space. All drawings, whether two-dimensional or three-dimensional should be thought of as models of a real-world entity (either a drawing or a 3D description of a real-world object). In either case, the description is maintained in model space. Paper space can be thought of as a model of a standard-size piece of paper on which you can establish view ports (rectangular regions) in which AutoCAD will display scaled views of the drawing you have created in model space. You can, of course, add additional linework in paper space to form borders and annotation.

In order to understand this, it is best to picture model space as a very large piece of paper located somewhere in two-dimensional space. (AutoCAD can actually draw anywhere in 3D space, but let's ignore that for the moment!) Since, the size and location of that piece of paper is entirely up to you, it would make sense to choose something that makes drawing as simple as possible. Now, Australian architects typically use millimetres as their unit of measurement and would draw objects in their true size. This means that when drawing a plan of a building that is, say, 15 metres square, the "paper" size (in model space) would be set at something greater than 15,000 × 15,000 units (where "units" equals millimetres). Strictly speaking, it is not necessary to set the model space drawing size, but it is helpful to do so in order to establish a context for the drawing.

When working on the drawing in model space, you should think of the graphics screen as a window through which you can view all or part of that drawing sheet. Thus, when viewing a drawing, a larger display scale will allow you to view only a part of the drawing on the screen. This is referred to as zooming in on the drawing: as you increase the scale, you can see less of your drawing, but what you can see will be in greater detail. If you zoom out, then you will be able to see more of the drawing, but in lesser detail. AutoCAD provides some fairly sophisticated tools for zooming in and out of your drawing and for panning back and forth across it. These are described later.

Although it is possible to plot from model space, it is normal to set up a sheet in paper space, and create one or more view ports showing different views of the drawing in model space. Each view is displayed at a fixed scale and the paper space drawing is then plotted at a scale of 1:1. In this case text notes and other annotation on the drawing is best added in paper space, and plotted at its actual size. Any text that is entered in model space has to be drawn at an artificially large size so that when it is scaled down for plotting, it ends up at the size required. For example, text on a 1:100 drawing might be set at 250 millimeters high in model space to create plotted text that is 2.5mm high on the plot.

DRAWING LAYERS

AutoCAD also supports the standard notion of layering. This means that any drawing entity can be assigned to any layer of the drawing. This allows separation of portions of the drawing. For example, all brickwork could be assigned to one layer, all electrical work to another and so on. In that way, when plotting, only selected layers need be included in the physical drawing that is produced from the one AutoCAD drawing.

Layering can also be used to advantage while editing a drawing. For example, suppose a plan drawing is substantially complete with only the brickwork cross-hatching to go. If all the brickwork is on one layer, each other layer could be turned off so that only the brickwork is visible and selectable. That makes it possible to cross-hatch the brickwork without inadvertently affecting something else.

Layering in AutoCAD is manipulated through the properties that can be assigned to each layer. Once the interaction between layer properties is understood, then these can be manipulated to great advantage.

3D GRAPHICS CONCEPTS

All graphic entities in AutoCAD are defined fully within 3D space. However, in the normal case, where the user makes no attempt to define them as 3D objects, they are assumed to lie on the base (Z=0) plane of the *world coordinate system* (WCS) defined by AutoCAD. In that case, the z- value of every point is assumed to be zero and the user has no need to be concerned about it.

In order to support the 3D user, AutoCAD provides five basic ways to enter 3D information :

- firstly, most of the basic graphic entities (lines, arcs and curves) can have a thickness associated with them which is effectively a height in the z-direction (this has always been a feature of AutoCAD and is sometimes referred to as 2.5D);
- secondly, when specifying the position of any point during the drawing process, all three coordinate values can be entered by the user (again, if only two coordinates are specified, the point is assumed to lie in the base plane - note also that some entities must be perfectly planar, so if you attempt to enter a 3D point that would make such an object non-planar, then AutoCAD will display an error message);
- thirdly, AutoCAD supports a number of specifically 3D graphic entities, including 3D polylines, faces and meshes, along with a set of commands that can be used to create 3D objects with them;
- fourthly and most significantly, AutoCAD allows the draftsman to set up a temporary *user coordinate system* (UCS) which can be positioned and orientated anywhere in space (relative to the WCS) - thus, you can picture the standard X, Y and Z axes of the WCS and then imagine an equivalent set of axes (the UCS) being moved away from the origin and then tilted and rotated to any orientation that you wish - once a UCS is established, all 2D drawing is done relative to those coordinates until a new UCS is defined or the user switches back to the WCS;

- lastly, from release 11 onwards, AutoCAD has provided an extension package called AME (Advanced Modelling Extension) which provides 3D solid modelling capabilities - these allow you to form complex solid objects by adding, subtracting and intersecting a set of simple solid primitives (such as, boxes, cone, cylinders, spheres, etc) - for example, you can form a box with a circular hole by subtracting a cylinder from a box and so on – we will not be concerned with these techniques in these notes.

Notice that the 3D characteristics of AutoCAD merge fairly neatly with the traditional 2D facilities such that it is possible (and not uncommon) to use AutoCAD as if it had no 3D facilities at all.

That now concludes the discussion of general concepts in AutoCAD. The remainder of this chapter is concerned with how to interact with AutoCAD in order to produce drawings.

INTERACTING WITH AUTOCAD

When you run AutoCAD, you are immediately switched to what has become known as the Drawing Editor. In this mode, the display screen is set up as shown diagrammatically in Figure.

LAYOUT OF THE AUTOCAD SCREEN

When creating or editing a drawing, a very simple, cyclical process is followed. In the most general case, this involves first forcing AutoCAD into a state where it can accept a command (referred to as command mode):

- **check that AutoCAD is in Command mode** (signified by the prompt "Command:" on the left) - if not, hold down the Ctrl key on the keyboard and press C to cancel the current operation and go back to command;
- **enter a command** - either by typing in the command word or selecting from a menu as explained later;
- **this activates Data Entry mode** - AutoCAD will prompt for information needed to complete the command;
- **enter data required by AutoCAD;**
- **AutoCAD will carry out the operation required by the command, update the displayed drawing and return to Command mode.**

Note that some of the commands have the particular feature that they can be executed during the data entry mode of other commands (as well as at the command prompt). These are referred to as transparent commands. They can be used whenever AutoCAD is expecting non-text input and are entered by prefixing the command name with an apostrophe (').

COMMAND ENTRY

There are a large number of commands (over 200 ??) which provide access to the facilities of the Drawing Editor. These are generally entered when the "Command:" prompt is displayed at the bottom of the command entry region. Many of these commands are very specific and rarely used: these notes cover most of the commonly-used ones. There are a number of ways of entering a command.

TYPING ON THE KEYBOARD

Simply type in the command word and press the space bar or the RETURN key. If a mistake is made, use the delete key to delete characters already typed or press Ctrl X (hold down Ctrl key and press X) to clear the whole entry.

To simplify command entry through the keyboard, AutoCAD permits the user to establish aliases, which are used most commonly as abbreviated forms of major commands. This is a customisation option which is set up outside AutoCAD and is therefore installation-specific. AutoCAD, as shipped from the vendor, has a number of aliases defined in this way in order to illustrate the concept. We make no attempt in these notes to identify the aliases, but examples will "crop up" in the tutorials section.

USING THE SCREEN MENU

The screen menu is displayed on the right side of the AutoCAD *graphics window*. This is more than just a list of available commands from which to choose. It actually represents a range of available operations that can be picked by the user (as will be explained shortly). You should also note that this screen menu (the one that you see when you use AutoCAD in this course) is the one set up by Autodesk: users can, and generally do, customize the menu to suit their own needs or preferences. For the moment, we are talking about the standard AutoCAD menu.

To pick an item from the screen menu, simply move the mouse until the required item is highlighted (displayed in rev video), and then press the *pick (left) button.*

There are three types of items included in the screen menu

- **pointers to sul menus** - these are displayed in all uppercase characters (not terminated by a colon ":") and cause a corresponding sub-menu to be called up;
- **command words** - these are displayed in uppercase characters terminated by ":" and cause the corresponding command to be entered at the "Command:" prompt as if it had been typed (including the *RETURN* key);
- **command options** - these are displayed in lower or mixed case and only appear when specific commands have been selected - they represent command options relevant to that command) that can be picked rather than typed at the keyboard om and option menus are often displayed automatically when a command is issued from some other source.

The best way to gain confidence in the use of AutoCAD is to explore the screen menus and experiment with the menu items. Feel free to do that when you get onto the machine: don't worry, you cannot do any harm by experimenting.

USING THE PULL-DOWN MENUS

These provide a second, alternative way to access the facilities of AutoCAD. In general, they are only used as a short-cut to command selection. They are generally not used to display command options in the way screen menus are. Pull-down menus tend to be implemented in different ways, depending on the kind of computer and workstation being used. Some systems will not even support this kind of menu.

To activate pull-down menus on a DOS-based PC system, move the cursor to the status line at the top of the graphics window (noting that the pull-down menus then appear in place of the status line) and highlight the menu that you wish to pull down. When you press the pick button, that menu will appear on the screen. The menu items are either commands or pointers to further sub- menus. Move the pointing device again until the desired item is highlighted and again press the pick button. Once a command is selected, it is entered into the Command line and executed. To remove a pull-down menu (without selecting an item), move the cursor away from the menu and click the left mouse button.

Under OpenLook, the pull-down menus are permanently displayed as a row of buttons above the status line in the AutoCAD graphics window. These are designed to function in exactly the same way as any other OpenLook menus, which may be confusing to first-time users because it involves using the mouse buttons in a different way to the rest of AutoCAD. To pull down an OpenLook menu, simply click it with the **right mouse button**. Items which are actually pointers to sub-menus are identified by a small arrow (triangle) pointing towards the right of the item. Clicking these items (again with the **right mouse button**) will open the sub-menu. Any command item in either the main menus or sub-menus can be selected by clicking (this time with either the left or right button, but normally the left). A nice feature of OpenLook menus is that they can be fixed semi-permanently to the screen and positioned anywhere that the user wishes. This is useful where you plan to re-use a menu frequently during some phase of a drawing task. To fix the menu in this way, first open it, then click (with the left button) on the "pin" displayed in the top left corner of the menu. The "pin" will change to appear as if it has been pinned into the screen. If you then position the cursor near the top of the pinned menu and **hold down** the left mouse button, you will be able to drag the menu to any part of the screen. Pinned menus can be removed by clicking (left button) on the pin. AutoCAD automatically removes pinned menus itself under various circumstances which can be a source of frustration to the user.

USING THE ICON MENUS

These are special *pop-up* menus which are displayed in the centre of the screen usually in response to a selection from one of the pull-down menus. They are used to show graphically a range of choices that can be made in a particular context. For example, you can obtain a display showing the full range of hatch patterns available by selecting "Hatch..." from the *Draw* pull-down menu. This selection initiates the *HATCH* command and then uses the icon menu to allow you to pick the hatch pattern that you would like to use. Icon menus are designed to allow you to choose an item from the menu by selecting a small box located beside each icon.

DATA ENTRY

Most AutoCAD commands require that some data be entered before or during command execution. For example, if the *LINE* command (to draw a series of straight lines) is issued, then the end-point coordinates of each line segment in the series must be specified.

AutoCAD will always prompt for the data that it requires. In general, your response will be either a piece of information (*e.g.* coordinates of a point, a distance or a string of text to be inserted into the drawing), or one choice out of a range of options associated with the command selected. For example, in response to the GRID command, AutoCAD should display the prompt...

```
Grid spacing (X) or ON/OFF/Snap/Aspect <.25>:
```

This prompt is an attempt by AutoCAD to tell you what it needs to know in order to carry out the GRID command. It means that you can enter either a numeric value representing the grid spacing (X) or one of the four *option keywords* (separated by slashes "/"). The angle brackets ("<...>") are used to signify the default that AutoCAD will assume if only the *RETURN* key is pressed: in this case, the default is a grid spacing of 0.25 units. Note that option keywords, when entered, may be abbreviated to only those letters shown in uppercase: thus, if you wished to select the Snap option in the above example, you would simply type s and then press the *RETURN* key.

All AutoCAD data entry prompts follow a similar pattern. Once that pattern becomes familiar, it is possible to almost guess your way through the system.

The following sub-sections explain briefly how to enter the most common types of data required by AutoCAD.

CARTESIAN COORDINATES

These are most "easily" entered by moving the mouse until the cross-hair cursor is positioned at the required point on the drawing and pressing the pick button. The difficulty with that, of course, is that it is impossible to accurately pick a point in that way. Therefore, AutoCAD supports a number of techniques designed to enable you to lock onto precise positions on your drawing. These generally revolve around snapping onto positions relative to existing graphic entities (such as snapping to the end or middle of a line) or snapping to an invisible (or visible) grid.

The technique which involves locking onto positions relative to existing graphic entities is called *object snapping* and is often used in conjunction with what are known as *X/Y/Z point filters* to make them even more powerful.

As an alternative to pointing and to provide absolute accuracy, AutoCAD allows the user to type in the coordinates as numbers. There are three types of values that can be entered this way:

- **absolute coordinates** - simply type two (or three) numbers separated by a comma (viz. 305.6, –232);
- **relative coordinates** - these represent offset distances in X, Y and Z (if required) relative to the last point entered - simply type "@" followed by the numbers separated by a comma (viz. @22, – 331.5);
- **polar coordinates** - these represent an angular distance from the last point entered - type "@" followed a number specifying distance, followed by "<" and a number specifying an angle about the Z axis in degrees (viz. @214.7<45 - by default, zero degrees is taken as directly to the right of the starting point and angles increase in an anti-clockwise direction).

DISTANCES AND NUMERIC VALUES

These are generally entered as numbers typed on the keyboard. They can be entered with decimal points, minus signs and/or in scientific notation.

Distances can also be specified by pointing with the cross-hairs. If the starting point (or anchor point) is obvious (such as when entering the radius of a circle once the centre is known), then one pointing operation is required. Otherwise, two pointing operations must be performed in order to specify the distance.

ANGLES

Angles are specified in decimal degrees and are generally typed through the keyboard.

Alternatively, AutoCAD can be "shown" the angle by pointing with the screen cross-hairs. To do this, first identify an *anchor point* and then show the end of a vector that defines the required angle. The angle is then measured by AutoCAD in an **anti-clockwise direction between an imaginary line pointing towards the right from the user's anchor point and the defined vector.**

DISPLACEMENTS

This is where AutoCAD needs to know how far to move both horizontally and vertically. The easiest way is to point to a base point and an end point. Alternatively, type in a distance for X and a distance for Y separated by a comma (if AutoCAD then prompts for a second point, simply press RETURN).

DIALOGUE BOXES

One of the new features of Release 12 are *dialogue boxes*. These pop up in response to several commands, allowing you to select various options (using the mouse and the keyboard) that are appropriate to that command. These generally circumvent the normal prompting process that was described in the previous section, making the use of many commands much more intuitive. The techniques for using dialogue boxes are very straightforward, particularly if you are already familiar with general window-based applications.

MAKING SELECTIONS OF OBJECTS FROM A DRAWING

Many AutoCAD operations require that one or more objects be selected from the displayed drawing. As an example, consider the ERASE command: it requires that all the items to be deleted are indicated **before** they are actually removed. To do that, the user points to each item in turn (*i.e.*, selects each item) to form what is called a selection set. As each item is selected, it is highlighted by AutoCAD (that is, its colour changes to show that AutoCAD has included it in the selection set). When the user indicates that the selection set is complete AutoCAD completes the operation by removing the selected items.

AutoCAD normally prompts you to create the selection set when it is actually required by a particular command. Thus, the normal process is to first issue the command and then select the objects to be effected by that command. However, under Release 12 of AutoCAD, you may choose to select the objects before issuing a command. The techniques for doing that will be explained later, but for the moment we will concentrate on the normal way of setting up selection sets after a command has been issued.

Once a command has been issued and AutoCAD requires the user to specify a selection set, it issues the prompt "Select objects:" and replaces the cross- hairs with a small box called the object selection target. A number of techniques (explained below) can then be used to select objects. Once those objects have been identified and highlighted, the prompt is re-issued and the process repeated until a solitary space bar or *RETURN* is pressed (in response to the prompt) to indicate that no more selections are required. At that point AutoCAD continues with the command that initiated the selection process.

The available techniques for selecting objects are as follows:

- **object pointing** - merely point to an individual object (it should then change colour);
- **multiple object pointing** - press **m** followed by *space bar* or *RETURN* - AutoCAD then allows the user to point to a number of objects until the *space bar* or *RETURN* is pressed again - at that point, AutoCAD searches for and highlights the selected objects before issuing the prompt again;
- **window selection** - press **w** followed by *space bar* or *RETURN* - AutoCAD then requires that the opposite corners of a rectangle be specified and it selects all the objects that lie wholly within that window;
- **window polygon selection** - press **wp** followed by *space bar* or *RETURN* - AutoCAD then requires that a series of points are entered that define a closed polygon and selects all the objects that lie wholly within that polygon;
- **crossing selection** - press **c** followed by *space bar* or *RETURN* - AutoCAD again requires that a rectangle be defined - this time, all objects that lie **partially or wholly** within the rectangle are selected;
- **crossing polygon selection** - press **cp** followed by *space bar* or *RETURN* - AutoCAD again requires that a polygon rectangle be defined - this time, all objects that lie *partially or wholly* within that polygon are selected;
- **fence selection** - press **f** followed by *space bar* or *RETURN* - AutoCAD allows you to pick any number of points to create a fence and any objects that intersect the fence are selected;
- **last object** - press **l** followed by *space bar* or *RETURN* to select the last object created (and still visible);
- **previous selection set** - press **p** followed by *space bar* or *RETURN* to re-select the last selection set that was constructed;
- **undo** - press **u** followed by *space bar* or *RETURN* to de-select the group of objects most recently added to the selection set - may be used repeatedly to step back through the selection process;
- **remove mode** - press **r** followed by *space bar* or *RETURN* to switch to "remove mode" such that further selections are removed from the current selection set;
- **add mode** - press **a** followed by *space bar* or *RETURN* to revert back to "add mode" after being in "remove mode";
- **cancel** - press *Ctrl C* to cancel the selection process (and the current command as well).

Before introducing the basic entity drawing commands, it is necessary to discuss a number of commands that are used to establish certain aspects of the drawing environment.

SETTING THE DRAWING ENVIRONMENT

The commands in this section can used at any time, but are generally used at the start of the drawing process to set up certain aspects of the drawing environment. This list is not exhaustive. A number of similar commands will be introduced later in their appropriate contexts. Still others will not be covered in these notes at all.

Units

Used to specify the drawing units. This is usually set by the prototype drawing, but may be set explicitly with this command for any drawing. The effect of this command is only to control the display format and precision (that is, whether it is a decimal number or a fraction, and the number of decimal places, etc.) rather than the meaning of the number (feet, metres, etc.). AutoCAD does not really "care" what the number means, but only how to represent it.

This command also prompts for the way in which angles are to be represented (decimal degrees, radians, etc.) and how angles are to be measured (normally anti-clockwise beginning from "east" taken as 0).

Limits

Used to set limits to the size of the drawing. The lower left corner and the top right corner must be specified. Limits checking may also be turned ON or OFF. If limits checking is on, then points cannot be specified outside the current limits.

Qtext

Sets quick text ON or OFF. If quick text is ON, then all text is represented on the drawing by simple boxes showing its extent only.

Viewres

This command performs two functions. The first is to allow the user to disable fast zoom. (There is little point in disabling fast zoom, except to conform to earlier versions of AutoCAD that had no fast zoom capability.) The second function is to permit control of the smoothness of circles and arcs as drawn on the display. There is a trade-off here between regeneration time (when zooming and panning) and quality of the displayed image. A circle zoom percent value of about 20 seems to be a good compromise. This command does not affect circles on plotted drawings.

Blipmode

Controls the use of blips (small crosses) by AutoCAD to mark any screen positions pointed to by the user. These blips can be useful reference points, but can also become irritating as they begin to clutter up the drawing. Note that blips are not part of the drawing, and are removed whenever a redraw is done.

Fill

Used to determine whether solids, doughnuts and wide polylines are solid filled (with colour) or simply outlined. Again, this represents a trade-off between regeneration time and quality of image. Note that this command does affect the plotted output of the drawing.

Status

Lists the environment settings for the current drawing.

ENTITY DRAWING COMMANDS

This section lists all the major commands that are used to produce entities on the drawing. The list is not quite exhaustive, but it certainly covers enough to meet all architectural needs.

Line

This command initiates the drawing of a sequence of one or more straight lines. The user is prompted "From point:" and should either specify a point or press RETURN to start at end of the previous line or arc that was drawn. The prompt "To point:" is then displayed repeatedly, permitting the user to either specify a sequence of points or type C to close the polygon, to undo last line segment or RETURN to complete the command.

Point

This command is used to draw a single marker or point. By default, the marker is a single "dot". Its major use in architectural drafting is probably as a means of setting up node points in blocks to be used by the NODE object snap operation. The AutoCAD screen menus provide a range of marker styles that can be selected instead of the "dot".

Circle

AutoCAD provides a number of alternative ways to construct a circle. The default way is to specify the centre point followed by the size of either the radius or the diameter. Alternatively, a user can specify three points on the circumference, two end-points of the circle's diameter, or the radius of the circle plus two other lines and/or circles (which already exist on the drawing) to which the new circle is to be tangential (option TTR in the prompt).

Arc

Arcs, like circles, can be constructed in a number of ways. The default method is to specify three points. The other methods are:

- start point, centre and end point;
- start point, centre and included angle;
- start point, centre and length of chord;
- start point, end point and radius;
- start point, end point and included angle;
- start point, end point and starting direction;
- start point and direction of previous line or arc plus end point.

The various methods are selected by following the prompts. The last method is selected by pressing space bar or RETURN in response to the initial prompt.

Ellipse

This command is used to construct ellipses. The simplest method requires that the two end points of one of the axes (major or minor) be specified followed by a distance value that defines half the length of the other axis. Alternatively, the same method is used only the first axis (major or minor) is specified by the centre of the ellipse and one of its end points. There are other options explained in the AutoCAD reference manual.

Pline

This command is used to draw what are known as polylines. These are continuous sequences of straight line and/or arc segments that can have varying line width. Individual segments can even have tapering thickness. Thick segments are bevelled at intersection points. Polylines can be closed to form a polygon. To construct a polyline, simply follow the prompts. Most options are quite clear.

Polylines are very important in AutoCAD because they are treated as single entities for many operations. For example, a single command can be used to fillet each corner of a polyline or to form a smooth curve from a polyline. Further, the area and perimeter of a polyline can be also calculated. Finally, polylines can be exploded into separate line and arc entities when necessary.

Polygon

This command is used to draw a regular polygon. After entering the number of edges, either specify its centre and "radius" (being the radius of either an inscribed or circumscribed circle about the polygon) or locate the end points of any one of its edges. Polygons are in fact closed polylines and can be treated as such, once constructed.

Hatch

This command is used to draw a cross-hatch pattern within a closed boundary or between closed boundaries. The boundaries must be defined by entities which are accurately connected at their endpoints (it does not cope well with "T" junctions). If the boundaries are not well defined, then the hatching can leak out in quite unexpected ways. AutoCAD comes with an extensive set of pre-defined patterns that can be selected. Alternatively, you can create your own patterns and add them to the standard set or even create a hatch pattern "on the fly" using the "User" option and following the prompts. If you select "Hatch..." from the Draw pull- down menu, then AutoCAD displays an icon menu to make it easier to select a pattern. Note that some caution has to be exercised when using standard hatch patterns as the whole pattern (as illustrated in the icon menu) is scaled to fit within a 1x1 unit square. Thus, when you are prompted for a scale factor, you need to visualise the size of a 1x1 square relative to the area you wish to fill in order to estimate the required scale to create the effect you want. If you do choose a scale factor which is too small, then you need to abort the cross-hatching process by pressing Ctrl-C (hold down the Control key and press c) and then erasing the abortive hatching by typing erase last followed by RETURN.

Bhatch

This is a new command with Release 12 and overcomes some of the boundary limitations of the normal HATCH command (above). It supports what is called boundary hatching, where you are able to pick a point adjacent to the boundary that you want and AutoCAD will search for the nearest entity (presumably on the boundary that you want) and then construct a closed boundary by tracing anti- clockwise looking for intersection points and connecting lines or arcs. This command is driven by a dialogue box and provides a great number of options, including the ability to preview the hatching before committing yourself. It is beyond the scope of these notes to detail all those options: there is on- line help available, and you really need to just experiment.

Dtext

Text can be entered anywhere on a drawing with any height (measured in drawing units) and with any rotation. It can be left justified (default), right justified, centred, stretched to fit neatly between two points (option F - with fixed height) or sized in order to align perfectly between two points (option A - where character size is adjusted to fill the available space). The text itself can be underscored or overscored and special characters like the degree symbol ("o") can be included (details in AutoCAD reference manual).

AutoCAD supports a variety of standard character fonts which can be combined with character attributes (height, width, obliquity angle, back-to- front, upside-down and orientation) to form user-defined styles. These are set up using the STYLE command. The "Fonts..." item in the Options pull-down menu causes AutoCAD to display the available fonts on the screen in the form of an icon menu.

In addition to these entity commands, there are commands to set up the following 3D objects: 3D polylines (3DPOLY); 3D faces (3DFACE); 3D meshes (3DMESH for any mesh, RULESURF for ruled surfaces, TABSURF for a tabulated surface mesh, REVSURF for surfaces of revolution and EDGESURF for surface meshes defined by 4 adjoining edges).

BASIC UTILITY COMMANDS

Redraw

This command forces AutoCAD to re-display the graphics on the screen. This has the effect of clearing away some extraneous graphics such as marker "blips" that are left behind by pointing operations.

Save

Causes all editing changes to the current drawing to be saved to the disk file. Should be done regularly during a long drawing session.

End

Terminates the drawing editor, saves the current drawing to a disk file and returns to the main AutoCAD menu.

Quit

Terminates the drawing editor without saving the changes made to the current drawing. Returns to the main AutoCAD menu.

DRAWING CONTROL AND MANIPULATION

Tools for Moving Around the Drawing Area

Most of the operations involved in moving around the drawing area are embodied in one command called ZOOM. This command has a number of options as set out in its data prompt:

```
All/Centre/Dynamic/Extents/Left/Previous/Vmax/Window/<Scale(X/XP)>:
```

Each of these options is described in the following paragraphs.

Zoom Scale

This is the default option and simply requires the entry of a number which represents a magnification factor. Note that the factor is applied to the entire drawing (as defined by the LIMITS command).

Numbers less than 1 will reduce the displayed size of the drawing, while numbers greater than 1 will enlarge it. If "x" is inserted after the number (viz. 0.8x) then the factor is applied to the current view. If "xp" is inserted after the scale factor, then the view is scaled relative to paper space (this is useful for zooming a view within a paper space viewport to a specific scale, for example, "0.1xp" will produce a view of model space at a scale of 1:10 relative to paper space).

Zoom Extents

This option causes AutoCAD to display all the graphics that is contained in the drawing (referred to as the drawing extent) with the largest image possible. It does not necessarily extend to the defined drawing limits.

Zoom All

This option causes AutoCAD to display the whole drawing as far as its drawing limits or drawing extents (whichever is greater).

Zoom Window

This option prompts the user to point to the lower left and upper right corners of a box on the existing view in order to define that part which is to be enlarged to fill the display.

Zoom Centre

This option requires a point which is taken to be the centre of the new display, followed by a value to be its new height in drawing units. The existing height is offered as the default for the new height to allow for panning across the drawing. If the new height is followed by "x" (viz. 2x), then it is taken as a magnification factor relative to the current height. If followed by "xp", then it is taken as a scale factor relative to paper space and can be used for scaling the contents of paper space viewports.

Zoom Left Corner

This option operates in the same way as "ZOOM Centre" except that the point specified is taken as the lower left corner of the new display.

Zoom Previous

This option reverts to the displayed view prior to the current one. For the purpose of this option, up to 5 views are "stacked" so that the last five views can be recalled.

Zoom Dynamic

This is the most powerful ZOOM option once it is understood. It permits very quick movement around the drawing.

Once selected, this option clears the graphics area of the screen and displays three rectangles. The solid white (or black) box denotes the extent of the current drawing. The magenta box shows the current view. The four corners shown in red indicate the region within which rapid views can be produced (there is a speed advantage in staying within these four corners).

Also on the screen will be a dynamic view box (with an "X" in the middle) which moves as the mouse is operated (this is referred to as pan mode). This view box should be positioned so that its lower left corner is at the lower left corner of the view required. By pressing the "pick" button on the mouse, the "X" is replaced by an arrow pointing to the right side of the view box. This indicates zoom mode. As the mouse is moved, the view box shrinks and expands so that the size of the required view can be set. The "pick button" toggles between PAN and ZOOM mode so that fine adjustments can be achieved. When the view required has been selected, press RETURN to cause AutoCAD to display it.

Another very useful command that can be used to alter the currently displayed view is the PAN command.

Pan

This command permits panning across the drawing without changing the display scale. A displacement must be specified either by pointing or typing.

Three other commands are available for creating 3D views of the drawing. These are really only of interest if you have taken the trouble to enter a three-dimensional description of an object. However, even if your drawing is only 2D, you can still look at it from any 3D point in space and view it as either a parallel projection or as a full perspective.

Vpoint

This command is used to establish a view from a viewpoint located anywhere in space. The viewpoint can be entered as a 3D point, a spherical point (horizontal and vertical angles relative to the target - normally the origin) or specified dynamically (by pressing RETURN instead of entering a point). The resultant view is always shown as a parallel projection and assumes that you are "looking at" the origin (which is then referred to as the target). The target can be changed, but the process involved is beyond the scope of these notes.

Dview

This command provides a dynamic tool for setting up a view of a 3D object as either a parallel projection or a perspective. It uses a camera and target concept to manipulate the viewing position, direction of view, focal length (effecting field of view) and viewing distance. This tool also supports front and back plane clipping and hidden line removal.

Plan

This command provides a convenient way of getting back to a normal plan view after working in 3D.

MODEL SPACE, PAPER SPACE AND VIEWPORTS

One of the fundamental concepts in AutoCAD is the distinction that is drawn between model space and paper space. The notion is that when you are drawing, whether in 2D or 3D, you are generally building a model of the entity that you wish to represent. A plan, elevation or section is simply a type of model which is drawn in model space in the same way as you might draw a 3D representation of the object you wish to represent. Whether the model is 2D or 3D, it is constructed in real units representing its actual size. Once the model is complete (or at least partially complete), AutoCAD allows you to switch to paper space where all drawing is done at full size in paper units. In paper space, you are able to construct one or more rectangular viewports, each containing an independent scaled view of the model (or part of the model). You can, of course, switch back and forth between paper and model space, and you can also draw directly in paper space to set up borders and title blocks, etc.

One of the confusing things in AutoCAD is that the term "viewport" has a different meaning depending on whether you are working in model space or paper space (though the two ideas are related).

When working in model space, viewports are used to sub-divide the drawing area on the screen so that the user can work with several views of their drawing (or model) at the same time (and move at will between them).

When working in paper space, viewports are used to represent rectangular areas of the paper (or sheet) in which views are displayed of the drawing contained in model space. These viewports are treated as editable entities which can be scaled, moved, stretched, copied or erased. These viewports can also overlap or have space between them.

To control this mechanism, AutoCAD maintains a system variable called TILEMODE. When this variable is equal to 1 ("on"), then one or more viewports are displayed on the screen in a "tiled" pattern and therefore serve to subdivide the drawing area to display different views of model space (equivalent to the first function described above). When this variable is set equal to 0 ("off"), then viewports are used to define regions in paper space where views of the model are displayed.

When TILEMODE is on, the user is necessarily working in model space (albeit with one or several viewports). When TILEMODE is off, the user can work in paper space or model space: use paper space to create, position and size viewports or to add/edit paper space graphics; or switch to model space and choose a (paper space) viewport and edit the model within it.

The commands available to manipulate these concepts are listed below.

Tilemode

This command is used to set the value of the system variable of the same name. Its primary purpose is to control the way in which AutoCAD handles viewports. If TILEMODE is switched off (set to 0), then AutoCAD switches to paper space. If no viewports have been created in paper space, then AutoCAD will remind the user to create at least one viewport. Once that has been done, the user can switch between paper space and model space as described above. If TILEMODE is switched on (set to 1), then AutoCAD switches to model space and displays the view (or set of tiled viewports) that was most recently active. Paper space entities are not visible when working in model space with TILEMODE "on".

Vports

This command only functions when TILEMODE is "on". It allows you to establish up to 16 viewports on the screen such that each viewport can hold a different view of your drawing. Once set up, you can only work in one viewport at a time, but it is easy to move between them: simply move the cursor to the desired viewport and click the left mouse button.

View

This command saves the current view of the drawing under a user-defined name or restores a view that was previously saved in that way. It can be used in both model space and paper space. For example, if you are currently zoomed in on a particular part of a drawing and you think that you will later want to get back to that view, then you would use this command. Viewport configurations (created by VPORTS) can be named, saved and restored in the same way as individual views.

Mview

This command is used when TILEMODE is "off" to create and define the characteristics of viewports in paper space. Once created, viewports can be turned "on" or "off": when off, there is no attempt to display the view that they contain, so that they can be manipulated without having to redraw their contents all the time. Viewports can also be linked to existing "views" saved using the VIEW command (see previous). Finally, viewports can be tagged so that AutoCAD automatically does a hide in that viewport every time the drawing is plotted.

Mspace

This command is used when TILEMODE is "off" (and paper space is active) to allow you to switch to model space and edit your drawing inside one of the paper space viewports. There must be at least one viewport "on" and active for this command to work. Control switches to one of the active viewports, displaying the cross-hair cursor and permitting you to edit your drawing within that viewport. You can switch between viewports simply by clicking on them (in the same way as for tiled viewports when TILEMODE is "on").

Pspace

This command is used when TILEMODE is "off", but model space is active (due to the use of the command MSPACE), to allow you to switch back to paper space and add or edit graphics within that drawing environment.

Drawing Tools

This section is concerned with a number of commands that set drawing modes which facilitate accurate drawing in one way or another.

UCS

This command is used to set up a user coordinate system (UCS) which can be positioned and orientated anywhere in 3D space. Once set up, all subsequent 2D drawing is done in the X-Y plane of the new UCS and relative to its origin and axes. This makes it possible to draw anywhere in space fairly easily. This command can also be used to store the current UCS under a user-defined name so that it can be later recalled. Although this command is designed primarily to assist with 3D work, it is very useful in 2D drafting when you wish to rotate the axes to work on buildings that are not orthogonal.

Snap

This command sets up an invisible, orthogonal grid onto which all points entered with the mouse are automatically locked. The grid may be square or rectangular (set by selecting the aspect option) and can be rotated. This command is also used to turn snapping ON or OFF.

Grid

This command turns a visible grid of points on the graphics area of the screen ON or OFF depending on its current state. This grid is for reference purposes only. It can, however, be optionally set to match or be a multiple of the SNAP grid.

Axis

This is almost the same as the GRID command except that two axes with tick marks replace the grid of dots.

Ortho

This command turns ortho mode ON or OFF. In this mode, all lines drawn with a mouse are kept parallel to the current axes.

Osnap

This command is used to set running object snap modes which are then in force for each subsequent pointing operation until another OSNAP command disables them. They can always be overridden for a specific point entry by selecting different object snap modes for that one entry.

Aperture

This command sets the size of the target box used whenever object snap is in force. Values in the range 1–50 screen units are valid.

Note that the various modes discussed in this section can be toggled ON or OFF at any time by using the following ctrl-keys. (A "ctrl-key" is activated by holding down the Control key on the keyboard and then pressing the corresponding alphabetic key.)

- CTRL B - Snap mode on/off.
- CTRL G - Grid on/off.
- CTRL O - Ortho mode on/off.

DRAWING EDITING COMMANDS

Deletion Operations

There are two commands in this category.

Erase

This command is used to remove a selected group of entities. The selection set can be built before or after the command is entered. After entry of this command, if there is not already a selection set, the user is required to construct one. Upon pressing the final RETURN, AutoCAD removes all the selected objects from the drawing. Since one of the selection options is "Last", it is possible to erase the most recent object added to the drawing. It is further possible to repeat that command any number of times in order to delete backwards through the whole drawing process.

Oops

This command restores the most recent group of objects that were deleted using the ERASE command. It will only restore one group of erased objects, so it cannot be repeated.

TRANSFORMATION OPERATIONS

There are a number of commands which permit the selection of a group of objects so that they can be transformed in some way. The following five commands work in this way.

Move

After selecting the objects to be moved, a displacement can be specified by picking two points which between them define a vector indicating the direction and length of the move.

Copy

This is similar to the MOVE command in operation, except that the original group of objects are not effected in any way. The copied objects are not scaled or rotated and are completely independent of the original (as if they had been drawn "manually"). A special "Multiple" option permits multiple copies to be made of the one group of objects.

Rotate

Used to rotate the selected group of objects about a specified base point through a given angle. Positive angles yield anti-clockwise rotation, while negative angles are taken as clockwise. The rotation angle can also be specified by "Reference". That is, the current angle in degrees is first specified (probably by pointing) and then the new angle is given (relative to the direction of the positive X-axis). This can be useful, as it allows AutoCAD to calculate the angle of rotation instead of the user.

Scale

The selected group of objects can be enlarged or shrunk by setting a base point for the scaling and applying an appropriate factor. As with rotation, the scaling factor can also be determined by "Reference". In this case, a reference length is set from the drawing and the required new length is specified. This is useful when scaling something to the same length as an existing entity on the drawing.

Mirror

With this command a mirror copy of a selected group of objects is produced by specifying the two ends of the mirror line. The original objects may be deleted or retained. The user can also control whether or not text is mirror inverted or kept readable during the mirroring process.

There are three other commands for moving and duplicating entities that are included in this group.

Stretch

This command permits a group of entities (generally selected with the "Crossing" option) to move through a given displacement (like the MOVE command), but with the difference that all other entities that connect to the "moved" ones are stretched or shrunk in order to maintain their connections. This would, for example, allow a door or window that is set into a wall to be moved while still maintaining its links to the wall.

Array

This command produces multiple copies of selected objects arranged in a rectangular or circular (polar) array or pattern.

Offset

This command is used to construct a new entity that is parallel to an existing entity. The entity can be any single line, polyline, arc, circle or curve. The user must either specify the side to offset from and the distance, or a point through which the offset entity is to pass.

EDITING AND CHANGING EXISTING ENTITIES

This group of commands permit various editing changes to be made to existing entities in the drawing.

Change

This is a general command that permits a wide variety of changes to existing entities. The options are too complex and varied to fully explain in these notes. However, in general there are two types of change that can be made: changes to properties that are possessed by all entities such as layer name, colour and line type; and changes to the geometry and attributes of specific types of entities (select "Change point" option). For example, if the entity is text, then this command allows the user to change its position, style, height, rotation angle and the actual text string itself.

Pedit

This command is used to make all kinds of editing changes to polylines. Options include: changing the uniform width of a whole polyline; changing width and taper of individual segments; closing an open polyline, or opening a closed one; breaking a polyline into two; assembling existing (connected) entities to form a new polyline; moving vertices of a polyline; adding and deleting vertices; and finally, fitting a curve to a polyline.

Break

This command is used to split an existing line, arc, circle or polyline into two parts, generally (though not necessarily) with an erased portion between.

Trim

This command may be used to trim parts of some objects in the drawing so that they finish precisely at some cutting edge (or edges) that are established by one or more other objects. One or more lines, arcs, circles or polylines must first be identified to serve as cutting edges (these may be selected by any of the available methods). Pointing is then used to select the parts of objects to be trimmed away. Any number of objects may be selected in this way for trimming, including those that had been specified as cutting edges.

Extend

This command is the complement of TRIM. It operates in exactly the same way, except that selected lines are extended to end precisely at the boundary edges that are specified.

Fillet

This command connects two existing lines, circles or arcs by means of a smoothly fitted arc of a specified radius (referred to as a fillet). The command allows the user to change the current default radius before filleting. This command can also be used to fillet all the corners in a selected polyline. If a fillet of zero radius is used, then two lines can be made to join at a single point (useful for closing corners in a plan drawing).

Chamfer

This command is similar to and operates in the same way as FILLET except that it chamfers the corners with a straight edge which intersects the two objects at a specified distance from their point of intersection. The two chamfer distances are specified separately and can be different values.

The next two commands permit the placement of points (as in the POINT command - using the current point style) at regular distances along a single line, arc, circle or polyline. These points can then be used as node points for object snap operations. Alternatively, these commands can insert instances of a block at each of the point positions, optionally rotated about their insertion points so that they are aligned with the object.

Divide

This divides the selected object into a specified number of equal divisions (number in range 2 to 32767).

Measure

This command starts at one end of the object and measures out segments of a specified length between each point or block.

ERROR RECOVERY

There are three commands in AutoCAD that can be used to recover from errors made during the editing process.

U

The U command can be used to undo the effect of the most recent editing or drawing operation. It can be used repeatedly to undo backwards through a whole drawing session.

Redo

This command is used immediately after any undo operation in order to redo what was undone.

Undo

This command is a more versatile version of the simplified U command. It supports the following operations: undo several commands at once; set Mark points and later undo Back to those points; Group operations together (terminated by End) so that they can be later undone as a group; and set various Controls and limitations on the undo process.

ENQUIRY OPERATIONS

The final section of this chapter lists a few commands that may be used in order to obtain information about the position and nature of the objects in a drawing.

List

This command will list a whole host of stored and derived information about any entities that are selected (using the normal method of selection) on the current drawing.

Dist

This command is used to calculate and display (in the command region) the distance and angle between two designated points on the drawing.

Id

This displays (in drawing units) the X Y and Z (height above the X-Y plane - used in 3D work) coordinates of a designated point on the drawing.

Area

This will calculate and display the area and perimeter of any region that is defined by a sequence of specified points on the drawing. The points are assumed to form a closed polygon.

GROUPING ENTITIES IN AUTOCAD

LAYERING

The AutoCAD extension package provides extensive facilities to aid in the use and management of layers. Therefore, this section need only introduce the basic commands that are used to define and select layers.

LAYER

This command supports the following operations.

Description of Operation	Option Keyword
obtain a list of existing layers	?
create new layers	New
select the current layer	Set
create a new layer and make it current	Make
set the colour for a specific layer	Colour
set the line type for a specific layer	Ltype
freeze or thaw a layer	Freeze/Thaw
make a layer visible or invisible	ON/OFF

Ddlmodes

This command performs the same function as the LAYER command just described except that it does it in a much more convenient fashion by making use of a pop-up dialogue box on the screen. This dialogue box also allows you to rename a layer which is not possible with he older, LAYER command. This command (since it has such an obscure name!!) is best called up by picking "Modify Layer..." from the Settings pull-down menu.

The colour and line style of entities drawn with AutoCAD are generally determined by the layer on which those objects reside. However, it is possible to override this by specifically defining these attributes for the objects in the drawing. This is done using the COLOR and LINETYPE commands. These commands are not discussed further in these notes, as it is unwise to mix the two methods of determining these attributes. Also note that the colour of an entity is used to determine which pen will be used when the drawing is plotted. This means that part of the function of layers can be to determine which pen is used for drawing on a multi-pen plotter.

Another important facility that is offered by AutoCAD is the opportunity to freeze and / or thaw layers on a per viewport basis when working in paper space with TILEMODE "off". This is achieved using the VPLAYER command. This facility allows you to have the same view of a drawing model in two viewports, where each displays a different set of layers. This is crucial if a single drawing is to contain, say, a reflected ceiling plan and a furniture layout plan of the same part of the model.

Vplayer

This command allows you to freeze and thaw layers in selected viewports. It will only operate if TILEMODE is set to 0 ("off"). Options associated with this command allow you to: list all layers that are frozen in a particular viewport; create layers which are frozen in all viewports; tag existing layers so that they are automatically frozen in any new viewports that are created; and reset selected layers in selected viewports back to their default state.

Blocks

Blocks in AutoCAD are used to group entities together so that they can be manipulated as a single unit. This concept should not be confused with the notion of selecting groups of objects and transforming or copying them. The use of blocks is best understood by considering the commands that are used to manipulate them.

Block

This command is used to create new blocks from parts of an existing drawing or to list all the defined blocks associated with the current drawing option. If creating a new block, AutoCAD prompts first for a name which can be up to 31 characters long, constructed from letters, digits and special characters ("$–_"). It then asks for an insertion base point which becomes the "anchor point" of the block for future manipulation. Finally, the user is prompted to select the objects to be included in the block using the normal methods. Once created, the graphics comprising the block is erased from the drawing (if desired, this can be restored using the OOPS command without affecting the block definition). The block can then be inserted anywhere using the INSERT command.

Wblock

This command is used to store a defined block from the current drawing on a disk file so that it can be used by another drawing. AutoCAD prompts first for a file name. It then asks for a block name. Valid responses are: a name entered on the keyboard; the character "=" denoting "same as file name"; "*" denoting "entire drawing"; or RETURN denoting a wish to select the objects in the normal fashion. If the entire drawing is to be saved as a block, then the BASE command should be used to set the base insertion point. If this command is not used, then the insertion point is assumed to be (0,0).

Insert

This command inserts a previously defined block into the current drawing or lists available blocks (option ?). If a specified block name is not on the list of available blocks for that drawing, then AutoCAD searches the disk for a file with the same name and, if found, loads that in as a new block before proceeding with the insert operation. Once a block has been found, AutoCAD supervises its insertion into the drawing. Options available include: X and Y scaling, rotation, fitting to a specified rectangle (if the block is defined in terms of a 1×1 box) and dragging.

A special case of the INSERT command is activated if the block name specified is preceded by an asterisk (*). This causes the block to be inserted as a single unit (using all the same insertion options) and then broken up into its separate graphic entities. These then lose their block characteristics and become like any other graphic entity.

Another special case is where a block has been defined from an external file, and that file has been subsequently changed. Those changes will not be automatically reflected in the block associated with the current drawing. To update the block definition in the current drawing, simply specify the block name for the INSERT command in the form "block name=file name" (or simply "name=" if the file name is the same as the block name). AutoCAD will then update the internal description of the block and regenerate the drawing to reflect those changes.

Explode

This command can be used to break up an existing instance of a block into its component graphic entities. These then lose their block characteristics and become like any other graphic entities. If a simple polyline entity is "exploded" (where it is not part of a block), then it breaks up into separate line and arc entities (and loses its thickness characteristics).

Minsert

This command is used to insert multiple instances of a block on a specified rectangular grid.

EXTERNAL REFERENCE BLOCKS

The insertion of an external drawing into another drawing, as described above, only creates a copy of that external drawing. A more powerful concept involves attaching that external drawing to the current drawing with a live link so that each time the current drawing is edited, the attached drawing is re-inserted. This arrangement can be achieved using the XREF command. Once the link is established, the external drawing is treated internally as a block. You can include multiple instances of that block with very little space penalty (in fact, the whole external drawing takes up little space in the local drawing). Although you cannot change the external block, you can access its parts. For example, you can snap onto entities in the drawing and you can temporarily change the visibility of its layers (layer changes are lost when the block is reloaded).

Xref

This command is used to manipulate external references. It allows you to: attach and detach external references; bind an external reference (which means severing the external link and making it a permanent block in the local drawing); relink an external reference whose path or name in the local file system has been altered (using the path option); or force an immediate reload of an external reference file.

APPENDIX-2

(More clipping methods and their mathematics)

Clipping refers to the removal of part of a scene. Internal clipping removes parts of a picture outside a given region; external clipping removes parts inside a region. We'll explore internal clipping, but external clipping can almost always be accomplished as a by-product.

There is also the question of what primitive types can we clip? We will consider *line* clipping and *polygon* clipping. A line clipping algorithms takes as input two endpoints of line segment and returns one (or more) line segments. A polygon clipper takes as input the vertices of a polygon and returns one (or more) polygons. There are several clipping algorithms. We'll study the Cohen-Sutherland line clipping algorithm to learn some basic concepts. Develop the more efficient Liang-Barsky algorithm and us its insights to culminate with Blinn's line clipping algorithm. The Sutherland-Hodgman polygon clipping algorithm will then be covered and plus the Weiler-Atherton algorithm. There are other issues in clipping that we will not have time to cover. Some of these are:

- Text character clipping
- Scissoring -- clips the primitive during scan conversion to pixels
- Bit (Pixel) block transfers (bitblts/pixblts)
  - o Copy a 2D array of pixels from a large canvas to a destination window
  - o Useful for text characters, pulldown menus, etc.

Cohen-Sutherland Line Clipping

The Cohen-Sutherland algorithm clips a line to an upright rectangular window. It is an application of *triage,* or make the simple case fast. The algorithm extended window boundaries to define 9 regions: top-left, top-center, top-right, center-left, center, center-right, bottom-left, bottom- center, and bottom-right.

See figure 1, these 9 regions can be uniquely identified using a 4 bit code, often called an ***outcode***. We'll use the order: left, right, bottom, top (LRBT) for these four bits. In particular, for $p = (x, y)$ each point

- Left (first) bit is set to 1 when p lies to left of window
- Right (second) bit is set to 1 when p lies to right of window
- Bottom (third) bit is set to 1 when p lies below window
- Top (fourth) bit set is set to 1 when p lies above window

The LRBT (Left, Right, Bottom, Top) order is somewhat arbitrary, but once an order is chosen we must stick with it. Note that points on the clipping window edge are considered inside (the bits are left at 0).

1001	0001	0101
1000	0000 Clip Window	0100
1010	0010	0110

Fig. 1 *The nine region defined by an up-right window and their outcodes*

Given a line segment with end points $p_0 = (x_0, y_0)$ and $p_1 = (x_1, y_1)$, here's the basic flow of the Cohen-Sutherland algorithm:

1. Compute 4-bit outcodes $LRBT_0$ and $LRBT_1$ for each end-point
2. If both outcodes are 0000, the ***trivially visible*** case, pass end-points to draw routine. This occurs when the bitwise OR of outcodes yields 0000.
3. If both outcodes have 1's in the same bit position, the ***trivially invisible*** case, clip the entire line (pass nothing to the draw routine). This occurs when the bitwise AND of outcodes is <u>not</u> 0000.
4. Otherwise, the ***indeterminate*** case, - line may be partially visible or not visible. Analytically compute the intersection of the line with the appropriate window edges

Let's explore the indeterminate case more closely. First, one of two end-points must be outside the window, pretend it is $p_0 = (x_0, y_0)$.

1. Read P_1's 4-bit code in order, say left-to-right
2. When a set bit (1) is found, compute intersection point I of corresponding window edge with line from p_0 to p_1.

As an example, pretend the right bit is set so we want to compute the intersection with the right clipping window edge, also, pretend we've already done the homogeneous divide, so the right edge is x=1, and we need to find y. The y value of the intersection is found by substituting x=1 into the line equation (from p_0 to p_1) $y - y_0 = \frac{y_1 - y_0}{x_1 - x_0}(x - x_0)$ and solving for $y = y_0 + \frac{y_1 - y_0}{x_1 - x_0}(1 - x_1)$.

Other cases are handled similarly.

Now this may not complete the clipping of the line, so we replace p_0 by the intersection point I and repeat Cohen-Sutherland algorithm. (Clearly we can save some state to avoid some computations)

- Define window by

$$x = 0 \text{ Left edge}$$
$$x = 1 \text{ Right edge}$$
$$y = 0 \text{ Bottom edge}$$
$$y = 1 \text{ Top edge}$$

- End-points $p_0 = (1/2, 1/2)$ and $p = (1/4, 3/4)$ both have 4-bit codes 0000. Logical bitwise OR: $0000 \vee 0000 = 0000 \Rightarrow$ line is completely visible - draw line between them.
- End-point $p_2 = (3, 3)$ has 4-bit code 0101 and end-point $p_3 = (-2, 5)$ has 4-bit code 1001. Logical bitwise AND: $0101 \wedge 1001 = 0001 \neq 0000 \Rightarrow$ both end-points to right of window. Therefore line is invisible.

- End-point $p_4 = (3, 3)$ has 4-bit code 0101 and end-point $p_5 = (0, 1/2)$ has 4-bit code 0000.
  - o Logical bitwise OR 0101 $\vee$ 0000 = 0101 $\Rightarrow$ no information.
  - o Logical bitwise AND 0101 $\wedge$ 0000 = 0000 $\Rightarrow$ no information.
  - o $p_4 = (3, 3)$ is outside.
  - o Reading p_4's 4-bit code from left-to-right, "right" bit is set.
  - o Intersection with right edge is at $I = (1, 4/3)$
  - o I has 4-bit code ...

The Cohen-Sutherland was one of, if not, the first clipping algorithm to be implemented in hardware. Yet the intersection was not computed analytically, as we have done, but by bisection (binary search) of the line segment.

Cohen-Sutherland in 3D

The Cohen-Sutherland algorithm extends easily to 3D. Extended the 3D clipping window boundaries to define 27 regions. Assign a 6 bit code to each region, that is, for each point (x, y, z)

- Left (first) bit set (1) $\Rightarrow$ point lies to left of window
- Right (second) bit set (1) $\Rightarrow$ point lies to right of window
- Bottom (third) bit set (1) $\Rightarrow$ point lies below window
- Top (fourth) bit set (1) $\Rightarrow$ point lies above window
- Near (fifth) bit set (1) $\Rightarrow$ point lies to in front of window (near)
- Far (sixth) bit set (1) $\Rightarrow$ point lies to behind of window (far)

The Left, Right, Bottom, Top, Near, Far (LRBTNF) outcode can be used to determine segments that are trivially visible, trivially invisible, or indeterminate. In the indeterminate case we intersect the line segment with faces of clipping cube determined by the outcode of an end-point that is outside of the clipping cube. More specifically, in the indeterminant case, use parametric form of the line

$$x = x_0 + t(x_1 - x_0)$$
$$y = y_0 + t(y_1 - y_0)$$
$$z = z_0 + t(z_1 - z_0)$$

To clip against a face, say y=1, compute $t = \dfrac{1 - y_0}{y_1 - y_0}$ and use it to evaluate the x and z intersections.

Liang-Barsky Line Clipping

The Liang-Barsky is optimized for clipping to an upright rectangular clip window (the Cyrus-Beck algorithms is similar but clips to a more general convex polygon). Liang-Barsky uses parametric equations, clip window edge normals, and inner products can improve the efficiency of line clipping over Cohen-Sutherland. Let $L(t) = p_0 + t(p_1 - p_0) = (1 - t)\, p_0 + tp_1, 0 \le t \le 1$ denote the parametric equation of the line segment from p_0 to p_1 Let $\vec{N}_e$ denote the outward pointing normal of the clip window edge e, and let p_e be an arbitrary point on edge e.

Consider the vector $L(t) - p_e$ from p_e to a point on the line $L(t)$ Figure <u>2</u> shows several of these vectors for different values of t. At the intersection of $L(t)$ and edge e the inner product of $\vec{N}_e$ and $L(t) - p_e$ is zero, see figure 2. In fact, we have

$$\vec{N}_e \cdot (L(t) - p_e) = \vec{N}_e \cdot (p_0 + t(p_1 - p_0) - p_e) = \vec{N}_e \cdot ((p_0 - p_e) + t\vec{N}_e \cdot (p_1 - p_0)) = 0$$

which if we Solve for t yields $t = \dfrac{\vec{N}_e \cdot (p_e - p_0)}{\vec{N}_e \cdot (p_1 - p_0)}$.

(Note that checks need to be made that the denominator above is not zero.)

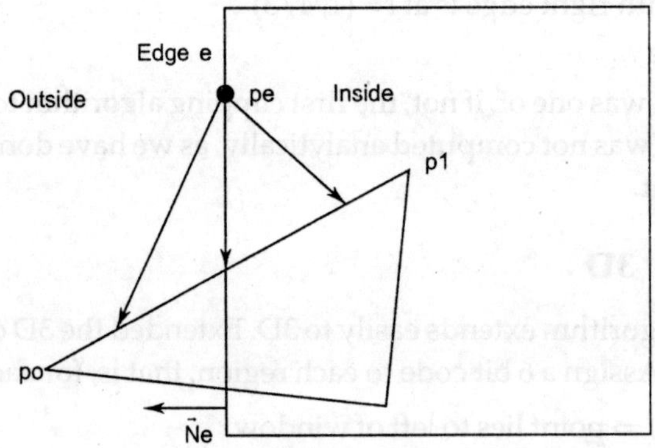

Fig. 2 *The setup for Liang-Barsky clipping*

Using the 4 edge normals for an upright rectangular clip window and 4 points, one on each edge, we can calculate 4 parameter values where $L(t)$ intersects each edge Let's call these parameter values t_L, t_R, t_B, t_T Note any of the t's outside of the interval [0, 1] can be discarded, since they correspond to points before p_0 (when $t < 0$) and points after p_1 (when $t > 1$). The remaining t values are characterized as "potentially entering" (PE) or "potentially leaving" (PL)

- The parameter t_i is PE if when traveling along the (extended) line from p_0 to p_1 we move from the outside to the inside of the window ***with respect to the edge i.***
- The parameter t_i is PL if when traveling along the (extended) line from p_0 to p_1 we move from the inside to the outside of the window ***with respect to the edge i.***

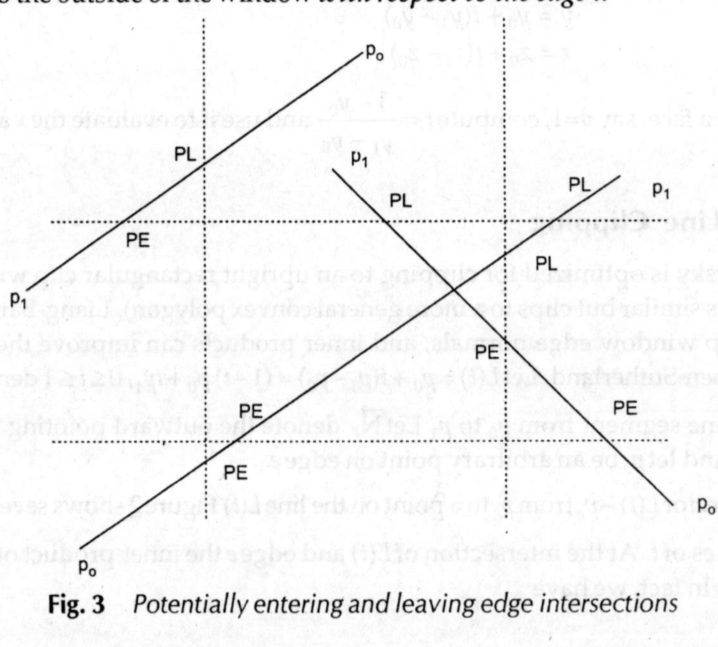

Fig. 3 *Potentially entering and leaving edge intersections*

The inner product of the outward pointing edge normal $\vec{N}_i$ with $p_1 - p_0$ can be used to classify the parameter t_i as either PE or PL.

1. If $\vec{N}_i \cdot (p_1 - p_0) < 0$ the parameter t_i is potentially entering (PE). The vectors $\vec{N}_i$ and $p_1 - p_0$ point in opposite directions. Since $\vec{N}_i$ is outward, the vector $p_1 - p_0$ from p_0 to p_1 points inward.
2. If $\vec{N}_i \cdot (p_1 - p_0) > 0$ the parameter t_i is potentially leaving (PL). The vectors $\vec{N}_i$ and $p_1 - p_0$ point in similar directions. Since $\vec{N}_i$ is outward, the vector $p_1 - p_0$ from p_0 to p_1 points outward too.
3. Let t_{pe} be the largest PE parameter value and t_{pl} the smallest PL parameter value
4. The clipped line extends from $L(t_{pe})$ to $L(t_{pl})$, where $0 \le t_{pe} \le t_{pl} \le 1$

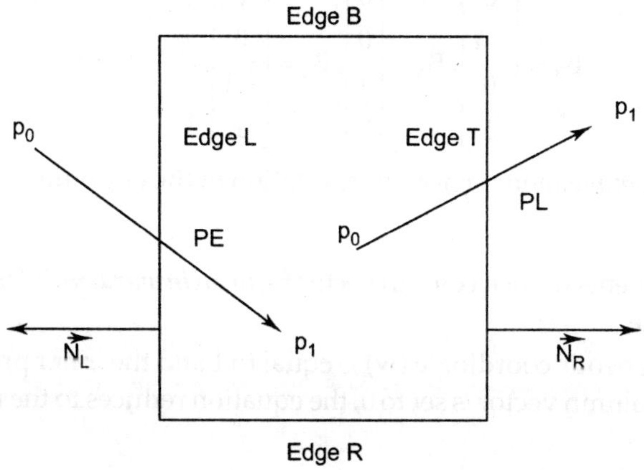

Blinn's Line Clipping

A clipping volume can be defined as set of bounding planes. Choosing simple planes is a good idea. We'll define the clipping volume by:

$$X = 0, X = 1, Y = 0, Y = 1, Z = 0, Z = 1$$

We'll call these the ***real*** space interpretation of the clipping volume bounding planes.

It is convenient to think of these in terms of inner products. More specifically, the $X = 0$ plane can be thought of at the column vector:

$$\begin{bmatrix} 1 \\ 0 \\ 0 \\ 0 \end{bmatrix}$$

A ***homogeneous point (x, y, z, w)*** is then "in the plane" if the inner product of the point and vector is zero, that is,

$$(x, y, z, w) \cdot \begin{bmatrix} 1 \\ 0 \\ 0 \\ 0 \end{bmatrix} = x = 0$$

To obtain the *real* plane we must divide x by w (whatever its value other than 0), but we'll still get $X = x/w = 0$ since $x = 0$.

(Recall the homogeneous divide necessary to map points after a perspective projection into real points: $X = x/w, Y = y/w, Z = z/w$.)

Using this notation, the six bounding planes become the six column vectors:

$$B_0 = \begin{bmatrix} 1 \\ 0 \\ 0 \\ 0 \end{bmatrix}, B_1 = \begin{bmatrix} -1 \\ 0 \\ 0 \\ 1 \end{bmatrix}, B_2 = \begin{bmatrix} 0 \\ 1 \\ 0 \\ 0 \end{bmatrix},$$

$$B_3 = \begin{bmatrix} 0 \\ -1 \\ 0 \\ 1 \end{bmatrix}, B_4 = \begin{bmatrix} 0 \\ 0 \\ 1 \\ 0 \end{bmatrix}, B_5 = \begin{bmatrix} 0 \\ 0 \\ -1 \\ 1 \end{bmatrix}$$

We'll call these the ***homogeneous*** space interpretation of the clipping volume bounding planes.

Nota bene:

1. The first three elements of each column vector form an ***inward, unit length normal vector*** to the plane in ***real*** space.
2. When the homogeneous coordinate (w) is equal to 1 and the inner product of a point with the bounding plane column vector is set to 0, the equation reduces to the real space equation. That is, for example,

$$(x, y, z, 1) \cdot \begin{bmatrix} 0 \\ 0 \\ -1 \\ 1 \end{bmatrix} = -z + 1 = 0$$

or

$$z = z/1 = Z = 1.$$

3. Or, better yet, dividing the equation by w produces the real equation, for example $w - z = 0$ becomes $1 - z/w = 1 - Z = 0$ or $Z = 1$.

Boundary coordinates

Following Blinn's terminology we'll call the inner products of a point with the bounding planes the ***boundary coordinates*** of a point. They are listed in the table below.

Boundary Number	*(Homogeneous Value) Boundary Coordinate*	*Real Plane*
0	x	$X = 0$
1	$w - x$	$X = 1$
2	y	$Y = 0$
3	$w - y$	$Y = 1$
4	z	$Z = 0$
5	$w - z$	$Z = 1$

Outcodes

The question we want to answer is:

Given two end points (P_0 and P_1) of a line segment, how can we use the boundary coordinates to determine a points Cohen-Sutherland outcode?

Let's assume the 6-bit outcode is in the order left, right, bottom, top, near, far (LRBTNF) so it corresponds to the order of the boundary coordinates. A particular bit is set (to 1) if the point is in the designated region and unset (to 0) otherwise.

We'll assume $w>0$. Recall that the value of w that comes out of the perspective transform is $w = z \sin(\theta)$ where θ is (half of) the field of view angle. Now both $\sin(\theta) > 0$ and $z>0$(provided we're looking at something in front of us) so $w>0$. The bottom line is division by a positive quantity does not affect the sense of an inequality!

Consider the left plane $X = 0$.

- if its boundary coordinate x is negative we're in the left region and L is set.
- if its boundary coordinate x is greater than or equal to zero, we're not in the left region and L is unset.

This works with the other planes too. Consider the right plane X=1.

- if its boundary coordinate $w - x<0$, then division by w yields $1 - X < 0$ and we're in the right region ($X > 1$) and R is set.
- if its boundary coordinate $w - x \geq 0$ we're not in the right region and R is unset.

All outcodes are set by testing inequality against 0.

$x < 0$ Set L (to 1)

$w - x < 0$ Set R

$y < 0$ Set B

$w - y < 0$ Set T

$z < 0$ Set N

$w - z < 0$ Set F

For a particular bounding plane (bit in the outcode) and a pair of line segment end points there are four cases.

Bit for P_0	Bit for P_1	Interpretation
0	0	Segment visible w.r.t. this boundary
1	0	Straddles boundary, P_0 outside
0	1	Straddles boundary, P_1 outside
1	1	Segment invisible w.r.t. this boundary

Given the outcodes LRBTNF for P_0 and P_1 (set by considering the boundary coordinates x, $w - x$, etc.) we can apply the trivial accept and reject tests:

1. If `outcode(`P_0`) | outcode(`P_1`)` == 000000 accept line segment. (All bits in both outcodes must be 0)
2. If `outcode(`P_0`) & outcode(`P_1`)` != 000000 reject line segment. (Some bit is set in both outcodes for some plane)

Interpolation

When the trivial tests fail we must calculate the intersections and this is best done by parametric linear interpolation, our old friend. Let

$$P(u) = P_0 + u(P_1 - P_0)$$

be the (directed) line segment from P_0 to P_1 as parameter u increases from 0 to 1. We need to calculate u and this is done by inner products with the boundary column vectors, say B_i, that is, $P(u) \cdot B_i = P0 \cdot B_i + u(P_1 - P_0) \cdot B_i$ and since we want the point P(u) to be on the boundary this inner product should be 0. Or $u = \dfrac{P_0 \cdot B_i}{(P_0 - P_1) \cdot B_i} = \dfrac{P_0 \cdot B_i}{P_0 \cdot B_i - P_1 \cdot B_i}$ but these inner products are just the boundary coordinates! To be explicit, $P(u) = (x_0 + u(x_1 - x_0), y_0 + u(y_1 - y_0), z_0 + u(z_1 - z_0), w_0 + u(w_1 - w_0))$ and let's assume the line straddles the X=1 plane, so we're working with boundary column vector $B_1 = \begin{bmatrix} -1 \\ 0 \\ 0 \\ 1 \end{bmatrix}$ and the inner product is $P(u) \cdot B_1 = -[x_0 + u(x_1 - x_0)] + [w_0 + u(w_1 - w_0)]$ which if we set to zero and solve for u yields $u = \dfrac{w_0 - x_0}{(w_0 - x_0) - (w_1 - x_1)}$.

Note this value of u will be in the range 0 to 1 only when boundary coordinates ($w_0 - x_0$ and $w_1 - x_1$ in the above example) have opposite signs. This is easy to interpret in real space. But you can also establish it algebraically by considering the inequality $0 < \dfrac{a}{a-b} < 1$.

If a is positive, then $a - b$ must be positive and greater than a, that is b is negative. Something similar happens when a is negative. The point is we only want to calculate u when the boundary coordinates differ in sign, that is the line segment straddles the boundary.

Polygon Clipping

Polygon clipping differs from line clipping in several respects.

1. The input to the clipper is a polygon, which for simplicity we will view as a list of $n \geq 3$ vertices $(v_0, v_1, \ldots, u_{n-1})$.
2. The output from the clipper is one or more polygons.
3. The clipping process may generate vertices that do not lie on any of the edges of the orginal polygon.
4. Complex polygons (that is, non-convex) may lead to strange artifacts.

Sutherland-Hodgman Polygon Clipping

Since polygons are basic primitives, algorithms have been developed for clipping them directly. The Sutherland-Hodgman algorithm is a polygon clipper. It was a basic component in James Clark's "Geometry Engine," which was the precursor to the first Silicon Graphics machines. This algorithm clips any ***subject polygon*** (convex or concave) against any ***convex clipping window,*** but we will usually pretend the clipping window is an upright rectangle.

Given a ***subject*** polygon with an ordered sequence of vertices $v_1, v_2, \ldots, v_{n-1}, n \geq 3$,

Sutherland-Hodgman compares each subject polygon edge against a single clip window edge, saving the vertices on the in-side of the edge and the intersection points when edges are crossed. The clipper is then re-entered with this intermediate polygon and another clip window edge.

Given a clip window edge and a subject polygon edge, there are four cases to consider:

1. The subject polygon edge goes from outside clip window edge to outside clip window edge. In this case we output nothing.
2. The subject polygon edge goes from outside clip window edge to inside clip window edge. In this case we save intersection and inside vertex.
3. The subject polygon edge goes from inside clip window edge to outside clip window edge. In this case we save intersection point.
4. The subject polygon edge goes from inside clip window edge to inside clip window edge. In this case we save second inside point (the first was saved previously).

To complete the description, we need to consider the first vertex of the subject polygon and its last edge. If the first vertex is inside the current edge we save it to the list of vertices in the intermediate polygon, otherwise we drop it out. For the last edge, note that if nothing has yet been saved in the intermediate polygon, the entire subject must not be visible in the clip window, so we can quit. Otherwise, if the last subject edge crosses clip window edge, the intersection point must be appended to the intermediate polygon.

Figure shows an example of the Sutherland-Hodgman clipping process. The clip window edge currently be used is solid, the others are dashed.

First Clip Window Edge

Starting with the original triangle (subject polygon), we set the intermediate polygon to null and find

1. Start vertex: p_0 is outside the edge, so not saved in the intermediate polygon vertex list.
2. Subject edge $p_0 p_1$ crosses the clip edge and so the intersection i_{01} is saved -- intermediate list (i_{01}).
3. p_1 is inside the edge, so it is saved -- intermediate list (i_{01}, p_1).
4. Subject edge $p_1 p_2$ does not crosses the clip edge and so no intersection is computed.
5. p_2 is inside the edge, so it is saved -- intermediate list (i_{01}, p_1, p_2).
6. Last edge $p_2 p_0$: We have output some data, so we'll continue.
   (*a*) Subject edge $p_2 p_0$ does crosses the clip edge and so the intersection i_{01} is saved -- intermediate list $(i_{01}, p_1, p_2, i_{20})$.

Second Clip Window Edge

Start vertex: i_{01} is inside the edge, so saved in the intermediate polygon vertex list -- intermediate list (i_{01}).

Subject edge $i_{01} p_1$ crosses the clip edge and so the intersection i_{011} is saved -- intermediate list (i_{01}, i_{011}).

p_1 is outside the edge, so it is not saved.

Subject edge p_1p_2 does crosses the clip edge and so the intersection i_{12} is saved -- intermediate list $(i_{01}, i_{011}, i_{12})$.

p_2 is inside the edge, so it is saved -- intermediate list $(i_{01}, i_{011}, i_{12}, p_2)$.

Subject edge p_2i_{20} does not cross the clip edge and so no interesection is computed.

i_{20} is inside the edge, so it is saved -- intermediate list $(i_{01}, i_{011}, i_{12}, p_2, i_{20})$.

Last edge $i_{20}i_{01}$: We have output some data, so we'll continue.

1. Subject edge $i_{20}i_{01}$ does not crosses the clip edge and so no intersection is saved.

As an exercise, you can complete the clipping process.

The Sutherland-Hodgman algorithm is not too difficult to code either.

Inside/Outside Testing

The Sutherland-Hodgman algorithm depends on our ability to determine that a point (vertex) is inside or outside of a given edge (line). This is a fairly common decision problem in computer graphics, yet due to the build up of floating point arithmetic errors, it may be difficult to answer the question exactly. We will declare that vertices that lie on the edge are ***inside***.

There are several ways to answer the question: Is point $p = (x, y)$ on the ***in*** or ***out*** side of a line determined by vertices $v_0 = (x_0, y_0)$ and $v_1 = (x_1, y_1)$. The one we present is based on inner products, but before we can begin, we must know what is meant by ***inside*** and ***outside***. A complete description of this topic and related one is included in the chapter on basic concepts. Recall, that our polygon vertices are listed in counter-clockwise when viewed from the front side, and this implies that the inside of the polygon is on our left as we traverse its vertices.

These assumption lead to the mathematical result that the outward edge normal from vertex v_0 to v_1 is given by $\vec{n}_{01} = \langle y_1 - y_0, -(x_1 - x_0)\rangle$.

Now, consider the vector $p \vec{-} v_0 = \langle x - x_0, y - y_0\rangle$ from v_0 to p. If the inner product of $\vec{n}_{01}$ and $p \vec{-} v_0$ is

1. positive, p is on the ***outside***.
2. zero, p is on the edge and consider ***inside***.
3. negative, p is on the ***inside***.

Crossings

We can use the inside/outside decision algorithm to determine whether or not two edges cross.

Intersections

The last task we must complete is developing the code to compute an intersection.

Sutherland-Hodgman Summary

The Sutherland-Hodgman polygon clipping algorithm clips polygons against convex clipping windows. It does so by clipping the subject polygon against each clip edge producing intermediate subject polygons. Although we have not done so, the Sutherland-Hodgman algorithm easily extends to 3 dimensions.

The Sutherland-Hodgman may produce connecting lines that were not in the original polygon. When the subject polygon is concave (not convex) these connecting lines may be undesirable artifacts.

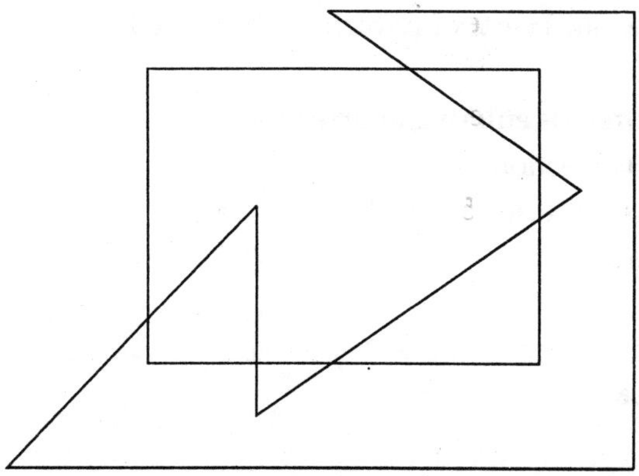

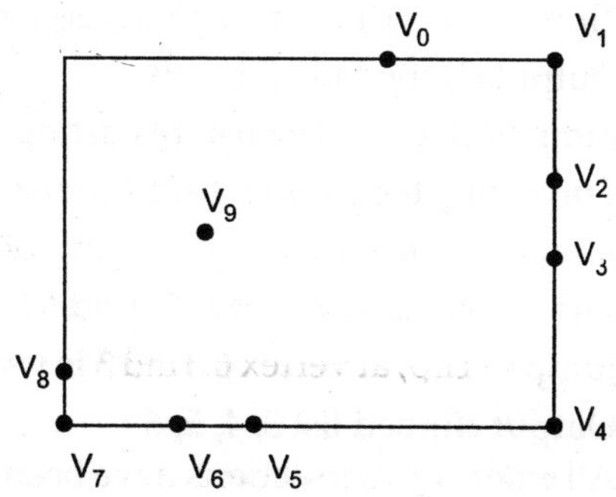

The Weiler-Atherton, which we will consider next, clips arbitrary polygons against arbitrary clipping windows, the price we pay for this generally is that Weiler-Atherton is only a 2D clipper.

Weiler-Atherton Polygon Clipper

- Assume the vertices of the subject polygon are listed in clockwise order (interior is on the right)
- Start at an entering intersection
- Follow the edge(s) of the polygon being clipped until an exiting intersection is encountered
- Turn right at the exiting intersection and following clip window edge until intersection is found
- Turn right and follow the subject polygon
- Continue until vertex already visited is reached
- If entire polygon has not be processed, repeat
- Consider the subject polygon with vertices a, b, c, d and the clip polygon with vertices A, B, C, D
- Insert the intersections in both vertex lists
    - o Subject list: $a, 1, b, 2, c, 3, 4, d, 5, 6,$
    - o Clip list: A, 6, 3, 2, B, 1, C, D, 4, 5,

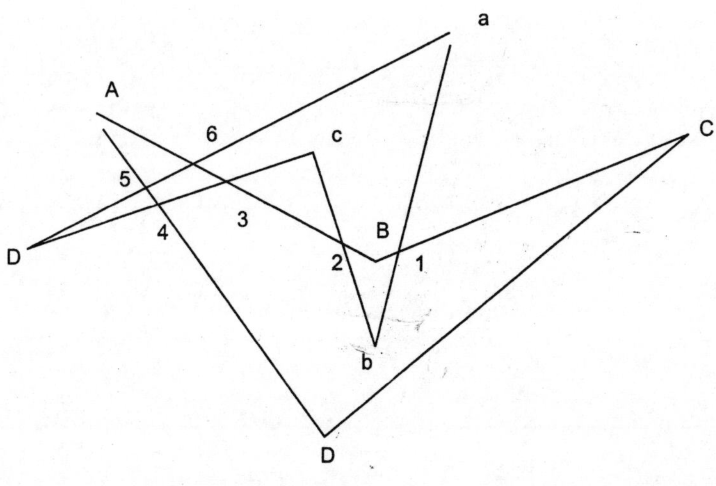

- Starting at vertex a of the clip polygon, find 1 is first entering intersection
- Traversing the subject, find 2 is exiting intersection
- "Jump" to vertex 2 in clip polygon, follow until vertex 1 (which has be visited)
- Output clipped list 1, *b*, 2, B
- Jump back to subject list, restarting at *c*, find 3 is entering intersection
- Traversing the subject, find 4 is exiting intersection
- Jump to vertex 4 in clip polygon, follow until vertex 5 (which is entering)
- Jump to subject, at vertex 5, find 6 is exiting
- Jump to clip, at vertex 6, find 3 is visited
- Output clipped list 3, 4, 5, 6

  All entering intersections have been visited.

APPENDIX-3

(Additional Topics)

1. Introduction to Aliasing

Aliasing is a potential problem whenever an analog signal is point sampled to convert it into a digital signal. It can occur in audio sampling, for example, in converting music to digital form to be stored on a CD-ROM or other digital device. Aliasing happens whenever an analog signal is not sampled at a high enough frequency. In audio, Aliasing manifests itself in the form of spurious low frequencies. An example is shown below of two sin waves.

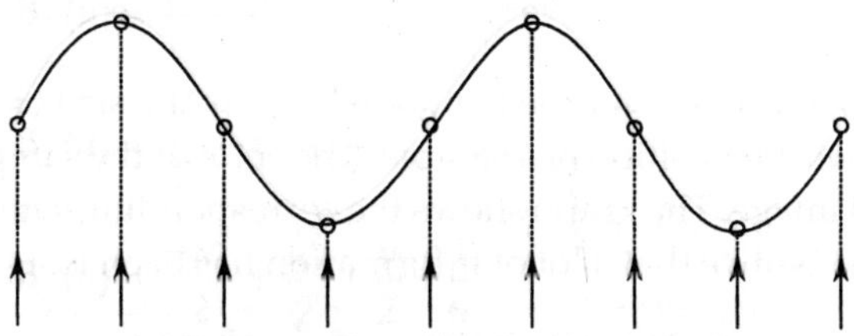

(a) Point sampling within the Nyquist limit

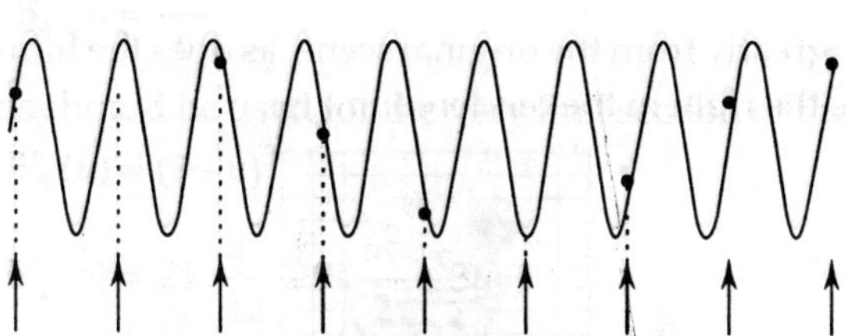

(b) Point sampling beyond the Nyquist limit

Image Reference

In the top sin wave, the sampling is fast enough that a reconstructed signal (the small circles) would have the same frequency as the original sin wave. In the bottom wave, with a higher frequency but the same point sampling rate, a reconstructed signal (the small circles) would appear to be a sin wave of a lower frequency, i.e., an *aliased signal*.

From Point Sampling Theory it turns out that to accurately reconstruct a signal, the signal must be sampled at a rate greater than or equal to two times the highest frequency contained in the signal. This is called the Nyquist Theorem and the highest frequency that can be accurately represented with a given sampling rate is called the Nyquist limit. For example, to produce a music CD-ROM the analog signal is sampled at a maximum rate of 44 Khz, therefore the highest possible audio frequency is 22khz. Any audio frequencies greater than 22Khz must be removed from the input signal or they will be aliased, i.e., appear as low frequency sounds.

Aliasing occurs in computer graphics, since we are point sampling an analog signal. The mathematical model of an image is a continuous analog signal which is sampled at discrete points (the pixel positions). When the sampling rate is less than Nyquist Limit then there are aliasing artifacts that are called "jaggies" in computer graphics. In general, aliasing is when high frequencies appear as low frequencies which produce regular patterns easy to see.

Original scene

The bowl of fruit was modeled using constructive solid geometry(CSG).

One scanline in the fruitbowl is highlighted. The graph shows the luminosity (brightness) function of the highlighted scan line.

Sampling the scene

The rectangular grid superimposed over the fruit bowl shows the size of the pixels. The dot in the middle of each square shows the position of a sample. The color at the sample point will be the color of the pixel in the rendered image. The graph shows the corresponding sampled luminosity function of the highlighted scanline. Notice that a lot of information has been lost.

Rendered image

The rendered image differs greatly from the original scene, as does the luminosity signal. Notice that the green leaf has moved to the right in the rendered image.

Effects caused by aliasing

The errors caused by aliasing are called artefacts. Common aliasing artefacts include jagged profiles, disappearing or improperly rendered fine detail, and disintegrating textures.

Jagged profiles

The picture above shows the sampling grid superimposed on the original scene. The picture above is the rendered image. A jagged profile is quite evident in the rendered image. Also known as "jaggies", jagged silhouettes are probably the most familiar effect caused by aliasing. Jaggies are especially noticeable where there is a high contrast between the interior and the exterior of the silhouette.

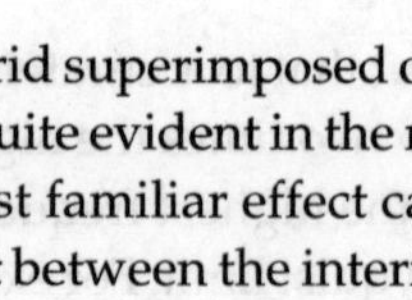

Antialiasing

Antialiasing methods were developed to combat the effects of aliasing. The two major categories of antialiasing techniques are prefiltering and postfiltering.

Prefiltering

Prefiltering methods treat a pixel as an area, and compute pixel color based on the overlap of the scene's objects with a pixel's area.

Basis for Prefiltering Algorithms

The original scene is a filled orange circle on a red background. All of the pixels inside the circle are 100 percent orange. All the pixels on the boundary of the circle have some area that is red and some area that is orange. Forty percent of the highlighted pixel is orange and 60 percent of its area is red. The computed color for the highlighted pixel is 40 percent orange and 60 percent red.

Prefiltering demonstration

Both phrases were rendered at a resolution of 512x512. Even at this resolution, the jaggies are apparent in the phrase that hasn't been antialiased.

Closeup

Without antialiasing, the jaggies are harshly evident.

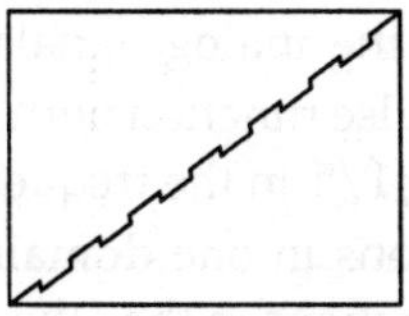

Closeup of Prefiltered image

Along the character's border, the colors are a mixture of the foreground and background colors.

Postfiltering

Postfiltering, also known as supersampling, is the more popular approach to antialiasing. For each displayed pixel, a postfiltering method takes several samples from the scene and computes an average of the samples to determine the pixel's color. The two steps in the postfiltering process are:

1. Sample the scene at n times the display resolution. For example, suppose the display resolution is 512x512. Sampling at three times the width and three times the height of the display resolution would yield 1536x1536 samples.

2. The color of each pixel in the rendered image will be an average of several samples. For example, if sampling were performed at three times the width and three times the height of the display resolution, then a pixel's color would be an average of nine samples. A filter provides the weights used to compute the average.

Sampling in the Postfiltering method

The display resolution is four pixels wide by three pixels high. The superimposed grid depicts the size of a pixel. Both figures show supersampling at three times the height and three times the width of the display resolution. In the right figure, the samples are regularly spaced. In the left figure, the positions of samples are displaced by a random amount. The random amount is small relative to the size of the pixel. This method of perturbing the sample positions is known as "jittering." Jittering adds noise to the rendered image. The advantage of jittering is that the human eye tolerates noise more easily than it tolerates aliasing artefacts, and as a result, humans perceive a higher quality in the rendered image.

Filters

Filters combine samples to compute a pixel's color. The weighted filter shown on the slide combines nine samples taken from inside a pixel's boundary. Each sample is multiplied by its corresponding weight and the products are summed to produce a weighted average, which is used as the pixel color. In this filter, the center sample has the most influence. The other type of filter is an unweighted filter. In an unweighted filter, each sample has equal influence in determining the pixel's color. In other words, an unweighted filter computes an unweighted average.

Point Sampling Theory

The key points are as follows:

- Point sampling in the spatial domain corresponds to the point by point multiplication of a sampling impulse function times the analog signal to be sampled.
- The Fourier Transform of an impulse function with spacing T in the spatial domain results in an impulse function with spacing 1/T in the frequency domain
- The multiplication of two functions in one domain corresponds to the convolution of the Fourier Transforms of the two functions in the other domain
- The convolution of an impulse function with another function is the second function instantiated at the impulse function positions.

Look at examples of point sampling without and with aliasing:

In the time domain: The top signal is sampled at the Nyquist limit and so is not aliased but the bottom signal is sampled at a rate below the Nyquist limit and is aliased.

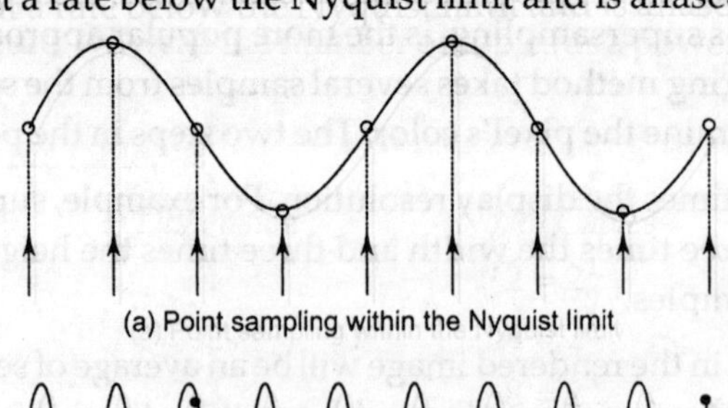

(a) Point sampling within the Nyquist limit

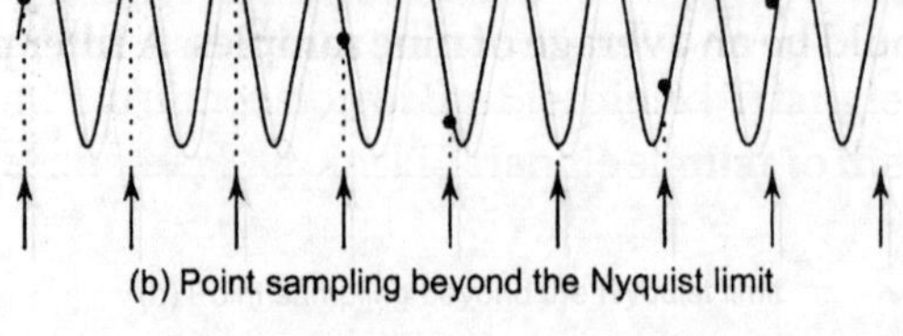

(b) Point sampling beyond the Nyquist limit

Image Reference

In the frequency domain: The left side corresponds to the top in the above image and the right side corresponds to the lower signal. Note that, for the left side case, after the reconstruction filter is applied, we obtain a signal identical to the initial signal, i.e., no aliasing has occurred. In the right side case, there is an overlap between the input signal instantiations and after the reconstruction filter is applied we do not have the original signal, but instead we now have two frequencies, both of which are lower than the original. This is aliasing.

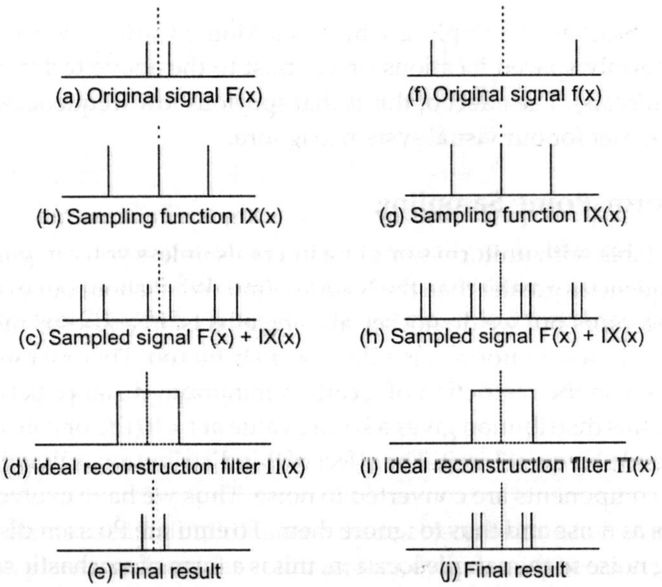

Note that the ideal reconstruction filter is a box in the frequency domain. This corresponds to a sinc filter (sin (x) / x) in the spatial domain. The sinc function is infinite, which means that it is impossible to have a perfect reconstruction filter in the spatial domain.

Poisson Distribution

Notice that if we use a Poisson distribution, then signals that are beyond the Nyquist limit become noise.

Super-Sampling

In supersampling we sample more than 1 sample per pixel. These samples can be at regularly spaced intervals. For example, we might compute an image at 2K by 2K or 4K by 4K points and display at 1K by 1K pixel resolution. Sampling at 2K x 2K for a 1K x 1K image increases the number of samples and graphics computations (and Z-buffer requirements for scan-line graphics) by a factor of 4. An alternative method would be to sample at the corners and center of each pixel. This only increases the number of computations by a factor of two but requires increased overhead for book-keeping (since the samples from the previous row must be stored). Supersampling has the effect of moving the Nyquist Limit to higher frequencies.

Rather than combining pixels with unweighted average (box filter) might use a weighted filter. We might even average pixel samples over several pixels , i.e. combine over a wider range with weighted average. This is an example of digital filtering. Even if we move the Nyquist Limit to higher frequencies, we will still have aliasing. Adaptive supersampling: additional sampling in region of high frequency, e.g. near edges. We continue supersampling as long as | Ic - Ii | > threshold variance. It does better but requires large number of rays/samples and it is a more complicated algorithm.

Stochastic Sampling in Anti-Aliasing

Rob Cook proposed Stochastic Sampling which is a Monte Carlo type technique. The image is sampled at nonuniformly spaced locations (in contrast to the above techniques which sample at regularly spaced intervals). The effect of this is that spurious low frequencies are replaced by random noise which is easier for our visual system to ignore.

Review of Uniform Point Sampling

Aliasing is not avoidable with uniform sampling intervals unless you can guarantee that the function contains no frequencies greater than the Nyquist limit. What about our eyes ? They have a finite number of photo receptors but we do not see aliasing effects. In a Rhesus monkey the eye photoreceptors distribution is non-uniform, it is a Poisson distribution. This is a random distribution but in a monkey there is also the restriction of a certain minimum distance between any two photoreceptors. The FT of this distribution gives a strong value at f = 0 (DC or constant component, with noise elsewhere outside Nyquist Limit. The effect of this distribution is that there is no aliasing but the high frequency components are converted to noise. Thus we have evolved to handle high frequency components as noise and thus to ignore them. To emulate Poisson disk distribution, we do "jittering" or adding noise to the sample location, this is a form of stochastic sampling.

Jittering in time (for a time sampled signal) was previously analyzed by Balakrishnan. i.e. rather than sample at nT, sample at nT + dn, where dn is the jittering factor. If the dn are uncorrelated (dn and dm are not correlated) and random, found results:

- high frequencies attenuated and energy appears as noise (energy conserved)
- basic composition of spectrum unchanged.

Analyzed two types of uncorrelated jittering - Gaussian and white noise.

In Gaussian jittering the values of d are chosen according to Gaussian distribution. For white noise d is uniformly distributed between some - dT and dT.

2. Ray Tracing: Another Important Topic in Graphics

Although three-dimensional computer graphics have been around for many decades, there has been a surge of general interest towards the field in the last couple of years. Just a quick glance at the latest blockbuster movies is enough to see the public's fascination with the new generation of graphics. As exciting as graphics are, however, there is a definite barrier which prevents most people from learning about them. For one thing, there is a lot of math and theory involved. Beyond that, just getting a window to display even simple 2D graphics can often be a daunting task. In this article, we will talk about a powerful yet simple 3D graphics method known as **ray tracing,** which can be understood and implemented without dealing with much math or the intricacies of windowing systems. The only math we assume is a basic knowledge of vectors, dot products, and cross products. We will skip most of the theory behind ray tracing, focusing instead on a general overview of the technique from an implementation-oriented perspective.

Ray tracing is a technique for rendering three-dimensional graphics with very complex light interactions. This means you can create pictures full of mirrors, transparent surfaces, and shadows, with stunning results. We discuss ray tracing in this introductory graphics article because it is a very simple method to both understand and implement. It is based on the idea that you can model reflection and refraction by recursively following the path that light takes as it bounces through an environment.

Some Terminology

Before presenting the full description of ray tracing, we should agree on some basic terminology. When creating any sort of computer graphics, you must have a list of objects that you want your software to render. These objects are part of a **scene** or **world** (Fig. 1), so when we talk about "looking at the world," we're not posing a philosophical challenge, but just referring to the ray tracer drawing the objects from a given viewpoint. In graphics, this viewpoint is called the **eye** or **camera**. Following this camera analogy, just like a camera needs film onto which the scene is projected and recorded, in graphics we have a **view window** on which we draw the scene. The difference is that while in cameras the film is placed ***behind*** the aperture or focal point, in graphics the view window is in ***front*** of the focal point. So the color of each point on real film is caused by a light ray (actually, a group of rays) that passes through the aperture and hits the film, while in computer graphics each pixel of the final image is caused by a simulated light ray that hits the view window on its path towards the eye. The results, however, are the same.

As you may have guessed, our goal is find the color of each point on the view window. We subdivide the view window into small squares, where each square corresponds to one pixel in the final image. If you want to create an image at the resolution of 640x400, you would break up the view window into a grid of 640 squares across and 400 square down. The real problem, then, is assigning a color to each square. This is what ray tracing does.

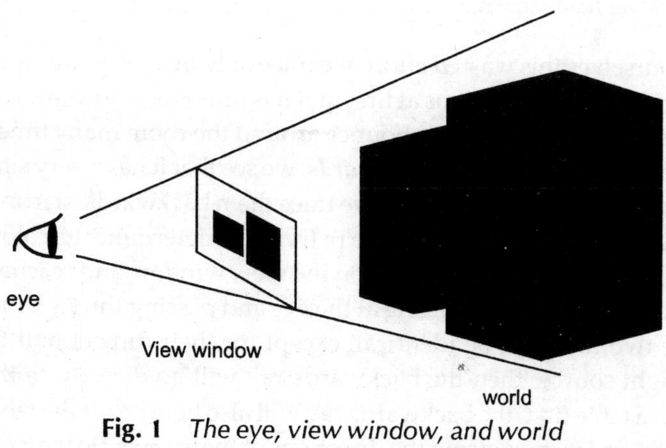

Fig. 1 *The eye, view window, and world*

How it works

Ray tracing is so named because it tries to simulate the path that light rays take as they bounce around within the world - they are *traced* through the scene. The objective is to determine the color of each light ray that strikes the view window before reaching the eye. A light ray can best be thought of as a single photon (although this is not strictly accurate because light also has wave properties - but I promised there would be no theory). The name "ray tracing" is a bit misleading because the natural assumption would be that rays are traced starting at their point of origin, the light source, and towards their destination, the eye (see Fig. 2). This would be an accurate way to do it, but unfortunately it tends to be very difficult due to the sheer numbers involved. Consider tracing one ray in this manner through a scene with one light and one object, such as a table. We begin at the light bulb, but first need to decide how many rays to shoot out from the bulb. Then for each ray we have to decide in what direction it is going. There is really an infinity of directions in which it can travel - how do we know which to choose? Let's say we've answered these questions and are now tracing a number of photons. Some will reach the eye directly, others will bounce around some and then reach the eye, and many, many more will probably never hit the eye at all. For all the rays that never reach the eye, the effort tracing them was wasted.

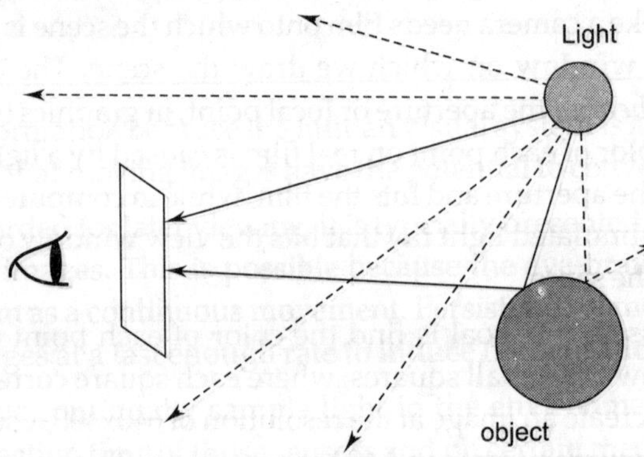

Fig. 2 *Tracing rays from the light source to the eye. Lots of rays are wasted because they never reach the eye*

In order to save ourselves this wasted effort, we trace only those rays that are ***guaranteed*** to hit the view window and reach the eye. It seems at first that it is impossible to know beforehand which rays reach the eye. After all, any given ray can bounce around the room many times before reaching the eye. However, if we look at the problem ***backwards***, we see that it has a very simple solution. Instead of tracing the rays starting at the light source, we trace them backwards, starting at the eye. Consider any point on the view window whose color we're trying to determine. Its color is given by the color of the light ray that passes through that point on the view window and reaches the eye. We can just as well follow the ray backwards by starting at the eye and passing through the point on its way out into the scene. The two rays will be identical, except for their direction: if the original ray came directly ***from*** the light source, then the backwards ray will go directly ***to*** the light source; if the original bounced off a table first, the backwards ray will also bounce off the table. You can see this by looking at Fig. 2 again and just reversing the directions of the arrows. So the backwards method does the same thing as the original method, except it doesn't waste any effort on rays that never reach the eye.

This, then, is how ray tracing works in computer graphics. For each pixel on the view window, we define a ray that extends from the eye to that point. We follow this ray out into the scene and as it bounces off of different objects. The final color of the ray (and therefore of the corresponding pixel) is given by the colors of the objects hit by the ray as it travels through the scene.

Just as in the light-source-to-eye method it might take a very large number of bounces before the ray ever hits the eye, in backwards method it might take many bounces before the ray every hits the light. Since we need to establish some limit on the number of bounces to follow the ray on, we make the following approximation: everytime a ray hits an object, we follow a single new ray from the point of intersection ***directly towards*** the light source (Fig. 3).

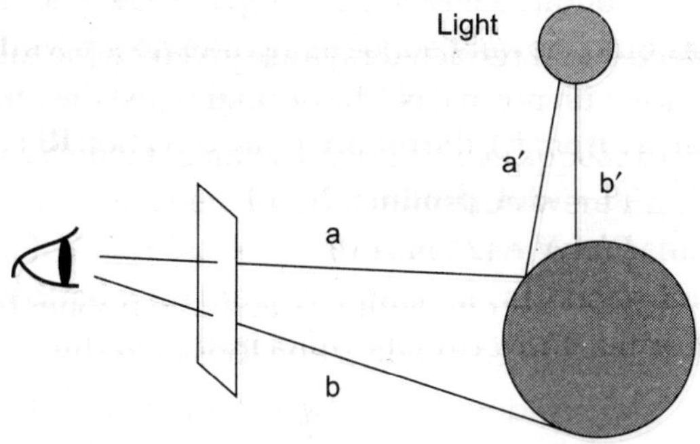

Fig. 3 *We trace a new ray from each ray-object intersection directly towards the light source*

In the figure we see two rays, **a** and **b**, which intersect the purple sphere. To determine the color of **a**, we follow the new ray **a′** directly towards the light source. The color of a will then depend on several factors, discussed in Color and Shading below. As you can see, **b** will be shadowed because the ray **b′** towards the light source is blocked by the sphere itself. Ray **a** would have also been shadowed if another object blocked the ray **a′**.

Reflection and Refraction

Just as shadows are easily handled, so are reflection and refraction. In the above example, we only considered a single bounce from the eye to the light source. To handle reflection we also consider multiple bounces from objects, and to handle refraction we consider what happens when a ray passes *through* a partially- or fully-transparent object.

If an object is reflective we simply trace a new **reflected ray** from the point of intersection towards the direction of reflection. The reflected ray is the mirror image of the original ray, pointing away from the surface. If the object is to some extent transparent, then we also trace a **refracted ray** into the surface. If the materials on either side of the surface have different **indices of refraction**, such as air on one side and water on the other, then the refracted ray will be bent, like the image of a straw in a glass of water. If the same medium exists on both sides of the surface then the refracted ray travels in the same direction as the original ray and is not bent.

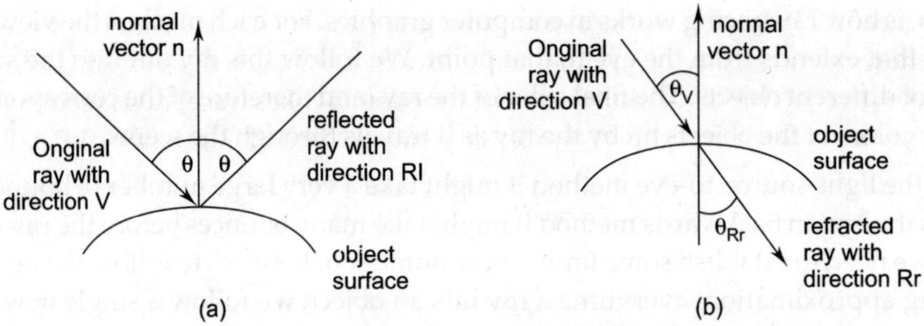

Fig. 4 *(a) Reflected ray (b) Refracted ray*

The directions of the reflected and refracted rays are given by the following formulas. For a ray with direction **V**, and a surface with normal **N** (the **normal** is just the direction perpendicular to the surface - pointing directly away from it), the reflected ray direction **Rl** is given by

$$c1 = \textbf{-dot\_product}(\,N, V\,)$$
$$Rl = V + (2 * N * c1\,)$$

Note that since **V**, **N**, and **Rl** are vectors with x, y, and z components, the arithmetic on them is performed per-component. The refracted ray direction **Rr** is given by

$$n1 = \text{index of refraction of original medium}$$
$$n2 = \text{index of refraction of new medium}$$
$$n = n1 \,/\, n2$$
$$c2 = \textbf{sqrt}(\,1 - n^2 * (1 - c1^2)\,)$$
$$Rr = (n * V) + (n * c1 - c2) * N$$

Recursive Reflection and Refraction

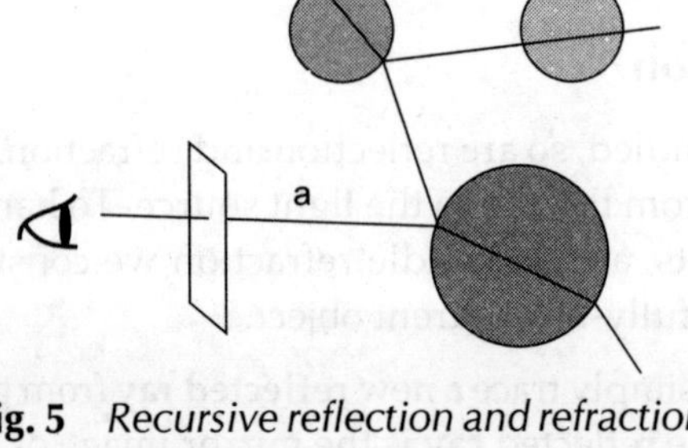

Fig. 5 *Recursive reflection and refraction*

Figure 6 shows an example of objects that are both reflective and refractive (it does not show the rays from each intersection to the light source, for the sake of clarity). Note how much more complicated the rays become once reflection and refraction are added. Now, each reflected and refracted ray can strike an object which spawns another two rays, each of ***these*** may spawn another two, and so on. This arrangement of rays spawning subrays spawning subrays leads to the idea of a ***tree of rays***. The root node of this tree is the original ray (**a** in the figure) from the eye, and each node in the tree is either a reflected or a refracted ray from the ray above it. Each leaf of the tree is either where the ray hit a non-reflective and non-transparent object, or where the tree depth reached a maximum. As complicated as it seems, there is actually a very simple way to implement this tree of rays: with **recursive function calls**. For each point on the view window we call a function trace_ray(), passing it the ray from the eye through the point. If the first object intersected by the ray is non-reflective and non-transparent, the function simply determines the color at the intersection point and returns this color. If this ray strikes a reflective object, however, the function invokes trace_ray() recursively, but with the reflected ray instead. If the intersected object is transparent, the function also calls trace_ray() with the refracted ray as a parameter. The colors returned by these two function calls are combined with the object color, and the combined color is returned. This can be easily expressed in pseudo-code as:

```
Color trace_ray( Ray original_ray )
{
        Color point_color, reflect_color, refract_color
        Object obj
        obj = get_first_intersection( original_ray )
        point_color = get_point_color( obj )
        if ( object is reflective )
        reflect_color = trace_ray(get_reflected_ray( original_ray, obj ) )
        if ( object is refractive )
        refract_color = trace_ray(get_refracted_ray(original_ray, obj ) )
        return ( combine_colors( point_color, reflect_color, refract_color ) )
}
```

where a **Color** is the triple (**R**, **G**, **B**) for the red, green, and blue components of the color, which can each vary between zero and one. This function, along with some intersection routines, is really all that is needed to write a ray tracer.

Intersections

One of the basic computations needed by the ray tracer is an intersection routine for each type of object in the scene: one for spheres, one for cubes, one for cones, and so forth. If a ray intersects an object, the object's intersection routine returns the distance of the intersection point from the origin of the ray, the normal vector at the point of intersection, and, if texture mapping is being used, a coordinate mapping between the intersection point and the texture image (discussed later in Texture Mapping). The distance to the intersection point is needed because if a ray intersects more than one object, we choose the one with the closest intersection point. The normal is used to determine the shade at the point, since it describes in which direction the surface is facing, and therefore affects how much light the point receives (see Color and Shading).

Intersecting a Sphere

For each type of object that the ray tracer supports, you need a separate intersection routine. We will limit our ray tracer to handling spheres only, since the intersection routine for a sphere is among the simplest. The following derivation of a sphere intersection is based on Glassner.

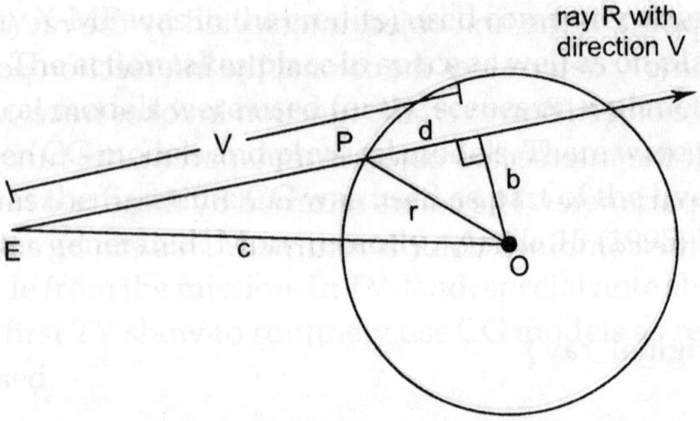

Fig. 6 *Intersection of a ray with a sphere*

Fig. 6 shows the geometry of a ray **R** (with origin at **E** and direction **V**) intersecting a sphere with center at **O** and radius r. According to the diagram,

$$v^2 + b^2 = c^2 \text{ and } d^2 + b^2 = r^2 \text{ (by simple geometry)}$$

and so $$d = \textbf{sqrt}(r^2 - (c^2 - v^2))$$

To determine whether an intersection occurs, we compute the value of **d**. If **d** >= 0, then a valid intersection occurs. If the ray does not intersect, then **d** will be less than zero. After finding the value of **d**, the distance from **E** to the intersection point **P** is (**v** – **d**). The pseudocode for all this is:

```
            v = dot_product( EO, V )
            disc = r^2 – ((dot_product( EO, EO ) – v^2 )
if ( disc < 0 )
no intersection
else        d = sqrt(disc )
            P = E + (v – d) * V
```

Color and Shading

There are many different ways to determine color at a point of intersection. Some methods are very simple - as in **flat shading**, where every point on the object has the same color. Some techniques - such as the **Cook-Torrance method** [Cook82] - are fairly complex, and take into account many physical attributes of the material in question. We will describe here a simple model known as **Lambertian shading or cosine shading**. It determines the brightness of a point based on the normal vector at the point and the vector from the point to the light source. If the two coincide (the surface directly faces the light source) then the point is at full intensity. As the angle between the two vectors increases, as when the surface is tilted away from the light, then the brightness diminishes. This model is known as "cosine shading" because that mathematical function easily implements the above effect: it returns the value 1 when given an angle of zero, and returns zero when given a ninety degree angle (when the surface and light source are perpendicular). Thus, to find the brightness of a point, we simply take the cosine of the angle between the two vectors. This value can be quickly computed because it is equal to the dot product of the two unit-length vectors. So by taking the dot product of the surface normal and the unit-length vector towards the light, we get a value between – 1 and 1. The values from – 1 to 0 indicate that the surface is ***facing away*** from the light source, so it doesn't receive any light. The value of 0 means the surface is directly perpendicular to the light source (it is at **grazing incidence**), and so again does not receive any light. Values above 0 indicate that the surface does receive some light, with maximum reception when the dot product is 1.

In case the result of the dot product is zero or below zero, we still may not want that part of the object to be pitch-black. After all, even when an object is completely blocked from a light source, there is still light bouncing around that illuminates it to some extent. For this reason we add a little bit of ambient light to every object, which means that the ***minimum*** amount of light that an object can receive is actually above zero. If we set the **ambient coefficient** to 20%, say, then even in total shadow an object will receive 20% illumination, and will thus be somewhat visible. If 20% illumination is always present, then the remaining 80% is determined by cosine shading. The value 80% in this case is known as the **diffuse coefficient**, which is just (1 - ambient coefficient). The final color computation is then:

```
        shade = dot_product( light_vector, normal_vector )
if ( shade < 0 )
        shade = 0
point_color = object_color * ( ambient_coefficient + diffuse_coefficient * shade )
```

Texture Mapping

So far we've assumed that every point on a given object has the same basic color, varied only through cosine shading to make it lighter or darker. However, there is another way to color objects, which assigns entire images to them instead of single colors. Known as **texture mapping**, in effect we "paste" images to the surfaces of objects. An example of this which certainly everyone will recognize is in the "Doom"-style games, where walls are drawn using stone or metal patterns instead of single colors. These program start off with small images of those patterns (called **textures**), and then cover the walls with these images. This covering is called a **mapping** because it maps pixels from the image onto the points comprising the walls. Texture mapping is much slower than assigning a single color to every object, since it requires determining and then fetching the appropriate texture pixel corresponding to every point we draw. It has become very common in the last few years, however, thanks to advances in processor speeds and faster graphics algorithms.

While texture mapping produces very nice effects, it is not a difficult feature to implement. All that is needed is a routine which returns the coordinates of a texture pixel given the coordinates of a point on an object. The texture coordinates are refered to as (**u**, **v**), where **u** is the horizontal location of the point in the image, and **v** is the vertical location of the point. The ray tracer then fetches the pixel at (**u**,**v**) from the texture image, and adjusts it as necessary using cosine shading to make it lighter or darker.

Texture Mapping Spheres

The easiest way to texture map onto a sphere is by defining **v** to be the latitude of the point and **u** to be the longitude of the point on the sphere. This way, the texture image will be "wrapped" around the sphere, much as a rectangular world map is wrapped around a globe.

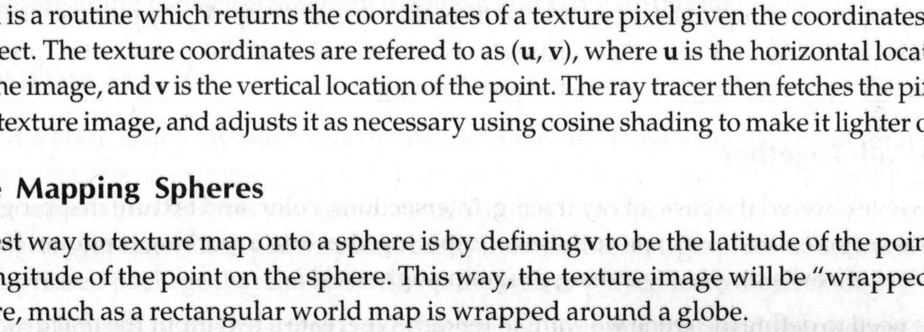

Fig. 7 *Mapping a rectangular world map onto a globe*

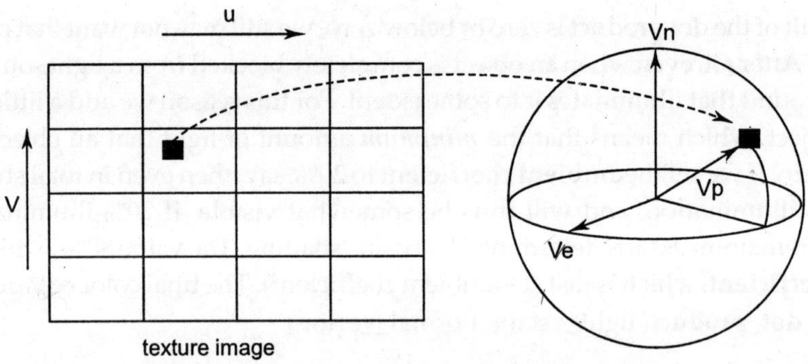

Fig. 8 *Mapping a texture image onto a sphere*

First we find the two unit-length vectors $\mathbf{V_n}$ and $\mathbf{V_e}$, which point from the center of the sphere towards the "north pole" and a point on the equator, respectively. We then find the unit-length vector $\mathbf{V_p}$, from the center of the sphere to the point we're coloring. The latitude is simply the angle between $\mathbf{V_p}$ and $\mathbf{V_n}$. Since we noted above that the dot product of two unit-length vectors is equal to the cosine of the angle between them, we can find the angle itself by

phi = **arccos(-dot_product(Vn, Vp))**

and since v needs to vary between zero and one, we let

v = phi / **PI**

We then find the longitude as

theta = (arccos(**dot_product(Vp, Ve) / sin(phi))) / (2 * PI)**

if **(dot_product(cross_product(Vn, Ve), Vp) > 0)**

u = theta

else u = 1 - theta

The last comparison simply checks on what side of the equator vector $\mathbf{V_e}$ the point is (clockwise or counterclockwise to it), and sets **u** accordingly. Now the color of the point is the pixel at (**u** * texture_width,**v** * texture_height) within the texture image.

Putting it all Together

Now that we've covered the basic of ray tracing, intersections, color, and texture mapping, it is still probably not very obvious how to piece these concepts together into a working program. Here, then, is an overview of how a simple ray tracing program might work:

First, we need to define the scene we want to render. We create a text input file that describes the objects in the scene by specifying the location, attributes (such as radius for spheres), color, and optional texture map of each object. We then specify where the camera and the view window should be located. For simplicity, we can assume that the camera is always on the Z axis pointing towards the origin, and that the view window is located at the origin. We also need to determine the size of the view window, which is specified by a **field of view** (FOV) parameter. The field of view determines the view window's size, and therefore how much of the scene is visible. Based on these parameters, we can calculate the top-left and bottom-right corners of the window.

Now that we have the top-left and bottom-right points, we divide the window into the resolution required for our output picture, e.g., 640 by 400. We step through each of the 640x400 points on the view window, defining a ray from the eye to that point. For each ray, we calculate its intersection with all the objects in the scene. If it does not intersect any objects, we set the ray - and therefore the corresponding pixel - to the background color. Otherwise, we choose the object with the closest intersection. If the object is reflective, we call the ray-tracing function again recursively, passing it the reflected ray direction. If the object is transparent, we do the same thing with the refracted direction. The calling function then computes the color for the object it is dealing with, and combines this color with the reflected and refracted rays' colors.

When the original ray-tracing call from the eye to the view window returns, the color will be the final color for that pixel - taking into account reflection, refraction, and shadows. This pixel color is then written out to the output file. When all points on the view window have been processed this way, you will have a finished ray-traced picture.

Internet Resources

There are many ray tracing resources on the Internet. Here's some of the best:

- There's a free, powerful ray tracing program called ***POV-Ray*** (for Persistence of Vision Ray Tracer), available for almost every platform at http://www.povray.org. It comes in both binary and source form, and their web page has links to other ray tracing information as well as a beautiful gallery of images created with POV-Ray.
- Radiance (http://radsite.lbl.gov/radiance/HOME.html) is a ray tracer geared towards analysis of lighting, rather than just making pretty pictures.
- Rayshade (http://www-graphics.stanford.edu/~cek/rayshade/rayshade.html) is a fast ray tracer with support for parallel processing.
- The Blue Moon Rendering Tools (http://www.seas.gwu.edu/student/gritz/bmrt.html) is a ray tracer that implements the Renderman shading language. This language is used by such companies as Industrial Light & Magic and Pixar to create just about every mind-blowing computer special effect in the last twenty years. The professional software is rather expensive, so this free package by Larry Gritz is an ideal way to play with the Renderman language.
- A good general ray tracing page can be found at http://www.cm.cf.ac.uk/Ray.Tracing/, with links to ray tracing information and more ray-tracing software.

3. Rendering: Another Important Topic in Graphics

Rendering is the process of generating an image from a model, by means of computer programs. The model is a description of three dimensional objects in a strictly defined language or data structure. It would contain geometry, viewpoint, texture, lighting, and shading information. The image is a digital image or raster graphics image. The term may be by analogy with an "artist's rendering" of a scene. 'Rendering' is also used to describe the process of calculating effects in a video editing file to produce final video output.

It is one of the major sub-topics of 3D computer graphics, and in practice always connected to the others. In the graphics pipeline, it is the last major step, giving the final appearance to the models and animation. With the increasing sophistication of computer graphics since the 1970s onward, it has become a more distinct subject.

Rendering has uses in architecture, video games, simulators, movie or TV special effects, and design visualization, each employing a different balance of features and techniques. As a product, a wide variety of renderers are available. Some are integrated into larger modeling and animation packages, some are stand-alone, some are free open-source projects. On the inside, a renderer is a carefully engineered program, based on a selective mixture of disciplines related to: light physics, visual perception, mathematics, and software development.

In the case of 3D graphics, rendering may be done slowly, as in pre-rendering, or in real time. Pre-rendering is a computationally intensive process that is typically used for movie creation, while real-time rendering is often done for 3D video games which rely on the use of graphics cards with 3D hardware accelerators.

When the pre-image (a wireframe sketch usually) is complete, rendering is used, which adds in bitmap textures or procedural textures, lights, bump mapping, and relative position to other objects. The result is a completed image the consumer or intended viewer sees.

For movie animations, several images (frames) must be rendered, and stitched together in a program capable of making an animation of this sort. Most 3D image editing programs can do this.

A rendered image can be understood in terms of a number of visible features. Rendering research and development has been largely motivated by finding ways to simulate these efficiently. Some relate directly to particular algorithms and techniques, while others are produced together.

- **shading** — how the color and brightness of a surface varies with lighting
- **texture-mapping** — a method of applying detail to surfaces
- **bump-mapping** — a method of simulating small-scale bumpiness on surfaces
- **fogging/participating medium** — how light dims when passing through non-clear atmosphere or air
- **shadows** — the effect of obstructing light
- **soft shadows** — varying darkness caused by partially obscured light sources
- **reflection** — mirror-like or highly glossy reflection
- **transparency** — sharp transmission of light through solid objects
- **translucency** — highly scattered transmission of light through solid objects
- **refraction** — bending of light associated with transparency
- **diffraction** — bending, spreading and interference of light passing by an object or aperture that disrupts the ray
- **indirect illumination** — surfaces illuminated by light reflected off other surfaces, rather than directly from a light source (also known as global illumination)
- **caustics (a form of indirect illumination)** — reflection of light off a shiny object, or focusing of light through a transparent object, to produce bright highlights on another object
- **depth of field** — objects appear blurry or out of focus when too far in front of or behind the object in focus
- **motion blur** — objects appear blurry due to high-speed motion, or the motion of the camera
- **photorealistic morphing** — photoshopping 3D renderings to appear more life-like
- **non-photorealistic rendering** — rendering of scenes in an artistic style, intended to look like a painting or drawing

Many rendering algorithms have been researched, and software used for rendering may employ a number of different techniques to obtain a final image.

Tracing every ray of light in a scene would be impractical and would take gigantic amounts of time. Even tracing a portion large enough to produce an image takes an inordinate amount of time if the sampling is not intelligently restricted.

Therefore, four loose families of more-efficient light transport modelling techniques have emerged: **rasterisation**, including **scanline rendering**, considers the objects in the scene and projects them to form an image, with no facility for generating a point-of-view perspective effect; **ray casting** considers the scene as observed from a specific point-of-view, calculating the observed image based only on geometry and very basic optical laws of reflection intensity, and perhaps using Monte Carlo techniques to reduce artifacts; **radiosity** uses finite element mathematics to simulate diffuse spreading of light from surfaces; and **ray tracing** is similar to ray casting, but employs more advanced optical simulation, and usually uses Monte Carlo techniques to obtain more realistic results at a speed that is often orders of magnitude slower.

Most advanced software combines two or more of the techniques to obtain good-enough results at reasonable cost.

Scanline rendering and rasterisation

A high-level representation of an image necessarily contains elements in a different domain from pixels. These elements are referred to as primitives. In a schematic drawing, for instance, line segments and curves might be primitives. In a graphical user interface, windows and buttons might be the primitives. In 3D rendering, triangles and polygons in space might be primitives.

If a pixel-by-pixel approach to rendering is impractical or too slow for some task, then a primitive-by-primitive approach to rendering may prove useful. Here, one loops through each of the primitives, determines which pixels in the image it affects, and modifies those pixels accordingly. This is called **rasterization**, and is the rendering method used by all current graphics cards.

Rasterization is frequently faster than pixel-by-pixel rendering. First, large areas of the image may be empty of primitives; rasterization will ignore these areas, but pixel-by-pixel rendering must pass through them. Second, rasterization can improve cache coherency and reduce redundant work by taking advantage of the fact that the pixels occupied by a single primitive tend to be contiguous in the image. For these reasons, rasterization is usually the approach of choice when interactive rendering is required; however, the pixel-by-pixel approach can often produce higher-quality images and is more versatile because it does not depend on as many assumptions about the image as rasterization.

Rasterization exists in two main forms, not only when an entire face (primitive) is rendered but when the vertices of a face are all rendered and then the pixels on the face which lie between the vertices rendered using simple blending of each vertex colour to the next, this version of rasterization has overtaken the old method as it allows the graphics to flow without complicated textures (a rasterized image when used face by face tends to have a very block-like effect if not covered in complex textures; the faces aren't smooth because there is no gradual color change from one pixel to the next), utilizing the graphics card's more taxing shading functions and still achieving better performance because the simpler textures stored in memory use less space. Sometimes designers will use one rasterization method on some faces and the other method on others based on the angle at which that face meets other joined faces, thus increasing speed and not hurting the overall effect.

Ray casting

Ray casting is primarily used for realtime simulations, such as those used in 3D computer games and cartoon animations, where detail is not important, or where it is more efficient to manually fake the details in order to obtain better performance in the computational stage. This is usually the case when a large number of frames need to be animated. The resulting surfaces have a characteristic 'flat' appearance when no additional tricks are used, as if objects in the scene were all painted with matte finish.

The geometry which has been modeled is parsed pixel by pixel, line by line, from the point of view outward, as if casting rays out from the point of view. Where an object is intersected, the color value at the point may be evaluated using several methods. In the simplest, the color value of the object at the point of intersection becomes the value of that pixel. The color may be determined from a texture-map. A more sophisticated method is to modify the colour value by an illumination factor, but without calculating the relationship to a simulated light source. To reduce artifacts, a number of rays in slightly different directions may be averaged.

Rough simulations of optical properties may be additionally employed: a simple calculation of the ray from the object to the point of view is made. Another calculation is made of the angle of incidence of light rays from the light source(s), and from these as well as the specified intensities of the light sources, the value of the pixel is calculated. Another simulation uses illumination plotted from a radiosity algorithm, or a combination of these two.

Radiosity

Radiosity, also known as Global Illumination, is a method which attempts to simulate the way in which directly illuminated surfaces act as indirect light sources that illuminate other surfaces. This produces more realistic shading and seems to better capture the 'ambience' of an indoor scene. A classic example is the way that shadows 'hug' the corners of rooms.

The optical basis of the simulation is that some diffused light from a given point on a given surface is reflected in a large spectrum of directions and illuminates the area around it.

The simulation technique may vary in complexity. Many renderings have a very rough estimate of radiosity, simply illuminating an entire scene very slightly with a factor known as ambiance. However, when advanced radiosity estimation is coupled with a high quality ray tracing algorithim, images may exhibit convincing realism, particularly for indoor scenes.

In advanced radiosity simulation, recursive, finite-element algorithms 'bounce' light back and forth between surfaces in the model, until some recursion limit is reached. The colouring of one surface in this way influences the colouring of a neighbouring surface, and vice versa. The resulting values of illumination throughout the model (sometimes including for empty spaces) are stored and used as additional inputs when performing calculations in a ray-casting or ray-tracing model.

Due to the iterative/recursive nature of the technique, complex objects are particularly slow to emulate. Advanced radiosity calculations may be reserved for calulating the ambiance of the room, from the light reflecting off walls, floor and celiing, without examining the contribution that complex objects make to the radiosity -- or complex objects may be replaced in the radiosity calculation with simpler objects of similar size and texture.

If there is little rearrangement of radiosity objects in the scene, the same radiosity data may be reused for a number of frames, making radiosity an effective way to improve on the flatness of ray casting, without seriously impacting the overall rendering time-per-frame.

Because of this, radiosity has become the leading real-time rendering method, and has been used from beginning-to-end to create a large number of well-known recent feature-length animated 3D-cartoon films.

Ray tracing

Ray tracing is an extension of the same technique developed in scanline rendering and ray casting. Like those, it handles complicated objects well, and the objects may be described mathematically. Unlike scanline and casting, ray tracing is almost always a Monte Carlo technique, that is one based on averaging a number of randomly generated samples from a model.

In this case, the samples are imaginary rays of light intersecting the viewpoint from the objects in the scene. It is primarily beneficial where complex and accurate rendering of shadows, refraction or reflection are issues.

In a final, production quality rendering of a ray traced work, multiple rays are generally shot for each pixel, and traced not just to the first object of intersection, but rather, through a number of sequential 'bounces', using the known laws of optics such as "angle of incidence equals angle of reflection" and more advanced laws that deal with refraction and surface roughness.

Once the ray either encounters a light source, or more probably once a set limiting number of bounces has been evaluated, then the surface illumination at that final point is evaluated using techniques described above, and the changes along the way through the various bounces evaluated to estimate a value observed at the point of view. This is all repeated for each sample, for each pixel.

In some cases, at each point of intersection, multiple rays may be spawned.

As a brute-force method, ray tracing has been too slow to consider for real-time, and until recently too slow even to consider for short films of any degree of quality, although it has been used for special effects sequences, and in advertising, where a short portion of high quality (perhaps even photorealistic) footage is required.

However, efforts at optimizing to reduce the number of calculations needed in portions of a work where detail is not high or does not depend on ray tracing features have led to a realistic possibility of wider use of ray tracing. There is now some hardware accelerated ray tracing equipment, at least in prototype phase, and some game demos which show use of real-time software or hardware ray tracing.

Optimisations used by an artist when a scene is being developed

Due to the large number of calculations, a work in progress is usually only rendered in detail appropriate to the portion of the work being developed at a given time, so in the initial stages of modelling, wireframe and ray casting may be used, even where the target output is ray tracing with radiosity. It is also common to render only parts of the scene at high detail, and to remove objects that are not important to what is currently being developed.

Common optimisations for real time rendering

For real-time, it is appropriate to simplify one or more common approximations, and tune to the exact parameters of the scenery in question, which is also tuned to the agreed parameters to get the most 'bang for the buck'.

Sampling and filtering

One problem that any rendering system must deal with, no matter which approach it takes, is the **sampling problem**. Essentially, the rendering process tries to depict a continuous function from image space to colors by using a finite number of pixels. As a consequence of the Nyquist theorem, the scanning frequency must be twice the dot rate, which is proportional to image resolution. In simpler terms, this expresses the idea that an image cannot display details smaller than one pixel.

If a naive rendering algorithm is used, high frequencies in the image function will cause ugly aliasing to be present in the final image. Aliasing typically manifests itself as jaggies, or jagged edges on objects where the pixel grid is visible. In order to remove aliasing, all rendering algorithms (if they are to produce good-looking images) must filter the image function to remove high frequencies, a process called antialiasing.

Academic core

The implementation of a realistic renderer always has some basic element of physical simulation or emulation - some computation which resembles or abstracts a real physical process.

The term *"physically-based"* indicates the use of physical models and approximations that are more general and widely accepted outside rendering. A particular set of related techniques have gradually become established in the rendering community.

The basic concepts are moderately straightforward, but intractable to calculate; and a single elegant algorithm or approach has been elusive for more general purpose renderers. In order to meet demands of robustness, accuracy, and practicality, an implementation will be a complex combination of different techniques.

Rendering research is concerned with both the adaptation of scientific models and their efficient application.

The rendering equation

This is the key academic/theoretical concept in rendering. It serves as the most abstract formal expression of the non-perceptual aspect of rendering. All more complete algorithms can be seen as solutions to particular formulations of this equation.

$$L_o(x, \vec{w}) = L_e(x, \vec{w}) + \int_{\Omega} f_r(x, \vec{w}', \vec{w})\, L_i(x, \vec{w}')\, (\vec{w}' \cdot \vec{n})\, d\vec{w}'$$

Meaning: at a particular position and direction, the outgoing light (L_o) is the sum of the emitted light (L_e) and the reflected light. The reflected light being the sum of the incoming light (L_i) from all directions, multiplied by the surface reflection and incoming angle. By connecting outward light to inward light, via an interaction point, this equation stands for the whole 'light transport' - all the movement of light - in a scene.

The Bidirectional Reflectance Distribution Function

The Bidirectional Reflectance Distribution Function (BRDF) expresses a simple model of light interaction with a surface as follows:

$$f_r(x, \vec{w}, \vec{w}) = \frac{dL_r(x, \vec{w})}{L_i(x, \vec{w}')(\vec{w}' \cdot \vec{n})\, d\vec{w}'}$$

Light interaction is often approximated by the even simpler models: diffuse reflection and specular reflection, although both can be BRDFs.

Geometric optics

Rendering is practically exclusively concerned with the particle aspect of light physics - known as geometric optics. Treating light, at its basic level, as particles bouncing around is a simplification, but appropriate: the wave aspects of light are negligible in most scenes, and are significantly more difficult to simulate. Notable wave aspect phenomena include diffraction - as seen in the colours of CDs and DVDs - and polarisation - as seen in LCDs. Both types of effect, if needed, are made by appearance-oriented adjustment of the reflection model.

Visual perception

Though it receives less attention, an understanding of human visual perception is valuable to rendering. This is mainly because image displays and human perception have restricted ranges. A renderer can simulate an almost infinite range of light brightness and color, but current displays - movie screen, computer monitor, etc. – cannot handle so much, and something must be discarded or compressed. Human perception also has limits, and so doesn't need to be given large-range images to create realism. This can help solve the problem of fitting images into displays, and, furthermore, suggest what short-cuts could be used in the rendering simulation, since certain subtleties won't be noticeable. This related subject is tone mapping.

Mathematics used in rendering includes: linear algebra, calculus, numerical mathematics, signal processing, monte carlo.

See also

- the painter's algorithm
- Scanline algorithms like Reyes
- Z-buffer algorithms
- Global illumination
- Radiosity
- Ray tracing
- Volume rendering

Rendering for movies often takes place on a network of tightly connected computers known as a render farm.

The current state of the art in 3-D image description for movie creation is the RenderMan scene description language designed at Pixar. (compare with simpler 3D fileformats such as VRML or APIs such as OpenGL and DirectX tailored for 3D hardware accelerators).

Movie type rendering software includes:

- RenderMan compliant renderers
- Mental Ray
- **Indigo**
- Brazil
- Blender (may also be used for modeling)

4. Color Models: Another Important Topic in Graphics

The **RGB color model** is an additive model in which red, green, and blue (often used in additive light models) are combined in various ways to reproduce other colors. The name of the model and the abbreviation 'RGB' come from the three primary colors, red, green, and blue and the technological development of cathode ray tubes which could display color instead of a monochrome phosphoresence (including grey scaling) such as black and white film and television imaging

The term **RGBA** is also used to mean Red, Green, Blue, Alpha. This is not a different color model, but a representation; the Alpha is used for transparency.

These three colors should not be confused with the primary pigments of red, blue, and yellow, known in the art world as 'primary colors', as the latter combine based on reflection and absorption of photons whereas RGB depends on emission of photons from (in the case of a Cathode ray tube display) a compound excited to a higher energy state by impact with an electron beam.

The RGB color model itself does not define what is meant by 'red', 'green' and 'blue' (spectroscopically), and so the results of mixing them are not specified as exact (but relative, and averaged by the human eye).

When the exact spectral make-up of the red, green and blue primaries are defined, the color model would then become what is known in science and engineering as an absolute color space, such as sRGB or Adobe RGB; see RGB color spaces for more details.

This topic discusses concepts common to all the different RGB color spaces that use the RGB color model, which are used in one implementation or another historically in color image producing electronics technology

An RGB image, along with its separate R, G and B components; Note that the white snow consists of strong red, green and blue; the brown barn is composed of strong red and green with little blue; the dark green grass consists of strong green with little red or blue; and the light blue sky is composed of strong blue and moderately strong red and green.

Additive primary colors

The choice of 'primary' colors is related to the physiology of the human eye; good primaries are stimuli that maximize the difference between the responses of the cone cells of the human retina to light of different wavelengths, and that thereby make a large **color triangle**.

A set of primary colors, such as the sRGB primaries, define a **color triangle**; only colors within this triangle can be reproduced by mixing the primary colors. Colors outside the color triangle are therefore shown here as gray. The primaries and the D65 white point of sRGB are shown.

The normal three kinds of light-sensitive photoreceptor cells in the human eye (cone cells) respond most to yellow (long wavelength or L), green (medium or M) and violet (short or S) light (peak wavelengths near 570 nm, 540 nm and 440 nm respectively[1]). The difference in the signals received from the three kinds allows the brain to differentiate a wide gamut of different colors, while being most sensitive (overall) to yellowish-green light and to differences between hues in the green-to-orange region.

As an example, suppose that light in the orange range of wavelengths (approximately 577 nm to 597 nm) enters the eye and strikes the retina. Light of these wavelengths would activate both the medium and long wavelength cones of the retina, but not equally–the long-wavelength cells will respond more. The difference in the response can be detected by the brain and associated with the concept that the light is 'orange'. In this sense, the orange appearance of objects is simply the result of light from the object entering our eye and stimulating the relevant kinds of cones simultaneously but to different degrees.

Use of the three primary colors is not sufficient to reproduce all colors; only colors within the color triangle defined by the chromaticities of the primaries can be reproduced by additive mixing of non-negative amounts of those colors of light.

RGB and displays

One common application of the RGB color model is the display of colors on a cathode ray tube, liquid crystal display or plasma display, such as a television or a computer's monitor. Each pixel on the screen can be represented in the computer or interface hardware (for example, a 'graphics card') as values for red, green, and blue. These values are converted into intensities or voltages via gamma correction, such that the intended intensities are reproduced on the display.

By using an appropriate combination of red, green, and blue intensities, many colors can be represented. Typical display adapters in 2007 use up to 24 bits of information for each pixel. This is usually apportioned with 8 bits each for red, green and blue, giving a range of 256 possible values, or intensities, for each hue. With this system, 16,777,216 (256^3 or 2^{24}) discrete combinations of hue, saturation, and lightness can be specified, though not necessarily distinguished.

Video electronics

RGB pixels in an LCD TV (on the right: an orange and a blue color; on the left: a closeup of pixels)

RGB is a type of component video signal used in the video electronics industry. It consists of three signals-red, green and blue-carried on three separate cables/pins. Extra cables are sometimes needed to carry synchronizing signals. RGB signal formats are often based on modified versions of the RS-170 and RS-343 standards for monochrome video. This type of video signal is widely used in Europe since it is the best quality signal that can be carried on the standard SCART connector. Outside Europe, RGB is not very popular as a video signal format; S-Video takes that spot in most non-European regions. However, almost all computer monitors around the world use RGB.

Nonlinearity

Due to gamma correction, the intensity of the color output on computer display devices is normally not directly proportional to the R, G, and B values in image files. That is, even though a value of 0.5

is very close to halfway between 0 and 1.0 (full intensity), the light intensity of a computer display device when displaying (0.5, 0.5, 0.5) is normally (on a standard 2.2-gamma CRT/LCD) only about 22% of that when displaying (1.0, 1.0, 1.0), instead of at 50%.

Professional color calibration

Proper reproduction of colors in professional environments requires extensive color calibration of all the devices involved in the production process. This results in several transparent conversions between device-dependent color spaces during a typical production cycle in order to ensure color consistency throughout the process. Along with the creative processing, all such interventions on digital images inherently damage it by reducing its gamut. Therefore the denser the gamut of the original digitized image, the more processing it can support without visible degradation. Professional devices and software tools allow for 48 bpp (bits per pixel) images to be manipulated (16 bits per channel) in order to increase the density of the gamut.

Representations

Numeric representations

The RGB color model mapped to a cube (with cut-away shown)

A color in the RGB color model can be described by indicating how much of each of the red, green and blue color is included. Each can vary between the minimum (no color) and maximum (full intensity). If all the colors are at minimum the result is black. If all the colors at maximum, the result is white. A confusing aspect of the RGB color model is that these colors may be written in several different ways.

- Color science talks about colors in the range 0.0 (minimum) to 1.0 (maximum). Most color formulae take these values. For instance, full intensity red is 1.0, 0.0, 0.0.
- The color values may be written as percentages, from 0% (minimum) to 100% (maximum). To convert from the range 0.0 to 1.0, see percentage. Full intensity red is 100%, 0%, 0%.
- The color values may be written as numbers in the range 0 to 255, simply by multiplying the range 0.0 to 1.0 by 255. This is commonly found in computer science, where programmers have found it convenient to store each color value in one 8-bit byte. This convention has become so widespread that many writers now consider the range 0 to 255 authoritative and do not give a context for their values. Full intensity red is 255,0,0.
- The same range, 0 to 255, is sometimes written in hexadecimal, sometimes with a prefix (e.g. #). Because hexadecimal numbers in this range can be written with a fixed two digit format, the full intensity red #ff, #00, #00 might be contracted to #ff0000. This convention is used in web colors and is also considered by some writers to be authoritative.

24-bit representation

When written, RGB values in 24 bits per pixel (bpp), also known as Truecolor, are commonly specified using three integers between 0 and 255, each representing red, green and blue intensities, in that order. For example, the following image shows the three "fully saturated" faces of the RGB cube, unfolded into a plane:

- (0, 0, 0) is black
- (255, 255, 255) is white
- (255, 0, 0) is red
- (0, 255, 0) is green
- (0, 0, 255) is blue
- (255, 255, 0) is yellow
- (0, 255, 255) is cyan
- (255, 0, 255) is magenta

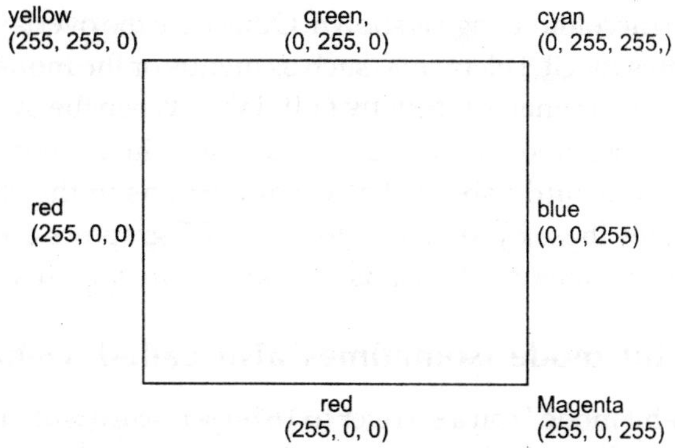

The above definition uses a convention known as *full-range* RGB. This convention is so often used that some people have come to view it as universal. This can be confusing because color values are also often considered to be in the range 0.0 through 1.0, rather than 0 to 255 (the latter range is used when colors are encoded in eight bits, which encoding permits 256 different values (sometimes written using two hexadecimal characters)). If in doubt, it is best to describe the range over which a color is specified.

Full-range RGB can represent up to two hundred and fifty-five shades of a given hue. (Only pure reds, greens, blues or greys have this full range of shades.)

Typically, RGB for digital video is not full range. Instead, video RGB uses a convention with scaling and offsets such that (16, 16, 16) is black, (235, 235, 235) is white, etc. For example, these scalings and offsets are used for the digital RGB definition in CCIR 601.

Memory space

The amount of memory space used by an uncompressed image is specified by the number of pixels in the image and the colour depth to which each pixel is specified. In a 24-bit image, each pixel is specified by a 24-bit allocation of memory, so the amount of space required in bits is 24 x the number of pixels. To calculate the memory required in bytes, the resulting number should be divided by 8 (8 bits in a byte).

E.g. A 24-bit image 640 x 480 pixels in size

24 x 640 x 480 = 7,372,800 bits
7,372,800 / 8 = 921,600 bytes

16-bit mode

There is also a 16 bpp mode (sometimes called Highcolor), in which there are either 5 bits per color, called 555 mode, or an extra bit for green (because the green component contributes most to the brightness of a color in the human eye), called 565 mode.

32-bit mode

The so-called 32 bpp mode is almost always identical in precision to the 24 bpp mode; there are still only eight bits per component, and the eight extra bits are often not used at all. The reason for the existence of the 32 bpp mode is the higher speed at which most modern hardware can access data that is aligned to byte addresses evenly divisible by a power of two, compared to data not so aligned.

Some graphics hardware allows the unused byte to be used as an 8-bit paletted overlay. A certain palette entry (often 0 or 255) is designated as being transparent, i.e., where the overlay is this value the truecolour image is shown. Otherwise the overlay value is looked up in the palette and used. This allows for GUI elements (such as menus or the mouse cursor) or information to be overlayed over a truecolour image without modifying it. When the overlay needs to be removed, it is simply cleared to the transparent value and the truecolour image is displayed again. This feature was often found on graphics hardware for Unix workstations in the 90s and later on some PC graphics cards (most notably those by Matrox). However, PC graphics cards (and the systems they are used in) now have plentiful memory to use as a backing store and this feature has mostly disappeared.

48-bit mode (sometimes also called 16-bit mode)

"16-bit mode" can also refer to 16 bit *per component*, resulting in 48 bpp. This modes makes it possible to represent 65536 tones of each color component instead of 256. This is primarily used in professional image editing, like Adobe Photoshop for maintaining greater precision when a sequence of more than one image filtering algorithms is used on the image. With only 8 bit per component, rounding errors tend to accumulate with each filtering algorithm that is employed, distorting the end result.

RGBA

With the need for compositing images came a variant of RGB which includes an extra 8-bit channel for transparency, thus resulting in a 32 bpp format. The transparency channel is commonly known as the alpha channel, so the format is named RGBA. Note that since it does not change anything in the RGB model, RGBA is not a distinct color model, it is only a file format which integrates transparency information along with the color information in the same file. This allows for alpha blending of the image over another, and is a feature of the PNG format. (Note: RGBA is not the only method to have transparency in graphics. See Transparency (graphic) for alternatives).

Digital cameras that use a CMOS or CCD image sensor often operate with the RGB system; the sensor can have a grid of red, green, and blue detectors arranged so that the first row is RGRGRGRG and the next is GBGBGBGB and so on. In a Bayer filter, green is given more detectors than red and blue in order to achieve higher luminance resolution than chrominance resolution. Demoasicing and matrixing processes are required to map the camera RGB measurements into a standard RGB color space.

Colors in web-page design

Colors used in web-page design are commonly specified using RGB; Initially, the limited color depth of most video hardware led to a limited color palette of 216 RGB colors, defined by the Netscape Color Cube. However, with the predominance of 24-bit displays, the use of the full 16.7 million colors of the HTML RGB color code no longer poses problems for most viewers.

In short, the web-safe color palette consists of the 216 combinations of red, green and blue where each color can take one of six values (in hexadecimal): #00, #33, #66, #99, #CC or #FF (based on the 0 to 255 range for each value discussed above). Clearly, $6^3 = 216$. These hexadecimal values = 0, 51, 102, 153, 204, 255 in decimal, which = 0%, 20%, 40%, 60%, 80%, 100% in terms of intensity. This seems fine for splitting up 216 colors into a cube of dimension 6. However, lacking gamma correction, the perceived intensity on a standard 2.5 gamma CRT / LCD is only: 0%, 2%, 10%, 28%, 57%, 100%. See the actual web safe color palette for a visual confirmation that the majority of the colors produced are very dark, or see Xona.com Color List for a side by side comparison of proper colors next to their equivalent lacking proper gamma correction.

The RGB color model for HTML was formally adopted as an Internet standard in HTML 3.2, however it had been in use for some time before that.

History of RGB color model

The RGB color model is based on the Young-Helmholtz theory of trichromatic color vision, and on Maxwell's color triangle that elaborated that theory.

The use of the RGB color model as the standard for presentation of color on the Internet has its roots in the 1953 RCA color-TV standards and in Edwin Land's use of an RGB standard in the Land/Polaroid camera.

5. OpenGl: Another Important Topic in Graphics

OpenGL is a library of functions for fast 3D rendering.

What OpenGL is not

OpenGL does not have any way to obtain input from the user. In order to do this you must use XLib calls or some sort of toolkit like Tcl/Tk or Motif.

Additional libraries

There are two libraries that we have that came with OpenGL. One is **glu** and the other is **glX**.

- **glu** is a set of utility functions. They are easy ways of doing things that are tedious with raw OpenGL.
- **glX** allows you to open up an X Window and link it up with OpenGL so that it will draw to that window.

A simple OpenGL program

The following program will open a window and render a red triangle in 3-space from a particular viewpoint:

```
#include "GL/glx.h"
#include "GL/gl.h"
#include "GL/glu.h"
#include "iostream.h"

void
OpenGLWindow(unsigned int width,
        unsigned int height,
        Display *&dpy,
        Window &win,
        GLXContext &cx)
```

```
{
    XVisualInfo *vi;
    Colormap cmap;
    XSetWindowAttributes swa;
    XEvent event;
    int attributeList[] = { GLX_RGBA, GLX_DOUBLEBUFFER,
                             GLX_DEPTH_SIZE, 24, None };
    /* get a connection */
    dpy = XOpenDisplay(0);

    /* get an appropriate visual */
    vi = glXChooseVisual(dpy, DefaultScreen(dpy), attributeList);
    if (vi == 0)
      {
        cout << "Couldn't get a spiffy visual -> no window" << endl;
      }

    /* create a GLX context */
    cx = glXCreateContext(dpy, vi, 0, GL_TRUE);

    /* create a color map */
    cmap = XCreateColormap(dpy, RootWindow(dpy, vi->screen),
                   vi->visual, AllocNone);

    /* create a window */
    swa.colormap = cmap;
    swa.border_pixel = 0;
    swa.event_mask = StructureNotifyMask;
    win = XCreateWindow(dpy, RootWindow(dpy, vi->screen), 0, 0, width, height,
                   0, vi->depth, InputOutput, vi->visual,
                   CWBorderPixel | CWColormap | CWEventMask, &swa);

    XMapWindow(dpy, win);

    /* Wait for it to be placed on the screen */
    while(1)
      {
        XNextEvent(dpy,&event);
```

```
    if ((event.type == MapNotify) && (event.xmap.window == win))
        break;
  }

  /* connect the context to the window */
  glXMakeCurrent(dpy, win, cx);
}

int
main()
{
  Display *dpy;
  Window win;
  GLXContext cx;

  // Need a pointer to the display and window being
  // used in order to do double buffering.
  // See glXSwapBuffers.
  OpenGLWindow(800,800,dpy,win,cx);

  glClear(GL_COLOR_BUFFER_BIT);
  glMatrixMode(GL_PROJECTION);
  glLoadIdentity();
  gluPerspective(40,1,1,50);
  glMatrixMode(GL_MODELVIEW);
  glLoadIdentity();
  gluLookAt(0,0,10,0,0,0,0,1,0);

  glBegin(GL_TRIANGLES);
  glColor3f(1,0,0);
  glVertex3f(-1,0,0);
  glVertex3f(1,0,0);
  glVertex3f(0,1,0);
  glEnd();
  glXSwapBuffers(dpy,win);

  sleep(10);
}
```

The function **OpenGLWindow()** opens up a window and returns three identifiers (**dpy, win,** and **cx**) which allow us to switch between different X Windows for OpenGL to draw on and different contexts (OpenGL state) in which to draw in.

We now clear the framebuffer with the **glClear(GL_COLOR_BUFFER_BIT)** statement.

Then we set up the perspective projection matrix. First we specify that we want to be working on the projection matrix with the **glMatrixMode(GL_PROJECTION)** statement. We then "clear" the matrix by loading the identity matrix onto it. Then we multiply the identity matrix with a matrix what will give us a 40 degree y field of view, a 1.0 x-y aspect ratio, a near clipping plane at 1, and a far clipping plane at 50.

We then switch to the ModelView matrix onto which we load the identity matrix and then specify that we want to look from (0,0,10) to (0,0,0) with an up vector of (0,1,0).

The **glBegin(GL_TRIANGLES)** statement tells OpenGL that we will now be describing triangles for it to be drawn on the screen.

The **glColor3f(1,0,0)** statement says that the current color to use is red.

The **glVertex3f(...)** statements describe the 3D vertices for our triangle.

The **glEnd()** statement matches the **glBegin(GL_TRIANGLES)** statement and says that we are finished describing the triangles to be drawn.

Finally, the **glXSwapBuffers()** call brings the back buffer to the front so we can see what we drew.

At this point, the triangle will be drawn. We then wait a while and finally exit the program.

Geometry

Geometric primitives are described by **glBegin()...glEnd()** pairs. For example, to draw a triangle you would use the following statements:

```
glBegin(GL_TRIANGLES);
glColor3f(...);
glVertex3f(...);
glVertex3f(...);
glVertex3f(...);
glEnd();
```

The argument to glBegin describes what type of primitive you want to draw. The possibilities are:

GL_POINTS

GL_LINES

GL_LINE_STRIP

GL_LINE_LOOP

GL_TRIANGLES

GL_TRIANGLE_STRIP

GL_TRIANGLE_FAN

GL_QUADS

GL_QUAD_STRIP

GL_POLYGON

glEnd() indicates when you wish to stop drawing that type of primitive. This is necessary because there can be an arbitrary number of vertices for a type of primitive (e.g. we could have used 6 **glVertex()** calls to describe 2 triangles or 9 to describe 3 triangles, etc.)

glVertex()

There are several **glVertex()** calls, one for each type and number of arguments you can specify a vertex with:

glVertex[234][dfis][v]

For example, if I wanted to describe a vertex with double precision floating point and only wanted to specify x,y, and z (no w), I would use

```
GLdouble x,y,z;
glVertex3d(x,y,z);
```

If I wanted to specify w, but using short integers and I already had an array in which the values were stored, I would use

```
GLshort array[4];
glVertex4sv(array);
```

Color

OpenGL has a concept of a current color, a current normal, and current texture coordinates. When you make a glVertex call, those values are associated with the vertex you just specified.

```
glBegin(GL_TRIANGLES);
glColor3f(1,0,0);
glVertex(...);
glVertex(...);
glColor3f(0,1,0);
glVertex(...);
glEnd()
```

In the preceeding code chunk, the first 2 vertices of the triangle would have the color (1,0,0) associated with them, while the last vertex would have the color (0,1,0).

The current color is specified with **glColor()**. It has all the forms of **glVertex()** and it has the additional forms of unsigned short, unsigned int and signed and unsigned byte (it does not however have the 2 component form). For example, if I wanted to specify the r,g,b, and alpha components of the current color with single unsigned bytes stored in an array, I would use

```
GLubyte array[4];
```

```
glColor4ubv(array);
```

Camera

OpenGL has a matrix called the ModelView matrix. This matrix is used to specify the viewing position, direction, and orientation. In order to operate on this matrix you use the

glMatrixMode(GL_MODELVIEW)

command. Any matrix operations you perform from now on will be performed on the ModelView matrix. The most common operation to perform on the ModelView matrix is to simply use the **gluLookAt()** command. The form of this command is:

```
gluLookAt(eye_x, eye_y, eye_z, target_x, target_y, target_z, up_x, up_y, up_z)
```

This will multiply the current matrix by the matrix necessary to be looking at **target** from **eye** with up vector **up**.

The following code fragment is a common use of the ModelView matrix:

```
glMatrixMode(GL_MODELVIEW);
glLoadIdentity();
gluLookAt(eye.x,eye.y,eye.z, target.x,target.y,target.z, 0,1,0);
```

OpenGL also has a projection matrix. This matrix is applied after the ModelView matrix and transforms coordinates from camera space to canonical projection space. Common use of this matrix is as follows:

```
glMatrixMode(GL_PROJECTION);
glLoadIdentity();
gluPerspective(40,1,.1,10);
```

The **gluPerspective(...)** call forms the correct matrix to do a projection transformation with a Y field of view of 40 degrees, an X to Y aspect ratio of 1, a near clipping plane at .1, and a far clipping plane at 10.

If you desire a parallel projection instead of a perspective projection, you would use the **glOrtho()** call instead of **gluPerspective()**. See the manual for use of this call.

Textures

Texturing is used to shade primitives by looking up color values from a 2D table instead of just linearly interpolating between vertex colors.

Turning on texture mapping

Texture mapping is turned on with **glEnable(GL_TEXTURE_2D)** and disabled with **glDisable (GL_TEXTURE_2D).**

Specifying the current texture

OpenGL has a concept of a current texture. The current texture is specified with the glTexture2D command:

```
glTexture2D(GLenum target,
        GLint level,
    GLint components,
    GLsizei width,
    GLsizei height,
    GLint border,
    GLenum format,
    GLenum type,
    const GLvoid *pixels)
```

- **target** : GL_TEXTURE_2D
- **level** : Used for mipmapping. Use 0 if you aren't doing mipmapping.
- **components** : How many data elements there are in each texture element. Use 3 for RGB, 4 for RGBA, and look at the manual for what other numbers mean.
- **width:** The width in texture elements of the image. This must be a power of 2.
- **height:** The height of the texture map. Must also be a power of 2.
- **border:** Set it to 0 if you are not using texture borders. If you do use texture borders, the texture width and height may be a power of 2 plus 2 pixels.
- **format:** The format of the pixel data (how the data is packed). You would usually use GL_RGB or GL_RGBA for this, but there are many other possible formats.
- **type:** The data type of the texture data (e.g. float, byte, etc.) The usual desired value for this is GL_UNSIGNED_BYTE (0–255 for each component).
- **pixels:** The actual texture data.

Texture coordinates

Once you have specified the current texture, you must give texture coordinates for each vertex (remember that there is always a current texture coordinate, so if you do not specify a texture coordinate for a vertex or a set of vertices, they will all get the last texture coordinates specified). Texture coordinate specification should be done before the vertex you want it to affect. It is done through the **glTexCoord[1234][dfis]()** call. Under most circumstances, you would choose **glTexCoord2[dfis]**

Changing texture mapping parameters

The **glTexEnv()** call allows you to change how rasterization is performed while using texture maps. Look at the manual for all possible modes, but some of the more interesting ones are the following:

Assuming you used 3 for the number of components in your glTexture2D call:

glTexEnvf(GL_TEXTURE_ENV,GL_TEXTURE_ENV_MODE,GL_MODULATE) The final RGB of a pixel will be the RGB it would have without texture mapping, multiplied by the RGB of the texture map. This allows the original primitive color to modulate the texture.

glTexEnvf(GL_TEXTURE_ENV,GL_TEXTURE_ENV_MODE,GL_DECAL) The final RGB of a pixel will be exactly that of the texture.

Assuming you used 4 for the number of components in your glTexture2D call:

glTexEnvf(GL_TEXTURE_ENV,GL_TEXTURE_ENV_MODE,GL_DECAL) The final RGB of the pixel will be an alpha blend (using the texture alpha) of the original RGB with the texture RGB.

The glTexParameter*() calls allow for further modification of texture behavior. The following are some of the more interesting parameters (see manual for complete list):

glTexParameterf(GL_TEXTURE_2D, GL_TEXTURE_MIN_FILTER, GL_NEAREST) When the pixel being textured is larger than one texture element, use the texture element closest to the center of the pixel.

glTexParameterf(GL_TEXTURE_2D, GL_TEXTURE_MIN_FILTER, GL_LINEAR) When the pixel being textured is larger than one texture element, use a weighted average of the four texture elements closest to the center of the pixel.

glTexParameterf(GL_TEXTURE_2D, GL_TEXTURE_MAG_FILTER, GL_NEAREST) When the pixel being textured is smaller than one texture element, use the texture element closest to the center of the pixel.

glTexParameterf(GL_TEXTURE_2D, GL_TEXTURE_MAG_FILTER, GL_LINEAR) When the pixel being textured is smaller than one texture element, use a weighted average of the four texture elements closest to the center of the pixel.

Display Lists

Display lists are lists of OpenGL commands to be called all at once. Display lists are useful because OpenGL has to process all the drawing commands only once. From then on, calling a display list causes OpenGL to quickly perform all the operations within the display list without having to go through the overhead of a function call for each operation. Display lists are also very useful if you have hardware texture memory and are using more than one texture, as this is the only way to guarantee the system that your texture memory has not changed and therefore the hardware texture memory can be used.

In order to create a display list, you must first get a display list identifier. This is simply an unsigned integer. Any time you refer to a display list, you will refer to it by this number. The function call **glGenLists(1)** will return an unused display list identifier. Use this call to guarantee that you will not be clobbering over some other display list that you previously allocated. A call to **glGenLists()** with a number greater than 1 will generate that many contiguous display list identifiers, returning the lowest numbered identifier.

Once you have a display list identifier, you must put "stuff" into the display list. This is done with the **glNewList()** command. The following code chunk puts a triangle into a display list:

```
GLuint displayList;
displayList = glGenLists(1);
glNewList(displayList,GL_COMPILE);
glBegin(GL_TRIANGLES);
glColor3f(1,0,0);
glVertex3f(1,0,0);
```

```
glVertex3f(0,1,0);
glVertex3f(0,0,1);
glEnd();
glEndList();
```

The **glNewList()** call must specify the display list identifier the following set of commands corresponds to. Note that if you specify a display list identifier that already has commands associated with it, these will be wiped out and replaced by the new commands. The **glEndList()** call marks the end of the display list specification.

Once you have created a display list you can execute the commands within it with the **glCallList()** call. You call this function with the display list identifier you used when creating your display list and it will call all the commands within the display list.

```
glCallList(displayList);
```

will execute the display list we created above.

Display lists can be hierarchical. In other words, you can have a **glCallList()** command within **glNewList()** and **glEndList()**.

Using Texture Maps with Display Lists

In order to place a texture map definition within a display list, simply place the glTexture2D() inside a display list definition:

```
GLuint textureDisplayList;
textureDisplayList = glGenLists(1);
glNewList(textureDisplayList,GL_COMPILE);
glTexture2D(...);
glEndList();
```

From now on, whenever you call glCallList(textureDisplayList), that texture will become the current texture.

Using the Z-Buffer

In order to turn on the Z-buffer, you must call

glEnable(GL_DEPTH_TEST)

To disable Z-Buffering, call

glDisable(GL_DEPTH_TEST)

Z-Buffer and the Freedoms

Curiously, turning on Z-buffering allows the Freedoms to perform much faster than with it off. This is because when Z-buffering is on, OpenGL allows the system to draw primitives in any order it wants, and not in the order the user specified them. This liberty allows the Freedoms to distribute primitive drawing among its processors, providing much better performance.

Shading

You can specify whether you want flat or smooth (Gouraud) shading with the **glShadeModel()** command.

glShadeModel(GL_FLAT)

will fill in your primitives with the color associated with the last vertex in each primitive.

glShadeModel(GL_SMOOTH)

will linearly interpolate the colors of the vertices.

Wireframe

In order to display primitives in wireframe use the

glPolygonMode(GL_FRONT_AND_BACK, GL_LINE)

function call. To turn off wireframe and solidly render primitives use

glPolygonMode(GL_FRONT_AND_BACK, GL_FILL).

OpenGL provides a set of commands to render a threedimensional scene. That means you provide the data in an OpenGL-useable form and OpenGL will show this data on the screen (render it). It is developed by many companies and it is free to use. You can develop OpenGL-applications without licencing.

OpenGL is a hardware- and system-independent interface. An OpenGL-application will work on every platform, as long as there is an installed implementation.

Because it is systemindependant, there are no functions to create windows etc., but there are helper functions for each platform. A very useful thing is GLUT.

What is GLUT?

GLUT is a complete API written by Mark Kilgard which lets you create windows and handle the messages. It exists for several platforms, that means that a program which uses GLUT can be compiled on many platforms without (or at least with very few) changes in the code.

How does OpenGL work?

OpenGL bases on the state variables. There are many values, for example the color, that remain after being specified. That means, you can specify a color once and draw several polygons, lines or what ever with this color then. There are no classes like in DirectX. However, it is logically structured. Before we come to the commands themselves, here is another thing:

To be hardware independent, OpenGL provides its own data types. They all begin with "GL". For example GLfloat, GLint and so on. There are also many symbolic constants, they all begin with "GL_", like GL_POINTS, GL_POLYGON. Finally the commands have the prefix "gl" like *glVertex3f()*. There is a utility library called GLU, here the prefixes are "GLU_" and "glu". GLUT commands begin with "glut", it is the same for every library. You want to know which libraries coexist with the ones called before? There are libraries for every system, Windows has the wgl*-Functions, Unix systems glx* and so on.

A very important thing is to know, that there are two important matrices, which affect the transformation from the 3d-world to the 2d-screen: The projection matrix and the modelview matrix. The projection matrix contains information, how a vertex - let's say a "point" in space - shall be mapped to the screen. This contains, whether the projection shall be isometric or from a perspective, how wide the field of view is and so on. Into the other matrix you put information, how the objects are moved, where the viewer is and so on.

Don't like matrices? Don't be afraid, you probably won't really see them, at least at the beginning. There are commands that do all the maths for you.

Some basic commands are explained later in this tutorial.

How can I use GLUT?

GLUT provides some routines for the initialization and creating the window (or fullscreen mode, if you want to). Those functions are called first in a GLUT application:

In your first line you always write ***glutInit(&argc, argv)***. After this, you must tell GLUT, which display mode you want - single or double buffering, color index mode or RGB and so on. This is done by calling ***glutInitDisplayMode()***. The symbolic constants are connected by a logical OR, so you could use ***glutInitDisplayMode(GLUT_RGB | GLUT_SINGLE)***. In later tutorials we will use some more constants here.

After the initialization you call ***glCreateWindow()*** with the window name as parameter.

Then you can (and should) pass some methods for certain events. The most important ones are "reshape" and "display". In reshape you need to (re)define the field of view and specify a new area in the window, where OpenGL is allowed to draw to.

Display should clear the so called color buffer - let's say this is the sheet of paper - and draw our objects.

You pass the methods by ***glut*Func()***, for example ***glutDisplayFunc()***. At the end of the main function you call ***glutMainLoop()***. This function doesn't return, but calls the several functions passed by ***glut*Func***.

Which commands do I need to work with OpenGL?

Here I'll explain the commands you need in "reshape" and at the beginning of "display".

As mentioned before, there are two (ok, in reality there are three, but let's make it easier) matrices. Which one is current is controlled by ***"glMatrixMode()"***. You can call it either with GL_PROJECTION or GL_MODELVIEW. In Reshape you specify a new projection matrix. After turning it current, you load an identity matrix into it, that means "deleting" the former projection matrix. Now you can apply a new field of view by using a glu* command: ***gluPerspective***. You pass the y-angle of view, the aspect ratio (the window's width / height), and a near and far clipping distance. The objects or parts of objects which are not between those distances will not be visible. Careful: Don't take a too small near clipping distance, you could get wrong-looking results! After this, you make the modelview matrix currrent and also load an identity matrix.

Display has to clear the color buffer. Therefore you call

glClear(GL_COLOR_BUFFER_BIT)

After the initialization of GLUT, you should have defined a clear color using ***glClearColor()***. It takes four arguments, red, green and blue and an alpha value. Set alpha = 0.0.

To get clear red, you would call ***glClearColor(1.0,0.0,0.0,0.0);***

Drawing the object is explained in the next section.

Last but not least you define the "viewport", the area on the window where OpenGL shall paint to.

Therefore you use ***glViewport(0,0,x,y);*** with x and y as the size of your window: You get them from the reshape parameters. Here is how to define the function headers of the two routines:

void Reshape (int x, int y);

void Display (void);

How can I draw a simple triangle with OpenGL?

Having cleared the colorbuffer, you can pass some data to OpenGL. It is very simple: You specify some vertices, which are used in a certain way. The way is defined by ***glBegin()***. For now let's use GL_POLYGON as parameter which tells OpenGL to use the following vertices as corners of one polygon.

After passing the data to OpenGL, you have to call ***glEnd()***. This method doesn't take any arguments.

To provide a vertex , you can call one of some ***glVertex*()*** routines. * stands for a combination of the number of arguments (two-dimensional, three-dimensional or four-dimensional) + the data type (f for float, d for double and i for int).

To specify a 3d vertex with integer coordinates, you call ***glVertex3i()***.

To finish rendering, you must call ***glFlush()*** at the end of your display-function.

That's all we need. Just call glVertex*() three times between ***glBegin*** and ***glEnd***.

To change the current color in RGB(A)-mode, you call ***glColor*()***. Again * stands for the number of arguments (three for RGB and four for RGBA)+ the data type. If you take a floating point type as parameters, note that 1.0 is full intensity for the color component. Also note, that colors are blended, when they are different for one or more vertices in the polygon.

One last thing: If you want to add some vertices to our polygon, you must note that OpenGL cannot render concave polygons (for performance reasons). Then you have to tesselate it, *i.e.*, make some smaller ones from it (add a new ***glBegin / glEnd*** pair).

Appendix-4

(Graphic Algorithms)

Line Generating Algorithms

```
//Line Generating Algorithm
//Digital Differential Analyzer
void line(int x1, int y1, int x2, int y2)
{
const double dx = x1 - x2;
const double dy = y1 - y2;
  if (dy == 0)
    for (int x=MIN(x1,x2); x<=MAX(x1,x2); ++x)
      putpixel(x, y1, getcolor());
  else if (dx == 0)
    for (int y=MIN(y1,y2); y<=MAX(y1,y2); ++y)
      putpixel(x1, y, getcolor());
  else
  {
  const double m = dy / dx;
  const double b = y1 - m * x1;
    if (fabs(dy) <= fabs(dx))
      for (int x=MIN(x1,x2); x<=MAX(x1,x2); ++x)
        putpixel(x, ROUND(m*x+b), getcolor());
    else
      for (int y=MIN(y1,y2); y<=MAX(y1,y2); ++y)
        putpixel(ROUND((y-b)/m), y, getcolor());
  }
}
//Line Generating Algorithm
//Bresenham's
```

```
void line(int x1, int y1, int x2, int y2)
{
const int dx = abs(x1 - x2);
const int dy = abs(y1 - y2);
int const1, const2, p, x, y, step;
 if (dx >= dy)
 {
 const1 = 2 * dy;
 const2 = 2 * (dy - dx);
  p = 2 * dy - dx;
  x = MIN(x1,x2);
  y = (x1 < x2) ? (y1) : (y2);
  step = (y1 > y2) ? (1) : (-1);
  putpixel(x, y, getcolor());
  while (x < MAX(x1,x2))
  {
    if (p < 0)
      p += const1;
    else
    {
      y += step;
      p += const2;
    }
   putpixel(++x, y, getcolor());
  }
 }
 else
 {
 const1 = 2 * dx;
 const2 = 2 * (dx - dy);
  p = 2 * dx - dy;
  y = MIN(y1,y2);
  x = (y1 < y2) ? (x1) : (x2);
  step = (x1 > x2) ? (1) : (-1);
  putpixel(x, y, getcolor());
```

```
  while (y < MAX(y1,y2))
  {
    if (p < 0)
      p += const1;
    else
    {
      x += step;
      p += const2;
    }
   putpixel(x, ++y, getcolor());
  }
 }
}
```

Circle Generating Algorithms

```
//Circle Generating Algorithm
//Simple Cartesian-Coordinate
void circle(int xc, int yc, int r)
{
double SQRT;
 for (int x=0; x<=(SQRT=sqrt(SQR(r)-SQR(x))); ++x)
 {
   putpixel(ROUND(xc + SQRT), yc + x, getcolor());
   putpixel(ROUND(xc + SQRT), yc - x, getcolor());
   putpixel(ROUND(xc - SQRT), yc + x, getcolor());
   putpixel(ROUND(xc - SQRT), yc - x, getcolor());
   putpixel(xc + x, ROUND(yc + SQRT), getcolor());
   putpixel(xc - x, ROUND(yc + SQRT), getcolor());
   putpixel(xc + x, ROUND(yc - SQRT), getcolor());
   putpixel(xc - x, ROUND(yc - SQRT), getcolor());
 }
}
//Circle Generating Algorithm
//Simple Polar-Coordinate
void circle(int xc, int yc, int r)
```

```
{
const double arc_size = PI / 4;
const int iterations = int(arc_size * r);
double RxCOS, RxSIN;
 for (int i=0; i<=iterations; ++i)
 {
  RxCOS = r * cos(arc_size*i/iterations);
  RxSIN = r * sin(arc_size*i/iterations);
  putpixel(ROUND(xc + RxCOS), ROUND(yc + RxSIN), getcolor());
  putpixel(ROUND(xc + RxCOS), ROUND(yc - RxSIN), getcolor());
  putpixel(ROUND(xc - RxCOS), ROUND(yc + RxSIN), getcolor());
  putpixel(ROUND(xc - RxCOS), ROUND(yc - RxSIN), getcolor());
  putpixel(ROUND(xc + RxSIN), ROUND(yc + RxCOS), getcolor());
  putpixel(ROUND(xc - RxSIN), ROUND(yc + RxCOS), getcolor());
  putpixel(ROUND(xc + RxSIN), ROUND(yc - RxCOS), getcolor());
  putpixel(ROUND(xc - RxSIN), ROUND(yc - RxCOS), getcolor());
 }
}
//Circle Generating Algorithm
//Bresenham's
void circle(int xc, int yc, int r)
{
int x = 0;
int y = r;
int p = 3 - 2 * r;
 while (x <= y)
 {
  putpixel(xc + x, yc + y, getcolor());
  putpixel(xc - x, yc + y, getcolor());
  putpixel(xc + x, yc - y, getcolor());
  putpixel(xc - x, yc - y, getcolor());
  putpixel(xc + y, yc + x, getcolor());
  putpixel(xc - y, yc + x, getcolor());
  putpixel(xc + y, yc - x, getcolor());
  putpixel(xc - y, yc - x, getcolor());
```

```
    if (p < 0)
      p += 4 * x++ + 6;
    else
      p += 4 * (x++ - y--) + 10;
  }
}
```

Ellipse Generating Algorithms

```
//Ellipse Generating Algorithm
//Simple Cartesian-Coordinate
void ellipse(int xc, int yc, int xr, int yr)
{
int len;
 if (xr > yr)
 {
 int y12, y22;
 int y11 = yc, y21 = yc;
  for (int x=xc-xr+1; x<=xc+xr; ++x)
  {
   len = yr * sqrt(1 - SQR((x - xc) / double(xr)));
   y12 = yc + len;
   y22 = yc - len;
   line(x-1, y11, x, y12);
   line(x-1, y21, x, y22);
   y11 = y12;
   y21 = y22;
  }
 }
 else
 {
 int x12, x22;
 int x11 = xc, x21 = xc;
  for (int y=yc-yr+1; y<=yc+yr; ++y)
  {
   len = xr * sqrt(1 - SQR((y - yc) / double(yr)));
```

```
        x12 = xc + len;
        x22 = xc - len;
        line(x11, y-1, x12, y);
        line(x21, y-1, x22, y);
        x11 = x12;
        x21 = x22;
      }
    }
  }
  //Ellipse Generating Algorithm
  //Simple Polar-Coordinate
  void ellipse(int xc, int yc, int xr, int yr)
  {
  const int ITERATIONS = 1000;
  double theta;
    moveto(xc + xr, yc);
    for (int i=1; i<=ITERATIONS; ++i)
    {
      theta = 2 * PI * i / ITERATIONS;
      lineto(ROUND(xc+xr*cos(theta)), ROUND(yc+yr*sin(theta)));
    }
  }
```

Fill Algorithms

```
  //Boundary Fill Algorithm
  void boundaryFill(int x, int y, int border)
  {
  #define IS_IN_X_RANGE(x) (((x) >= 0) && ((x) <= getmaxx()))
  #define IS_IN_Y_RANGE(y) (((y) >= 0) && ((y) <= getmaxy()))
    if (IS_IN_X_RANGE(x) && IS_IN_Y_RANGE(y) &&
      (getpixel(x,y) != border) && (getpixel(x,y) != getcolor()))
    {
      putpixel(x, y, getcolor());
      boundaryFill(x+1, y, border);
      boundaryFill(x-1, y, border);
```

```
    boundaryFill(x, y+1, border);
    boundaryFill(x, y-1, border);
  }
#undef IS_IN_X_RANGE
#undef IS_IN_Y_RANGE
}
//Note: the 4-connected approach is implemented rather
//than the 8-connected approach.
//Flood Fill Algorithm
void floodFill(int x, int y, int old_color)
{
#define IS_IN_X_RANGE(x) (((x) >= 0) && ((x) <= getmaxx()))
#define IS_IN_Y_RANGE(y) (((y) >= 0) && ((y) <= getmaxy()))
  if (IS_IN_X_RANGE(x) && IS_IN_Y_RANGE(y) &&
     getpixel(x,y) == old_color)
  {
    putpixel(x, y, getcolor());
    floodFill(x+1, y, old_color);
    floodFill(x-1, y, old_color);
    floodFill(x, y+1, old_color);
    floodFill(x, y-1, old_color);
  }
#undef IS_IN_X_RANGE
#undef IS_IN_Y_RANGE
}
//Note: the 4-connected approach is implemented rather
//than the 8-connected approach.
```

Scan-Line Fill Algorithms

```
//Scan-Line Rectangle Fill Algorithm
void rectangleFill(int x1, int y1, int x2, int y2)
{
  for (int y=MIN(y1,y2); y<=MAX(y1,y2); ++y)
    line(x1, y, x2, y);
}
```

```
//Scan-Line Circle Fill Algorithm
//Utilizing Cartesian-Coordinate
void circleFill(int xc, int yc, int r)
{
int x1, x2;
 for (int y=yc-r; y<=yc+r; ++y)
 {
  x1 = ROUND(xc + sqrt(SQR(r) - SQR(y - yc)));
  x2 = ROUND(xc - sqrt(SQR(r) - SQR(y - yc)));
  line(x1, y, x2, y);
 }
}
//Scan-Line Circle Fill Algorithm
//Utilizing Polar-Coordinate
void circleFill(int xc, int yc, int r)
{
const int ITERATIONS = 2 * PI * r;
double theta;
int x, y;
 for (int i=0; i<=ITERATIONS; ++i)
 {
  theta = 2 * PI * i / ITERATIONS;
  x = ROUND(xc + r * cos(theta));
  y = ROUND(yc + r * sin(theta));
  line(xc, yc, x, y);
 }
}
```

Line Clipping Algorithms

```
//Line Clipping Algorithm
//Sutherland-Cohen
int ABRL(int x, int y)
{
int code = 0;
 if (x < XS_MIN)
```

```
    code = 1;
  else if (x > XS_MAX)
    code = 2;
  if (y < YS_MIN)
    code |= 4;
  else if (y > YS_MAX)
    code |= 8;
  return code;
}
void intersection(int& x1, int& y1, int x2, int y2)
{
  if (y1 > YS_MAX)
  {
    x1 += (x2 - x1) * (YS_MAX - y1) / (y2 - y1);
    y1 = YS_MAX;
  }
  else if (y1 < YS_MIN)
  {
    x1 += (x2 - x1) * (YS_MIN - y1) / (y2 - y1);
    y1 = YS_MIN;
  }
  if (x1 > XS_MAX)
  {
    y1 += (y2 - y1) * (XS_MAX - x1) / (x2 - x1);
    x1 = XS_MAX;
  }
  else if (x1 < XS_MIN)
  {
    y1 += (y2 - y1) * (XS_MIN - x1) / (x2 - x1);
    x1 = XS_MIN;
  }
}
void clipping(int& x1, int& y1, int& x2, int& y2)
{
  intersection(x1, y1, x2, y2);
```

```
 intersection(x2, y2, x1, y1);
}
void drawClippedLine(int x1, int y1, int x2, int y2)
{
 if (ABRL(x1, y1) == 0 && ABRL(x2, y2) == 0)
   line(x1, y1, x2, y2);
 else if (ABRL(x1, y1) && ABRL(x2, y2) != 0)
   return;
 else
 {
   clipping(x1, y1, x2, y2);
   if (ABRL(x1, y1) == 0 && ABRL(x2, y2) == 0)
     line(x1, y1, x2, y2);
 }
}
//Line Clipping Algorithm
//Midpoint
int ABRL(int x, int y)
{
int code = 0;
 if (x < XS_MIN)
   code = 1;
 else if (x > XS_MAX)
   code = 2;
 if (y < YS_MIN)
   code |= 4;
 else if (y > YS_MAX)
   code |= 8;
 return code;
}
void intersection(int& x1, int& y1, int x2, int y2)
{
int xm, ym;
 if (y1 > YS_MAX)
 {
```

```
  while (y1 != YS_MAX)
  {
    xm = (x1 + x2) >> 1;
    ym = (y1 + y2) >> 1;
    if (ym >= YS_MAX)
      x1 = xm, y1 = ym;
    else
      x2 = xm, y2 = ym;
  }
}
else if (y1 < YS_MIN)
{
  while (y1 != YS_MIN)
  {
    xm = (x1 + x2) >> 1;
    ym = (y1 + y2) >> 1;
    if (ym <= YS_MIN)
      x1 = xm, y1 = ym;
    else
      x2 = xm, y2 = ym;
  }
}
if (x1 > XS_MAX)
{
  while (x1 != XS_MAX)
  {
    xm = (x1 + x2) >> 1;
    ym = (y1 + y2) >> 1;
    if (xm >= XS_MAX)
      x1 = xm, y1 = ym;
    else
    x2 = xm, y2 = ym;
  }
}
else if (x1 < XS_MIN)
```

```
  {
    while (x1 != XS_MIN)
    {
      xm = (x1 + x2) >> 1;
      ym = (y1 + y2) >> 1;
      if (xm <= XS_MIN)
        x1 = xm, y1 = ym;
      else
        x2 = xm, y2 = ym;
    }
  }
}
void clipping(int& x1, int& y1, int& x2, int& y2)
{
  intersection(x1, y1, x2, y2);
  intersection(x2, y2, x1, y1);
}
void drawClippedLine(int x1, int y1, int x2, int y2)
{
  if (ABRL(x1, y1) == 0 && ABRL(x2, y2) == 0)
    line(x1, y1, x2, y2);
  else if (ABRL(x1, y1) && ABRL(x2, y2) != 0)
    return;
  else
  {
    clipping(x1, y1, x2, y2);
    if (ABRL(x1, y1) == 0 && ABRL(x2, y2) == 0)
      line(x1, y1, x2, y2);
  }
}

//Line Clipping Algorithm
//Liang-Barsky

int clipTest(int p, int q, double& u1, double& u2)
{
double r;
```

```
 if (p < 0)
 {
   r = q / p;
   if (r > u2)
     return 0;
   else if (r > u1)
     u1 = r;
 }
 else if (p > 0)
 {
   r = q / p;
   if (r < u1)
     return 0;
   else if (r < u2)
     u2 = r;
 }
 else if (q < 0)
   return 0;
 return 1;
}
void clipping(int& x1, int& y1, int& x2, int& y2)
{
const int dx = x2 - x1;
const int dy = y2 - y1;
double u1 = 0;
double u2 = 1;
 if ((clipTest(-dx, x1-XS_MIN, u1, u2)) &&
    (clipTest( dx, XS_MAX – x1, u1, u2)) &&
    (clipTest(-dy, y1-YS_MIN, u1, u2)) &&
    (clipTest( dy, YS_MAX-y1, u1, u2)))
  {
    if (u2 < 1)
      x2 = x1 + ROUND(u2 * dx),
      y2 = y1 + ROUND(u2 * dy);
    if (u1 > 0)
      x1 += ROUND(u1 * dx),
      y1 += ROUND(u1 * dy);
  }
}
```

Curve Generating Algorithm

```
//Curve Generating Algorithm
//Bezier-Spline
long C(int n, int k)
{
 return k != 0 && n != k ? C(n-1, k-1) + C(n-1, k) : 1;
}
double power(double x, double y)
{
 return x == 0 && y == 0 ? 1 : pow(x, y);
}
double BEZ(int k, int n, double u)
{
 return C(n, k) * power(u, k) * power(1-u, n-k);
}
void bezierCurve(int n, pointType* point)
{
double u, x, y;
 for (int i=0; i<=ITERATIONS; ++i)
 {
  u = double(i) / ITERATIONS;
  x = y = 0;
  for (int k=0; k<=n; ++k)
  {
  double BEZvalue = BEZ(k, n, u);
    x += point[k].x * BEZvalue;
    y += point[k].y * BEZvalue;
  }
  if (i == 0)
    moveto(x, y);
  lineto(x, y);
 }
}
```

APPENDIX-5

Multimedia File Formats on the Internet

***B:** binary file

***A:** ASCII file

<>: Recommend software

Extension	Description	File type	How to use the file
.acr	ACR-NEMA medical	B	image file
.aif(c)	sound (Apple, SGI)	B	sound player
.aif(f)	sound (Apple, SGI)	B	sound player
.arc	DOS compression	B	decompress
.arj	compressed	B	decompress
.art	First Publisher		Clip Art file
.ASC	image	B	image viewer
.au	music	B	ULAW player
.avi	video (MS Windows)	B	avi viewer
.avr	sound	B	sound player
.avs	animation	B	image viewer
.bac	binary backup	B	
.bas	Basic file	B	run in QBasic
.BBM	image	B	image viewer
.bck	VMS backup		depends
.BIG	Chinese (old version)	B	Chinese viewer
.BIG5	Chinese (old version)	B	Chinese viewer
.BMF	image	B	image viewer
.bmp	picture (Bitmap)	B	picture viewer
.BOO	image	B	image viewer
.byu	movie byu file	B	
.CGM	Computer Graphics		
.cmf	music	B	music player
.com	compressed	B	decompress
.com	executable file	B	type the file name to run
.com	VMS command file	B	
.cpt	Macintosh Compressed	B	decompress

.CUR	image	B	image viewer
.CUT	image	B	image viewer
.dat	VMS data file		
.des	text	A	word processor
.DCS	image	B	image viewer
.DIB	picture (Bitmap)	B	picture viewer
.dig	text	A	word processor
.dl	animated picture	B	dl viewer
.dlg	image	B	image viewer
.DMS	compressed	B	decompress
.doc	text	A	word processor
.dvi	special TeX text	A	
.dwc	archive	B	decompress
.DWG	image	B	image viewer
.dxf	ASCII Drawing Interchange	A	
.eps	Encapsulated Post-Script image	B	PostScrip viewer
.euc	Japanese (Kanji)	B	Japanese reader
.exe	self-extracting file	B	type "filename" to run
.exe	executable file	B	type "filename" to run
.F	Freeze for UNIX	B	unfreeze
.fac	picture	B	picture viewer
.fit(s)	image	B	image viewer
.flc	animated picture	B	picture viewer
.fli	animated picture	B	picture viewer
.flx	image	B	image viewer
.fssd	sound	B	sound player
.gds	image	B	image viewer
.gb	Chinese	B	Chinese viewer
.gif	picture	B	picture viewer
.gl	animated picture	B	picture viewer
.gry	picture	B	picture viewer
.gz	compressed	B	decompress
.gzip	compressed	B	decompress
.h	text	A	word processor
.ha	compressed	B	decompress
.ham	image	B	image viewer
.hlb	VMS help libraries	A	
.hlp	VMS help files	A	
.HPK	compressed	B	decompress

.hqx	Macintosh compressed	B	decompress
.HRZ	image	B	image viewer
.HYP	compressed	B	decompress
.hz	Chinese	B	Chinese viewer
.ibm	picture	B	picture viewer
.ice	archive	B	decompress
.ico	image	B	image viewer
.ief	image	B	image viewer
.iff	many types of binary data	B	image viewer
.IMG	picture	B	picture viewer
.ish	compressed	B	decompress
.jas	image	B	image viewer (Paint Shop Pro>
.JBIG	image	B	image viewer
.JFI	image	B	image viewer
.jis	Japanese	B	Japanese reader
.jpc	picture	B	picture viewer
.jpg	picture	B	picture viewer
.LBM	image	B	image viewer
.lbr	archive	B	decompress
.lha	compressed	B	decompress
.lis	program listing	A	DOS editor
.lm8	picture	B	picture viewer
.LZH	compressed	B	decompress
.LZS	compressed	B	decompress
.LZX	compressed	B	decompresse
.lzw	LHWarp archive	B	decompress
.MAC	picture	B	picture viewer
.mag	picture	B	picture viewer
.man	text manual	A	word processor
.map	image	B	image viewer
.MAT	sound	B	sound player
.md	compressed	B	decompress
.mgf	image	B	image viewer
.mhg	multimedia	B	multimedia player
.mid	music	B	midi player
.mki	picture	B	picture viewer
.mod	music	B	mod player
.mp2	audio	B	audio player
.mpa	audio	B	audio player
.mpg	multimedia	B	mpeg player

.mps	multimedi	B	mpeg player
.mrb	image	B	image viewer
.MSP	image	B	image viewer
.MTM	sound	B	sound player
.mtv	picture	B	picture viewer
.nff	image	B	image viewer
.nst	sound	B	sound player
.off	image	B	image viewer
.omf	image	B	image viewer
.pak	compressed	B	decompress
.pbm	picture	B	picture viewer
.pcd	Kodak photo CD	B	picture viewer
.pcc	image	B	image viewer
.pcm	sound	B	sound player
.pct	picture	B	picture viewer
.pcx	picture(Paintbrush)	B	picture viewer
.pdf	image	B	Acrobat Reader
.pds	picture	B	picture viewer
.pgm	picture	B	picture viewer
.pic	picture	B	picture viewer
.pict	picture (Macintosh)	B	picture viewer
.pit	Macintosh compressed	B	decompress
.pm	picture	B	picture viewer
.png	image	B	image viewer
.pnt	MacPaint	B	image viewer
.pol	music	B	music player
.pp	Amiga compressed	B	decompress
.ppm	video	B	picture viewer
.ps/.psid	picture/text	B	picture viewer
.ps	laser printer file	A	word processor
.ras	picture	B	picture viewer
.RAX	image	B	image viewer
.RAW	animated picture	B	picture viewer
.rgb	picture	B	picture viewer
.rmi	sound	B	sound player
.rle	picture	B	picture viewer
.ROL	sound	B	sound player
.s3m	sound	B	sound player
.scx	image	B	image viewer (CShow>
.sdn	shell archive	B	decompress
.sea	self-extracting (Mac)	B	type "filename" to run

.sf	sound	B	sound player
.sgi	picture	B	picture viewer
.shar	shell archive	A	unshell
.shg	image	B	image viewer
.SHK	compressed (Mac)	B	decompress
.sit	compressed (Mac)	B	decompress
.snd	music	B	music player
.sqz	squeeze for MSDOS	B	decompress
.?q?	squeeze	B	decompress
.stm	sound	B	sound player
.tar	tape archive	B	untar
.tar.gz	compressed tar	B	decompress and untar
.tar.Z	compressed tar	B	decompress and untar
.tdo	compressed	B	decompress
.TGA	picture	B	picture viewer
.tif(f)	image	B	image viewer
.txt	text	A	word processor
.uc2	compressed	B	decompress
.ul	sound	B	sound player
.UTL	sound	B	sound player
.uue	uuencoded	A	decode
.uud	uudecoded	B	
.vic	picture	B	picture viewer
.vik	picture	B	picture viewer
.vis	picture	B	picture viewer
.voc	sound	B	sound player
.WAV	sound	B	sound player
.WMF	image	B	image viewer
.XBM	picture (X Windows)	B	picture viewer
.xm	sound	B	sound player
.xpm	picture	B	picture viewer
.XWD	image	B	image viewer
.Y	compressed	B	decompress
.yuv	image	B	image viewer
.Z	compressed	B	decompress
.zip	compressed	B	decompress
.zoo	compressed	B	decompress
.zw	Chinese	B	Chinese viewer